GREEN LANTERN

AGENT ORANGE

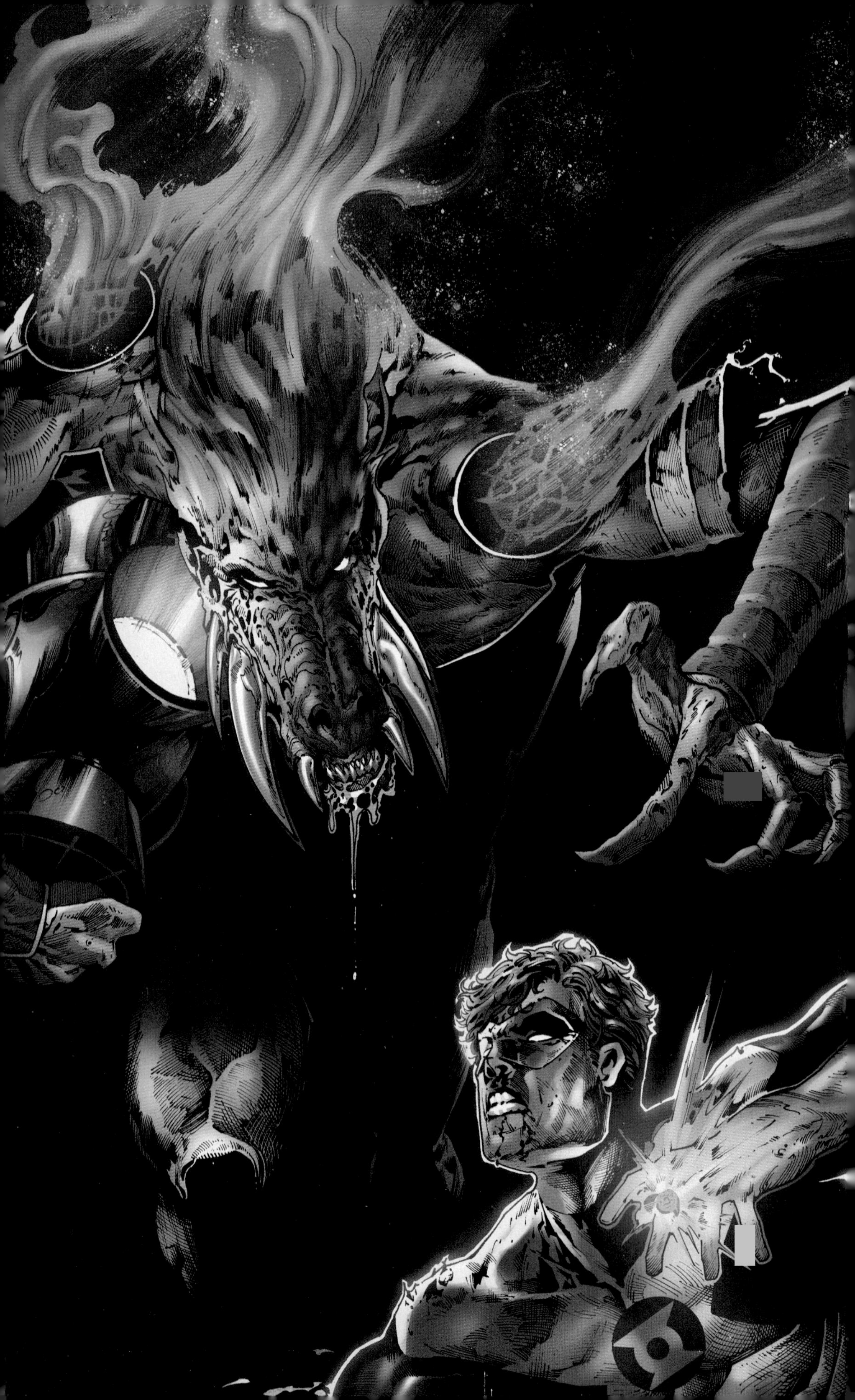

GREEN LANTERN

AGENT ORANGE

Geoff Johns
Writer

Philip Tan Eddy Barrows Ivan Reis Rafael Albuquerque Doug Mahnke
Pencillers

Jonathan Glapion Ruy José Julio Ferreira Oclair Albert
Rafael Albuquerque Christian Alamy Doug Mahnke Tom Nguyen
Inkers

Nei Ruffino Rod Reis Randy Mayor Gabe Eltaeb Hi-Fi
Colors

Rob Leigh
Letters

Dan DiDio SVP-Executive Editor
Eddie Berganza Editor-original series
Adam Schlagman Associate Editor-original series
Georg Brewer VP-Design & DC Direct Creative
Bob Harras Group Editor-Collected Editions
Sean Mackiewicz Editor
Robbin Brosterman Design Director-Books

DC COMICS
Paul Levitz President & Publisher
Richard Bruning SVP-Creative Director
Patrick Caldon EVP-Finance & Operations
Amy Genkins SVP-Business & Legal Affairs
Jim Lee Editorial Director-WildStorm
Gregory Noveck SVP-Creative Affairs
Steve Rotterdam SVP-Sales & Marketing
Cheryl Rubin SVP-Brand Management

Cover by Philip Tan, Jonathan Glapion and Nei Ruffino

GREEN LANTERN: AGENT ORANGE

Published by DC Comics.

Originally published in single magazine form in GREEN LANTERN 38-42, BLACKEST NIGHT 0.

DC Comics, 1700 Broadway, New York, NY 10019
A Warner Bros. Entertainment Company
Printed by RR Donnelley, Roanoke, VA, USA
10/14/09. First Printing.

ISBN: 978-1-4012-2421-9
SC ISBN: 978-1-4012-2420-2

SUSTAINABLE FORESTRY INITIATIVE
Certified Chain of Custody
Promoting Sustainable Forest Management

Fiber used in this product line meets the sourcing requirements of the SFI program. www.sfiprogram.org NSF-SFICOC-C0001801

GREEN LANTERN 39 Cover by Ivan Reis, Oclair Albert and Nei Ruffino

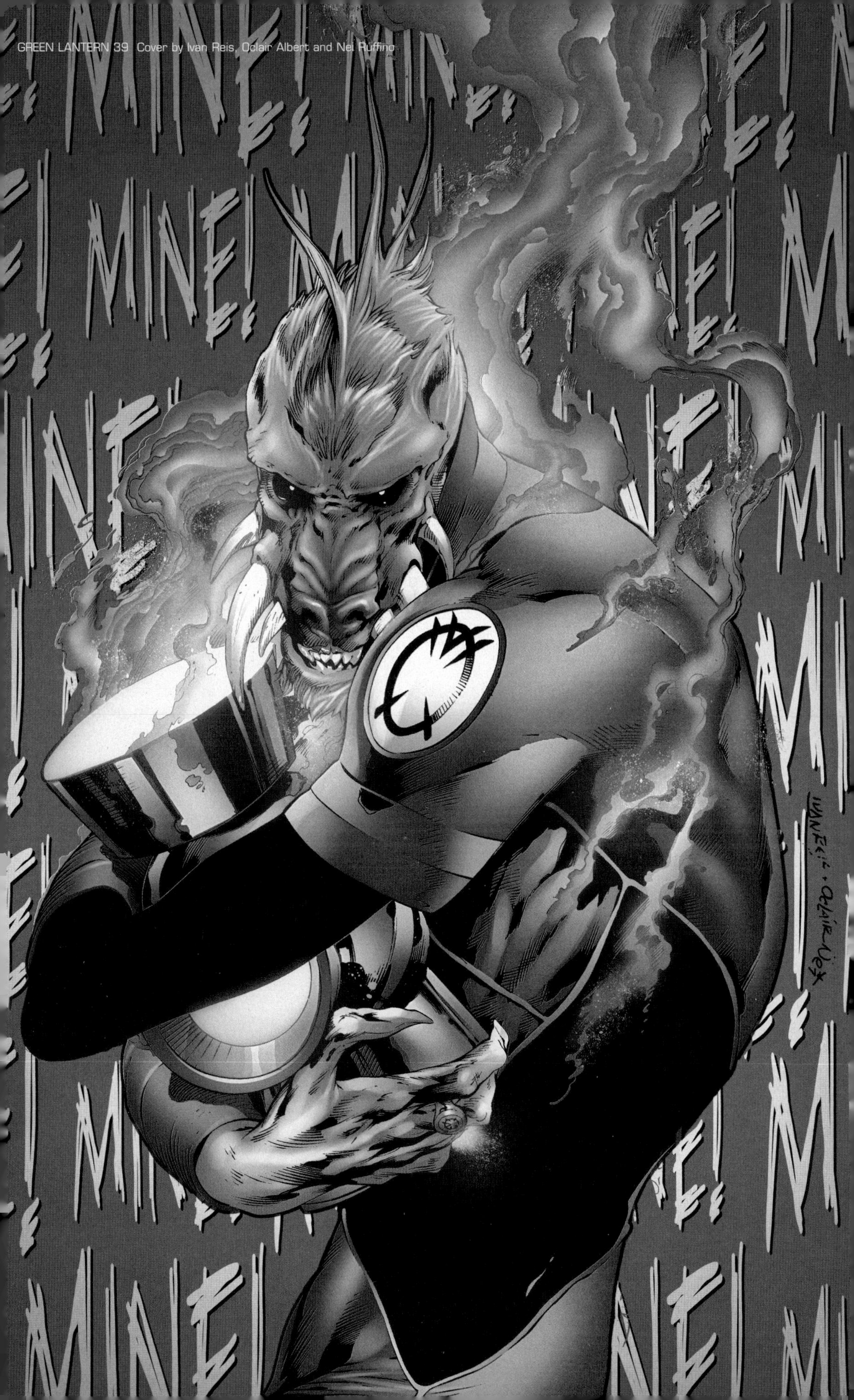
MINE!

AGENT ORANGE
Part 1

Philip Tan Pencils
Jonathan Glapion Inks

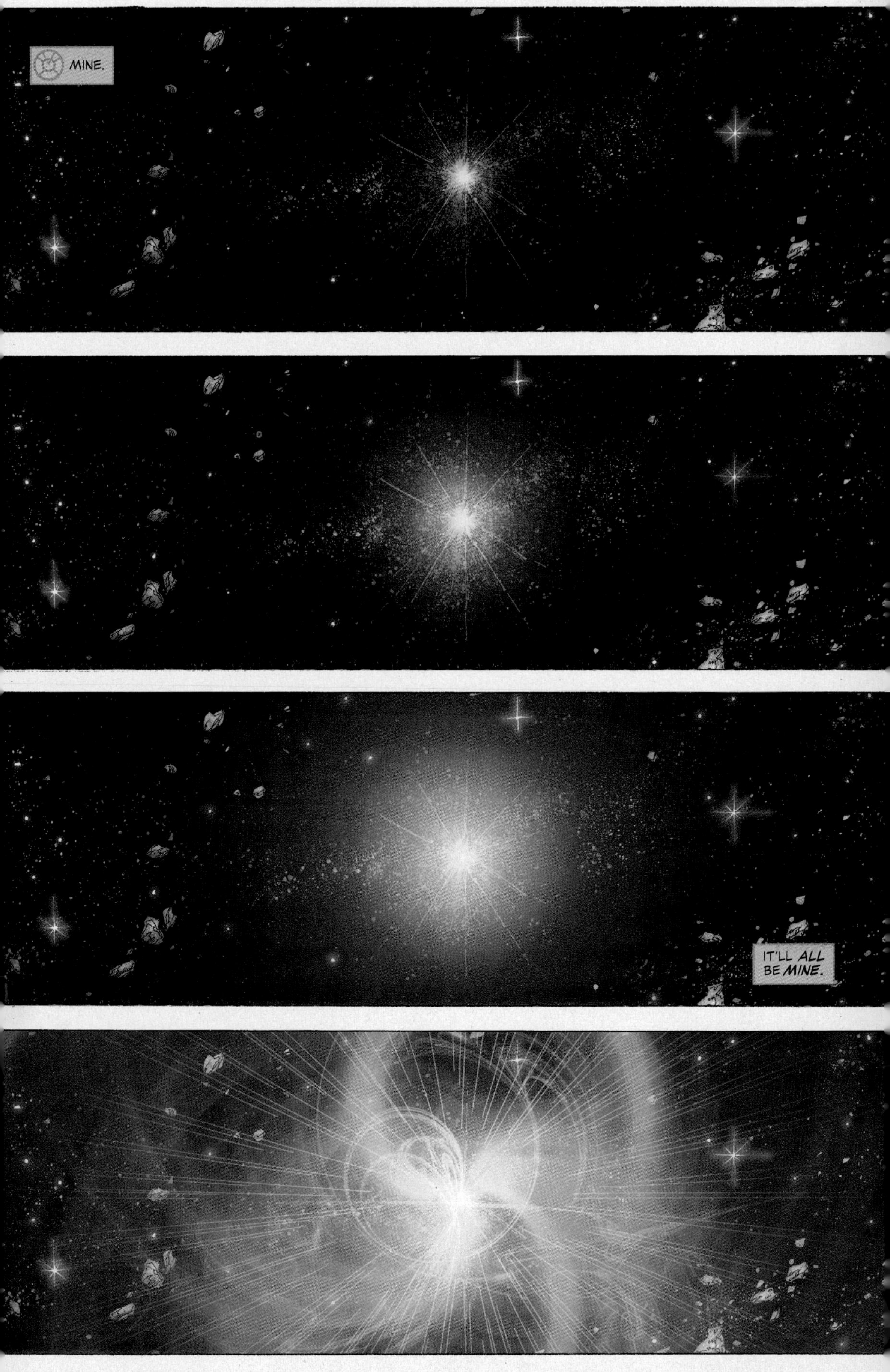
MINE.
IT'LL ALL BE MINE.

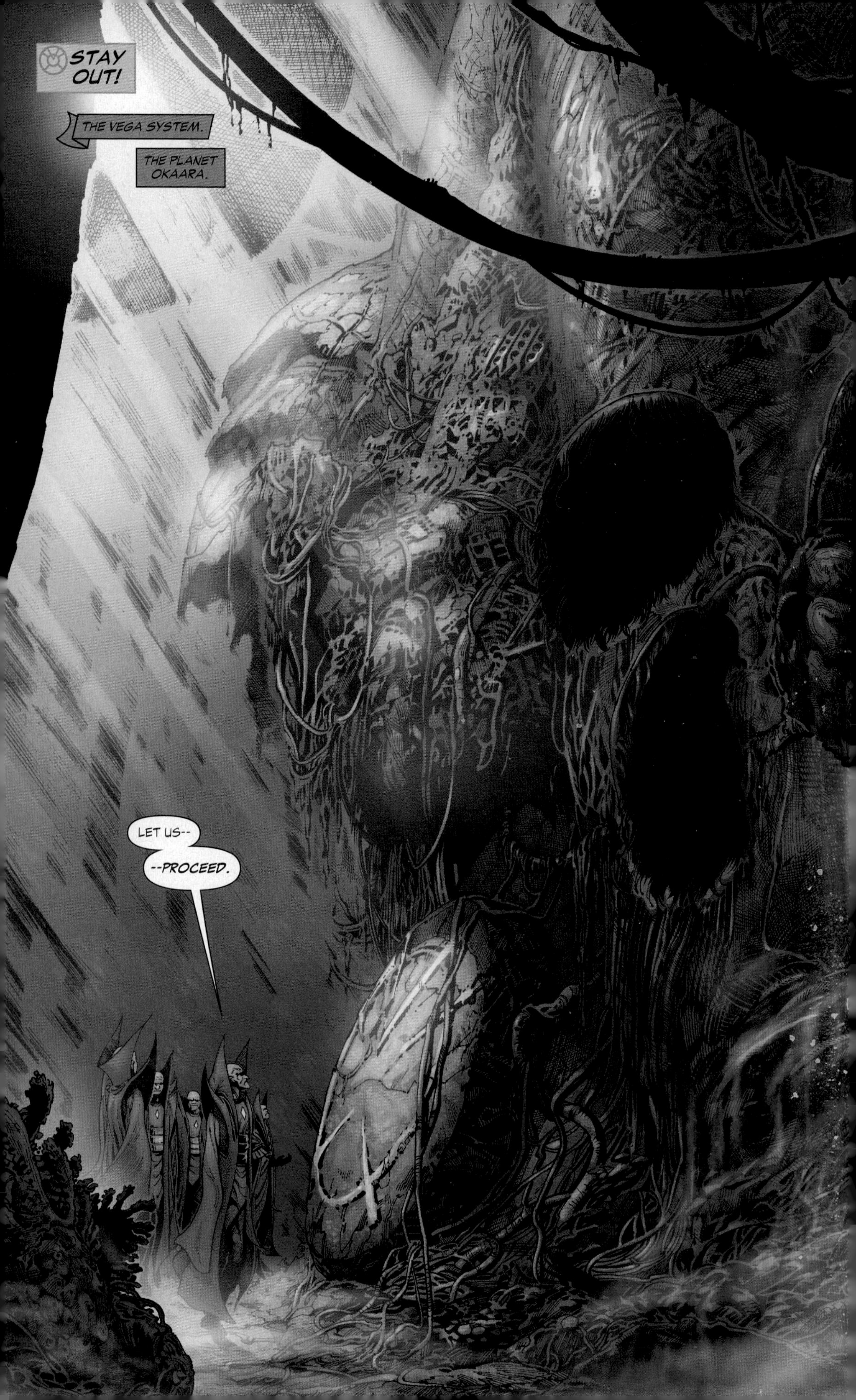
STAY OUT!
THE VEGA SYSTEM.
THE PLANET OKAARA.
LET US--
--PROCEED.

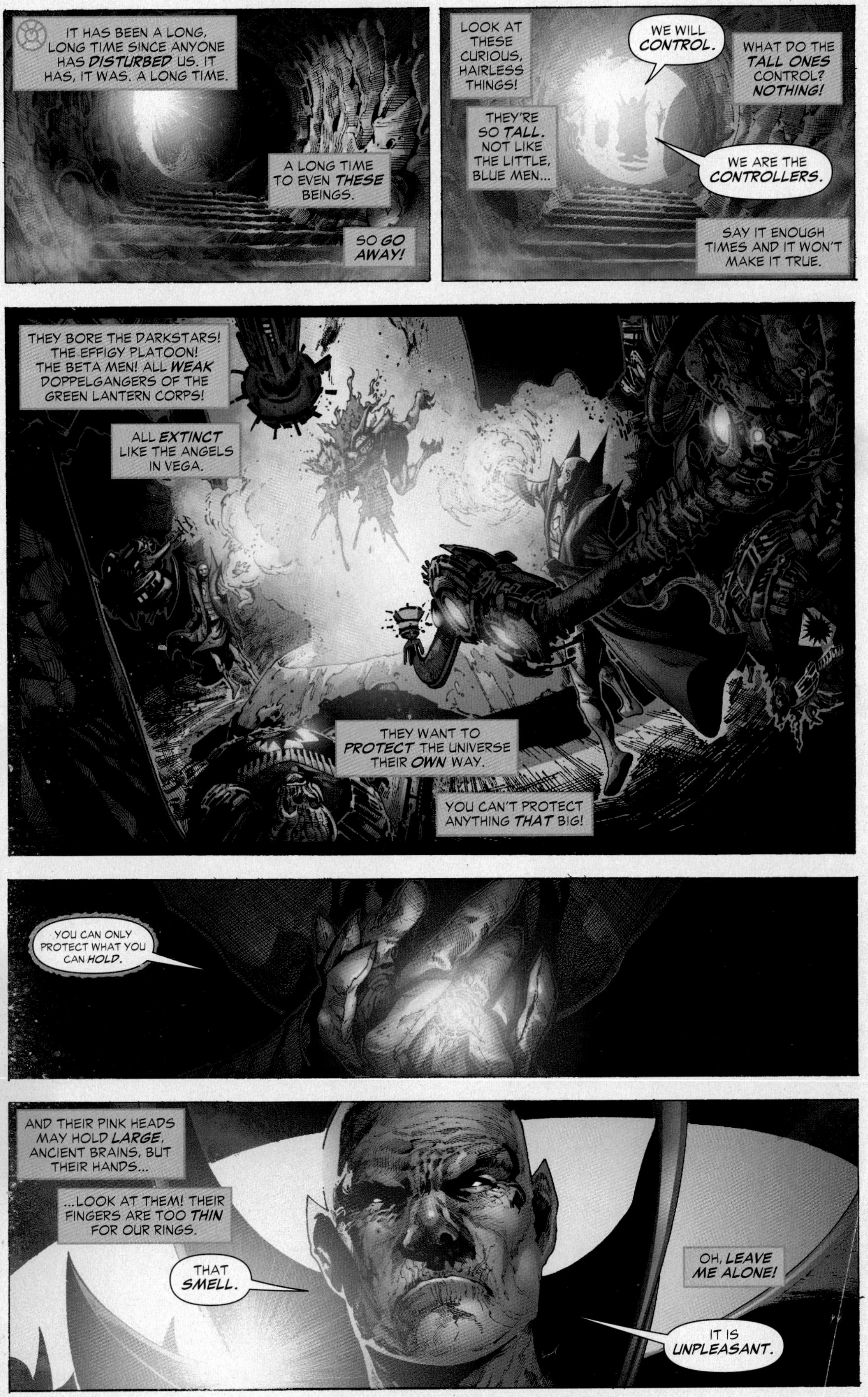
IT HAS BEEN A LONG, LONG TIME SINCE ANYONE HAS DISTURBED US. IT HAS, IT WAS. A LONG TIME.
A LONG TIME TO EVEN THESE BEINGS.
SO GO AWAY!
LOOK AT THESE CURIOUS, HAIRLESS THINGS!
WE WILL CONTROL.
WHAT DO THE TALL ONES CONTROL? NOTHING!
THEY'RE SO TALL. NOT LIKE THE LITTLE, BLUE MEN...
WE ARE THE CONTROLLERS.
SAY IT ENOUGH TIMES AND IT WON'T MAKE IT TRUE.
THEY BORE THE DARKSTARS! THE EFFIGY PLATOON! THE BETA MEN! ALL WEAK DOPPELGANGERS OF THE GREEN LANTERN CORPS!
ALL EXTINCT LIKE THE ANGELS IN VEGA.
THEY WANT TO PROTECT THE UNIVERSE THEIR OWN WAY.
YOU CAN'T PROTECT ANYTHING THAT BIG!
YOU CAN ONLY PROTECT WHAT YOU CAN HOLD.
AND THEIR PINK HEADS MAY HOLD LARGE, ANCIENT BRAINS, BUT THEIR HANDS...
...LOOK AT THEM! THEIR FINGERS ARE TOO THIN FOR OUR RINGS.
THAT SMELL.
OH, LEAVE ME ALONE!
IT IS UNPLEASANT.

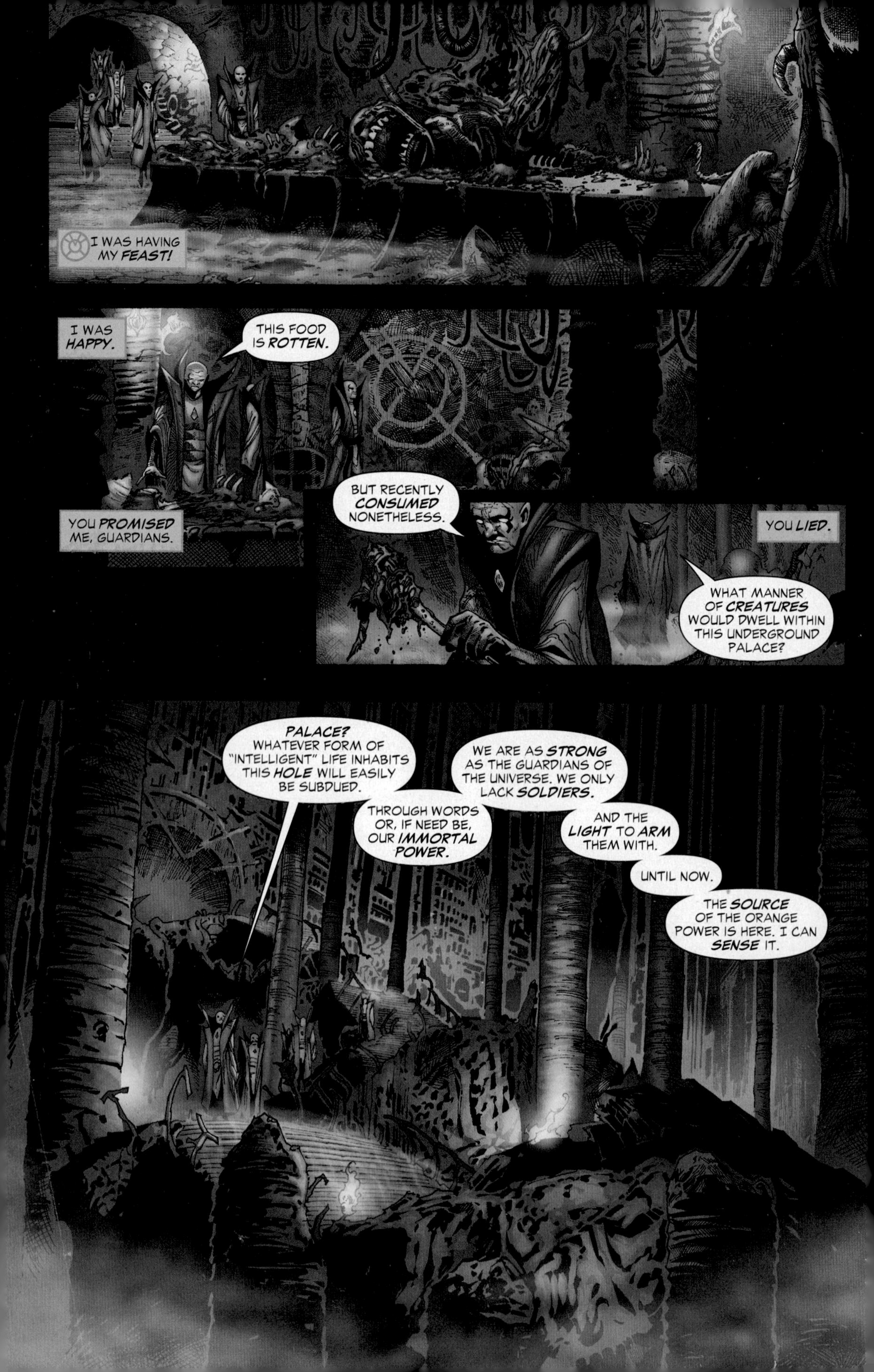

I WAS HAVING MY FEAST!
I WAS HAPPY.
THIS FOOD IS ROTTEN.
YOU PROMISED ME, GUARDIANS.
BUT RECENTLY CONSUMED NONETHELESS.
YOU LIED.
WHAT MANNER OF CREATURES WOULD DWELL WITHIN THIS UNDERGROUND PALACE?
PALACE? WHATEVER FORM OF "INTELLIGENT" LIFE INHABITS THIS HOLE WILL EASILY BE SUBDUED.
THROUGH WORDS OR, IF NEED BE, OUR IMMORTAL POWER.
WE ARE AS STRONG AS THE GUARDIANS OF THE UNIVERSE. WE ONLY LACK SOLDIERS.
AND THE LIGHT TO ARM THEM WITH.
UNTIL NOW.
THE SOURCE OF THE ORANGE POWER IS HERE. I CAN SENSE IT.

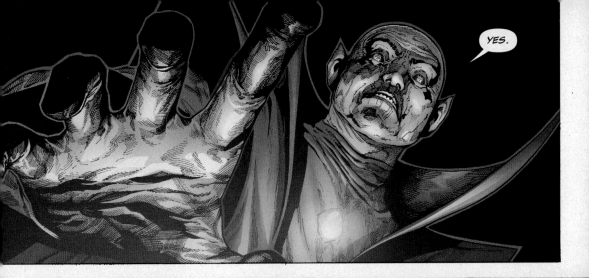

YES.

IT BURNS BRIGHT.

WHATEVER LIGHT IT CONTAINS, IT IS STRONG.

LET US TAKE CONTROL OF IT.

NO!

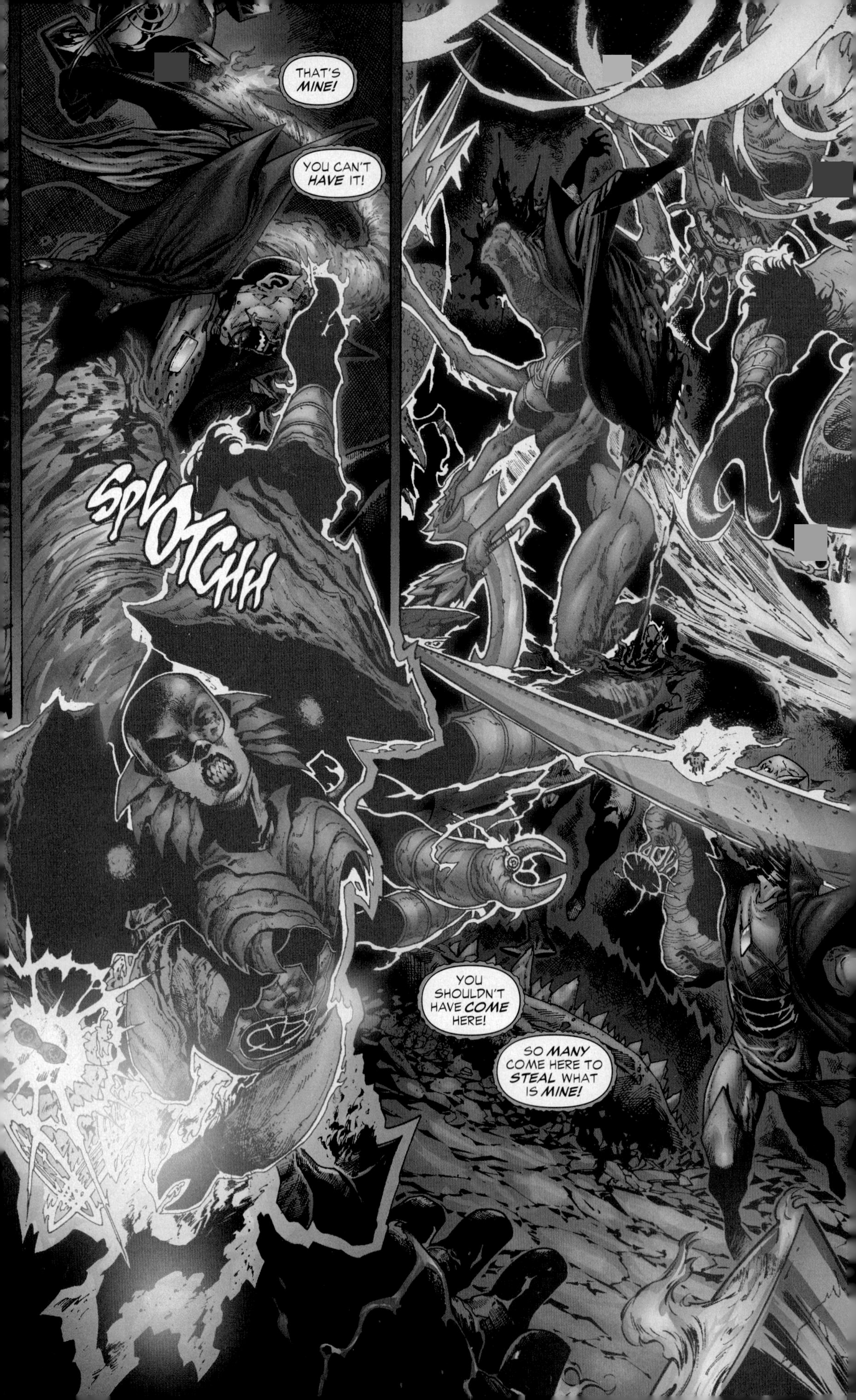
THAT'S MINE!
YOU CAN'T HAVE IT!
SPLOTCHH
YOU SHOULDN'T HAVE COME HERE!
SO MANY COME HERE TO STEAL WHAT IS MINE!

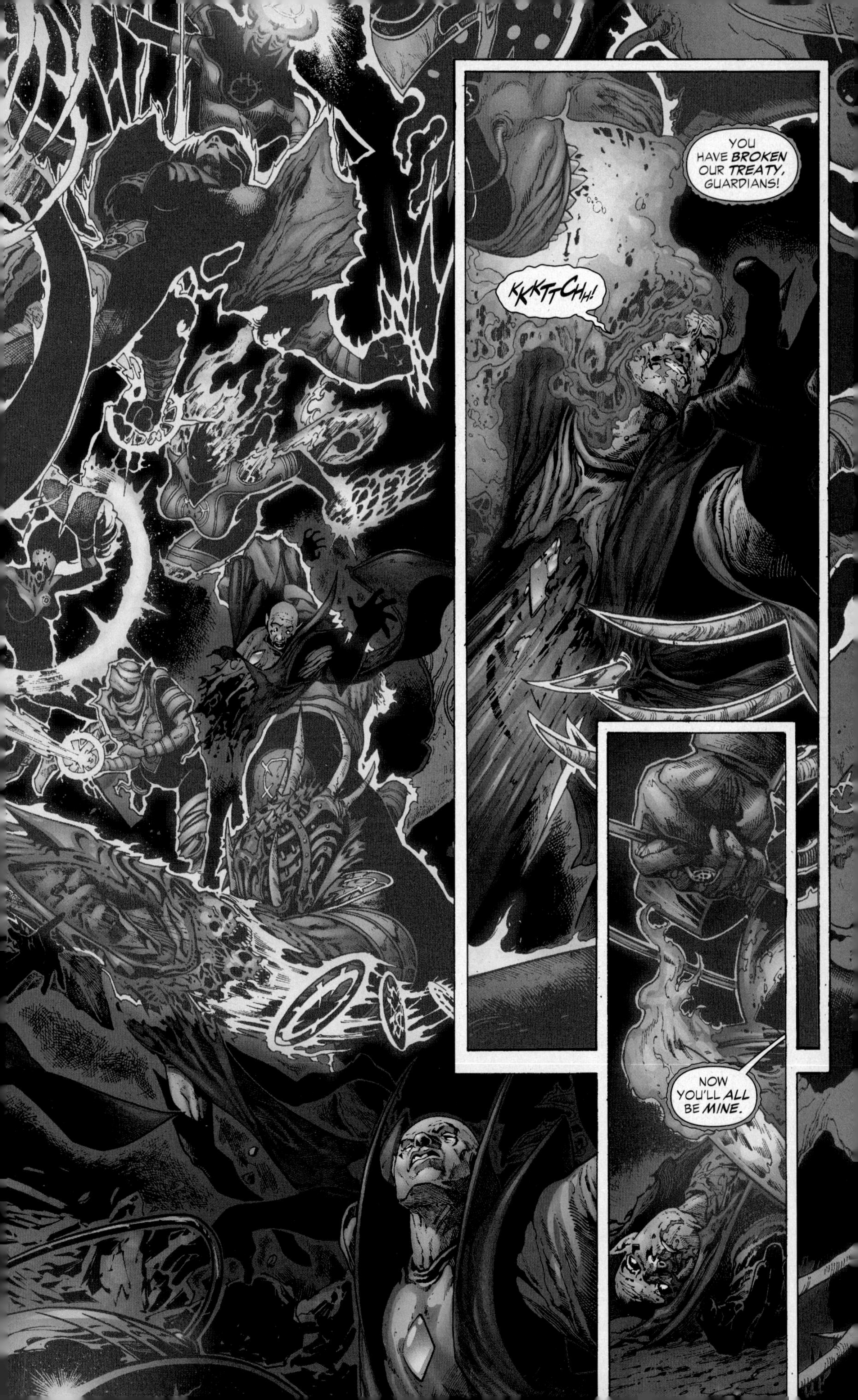

YOU HAVE BROKEN OUR TREATY, GUARDIANS!
KKKTTCHH!
NOW YOU'LL ALL BE MINE.

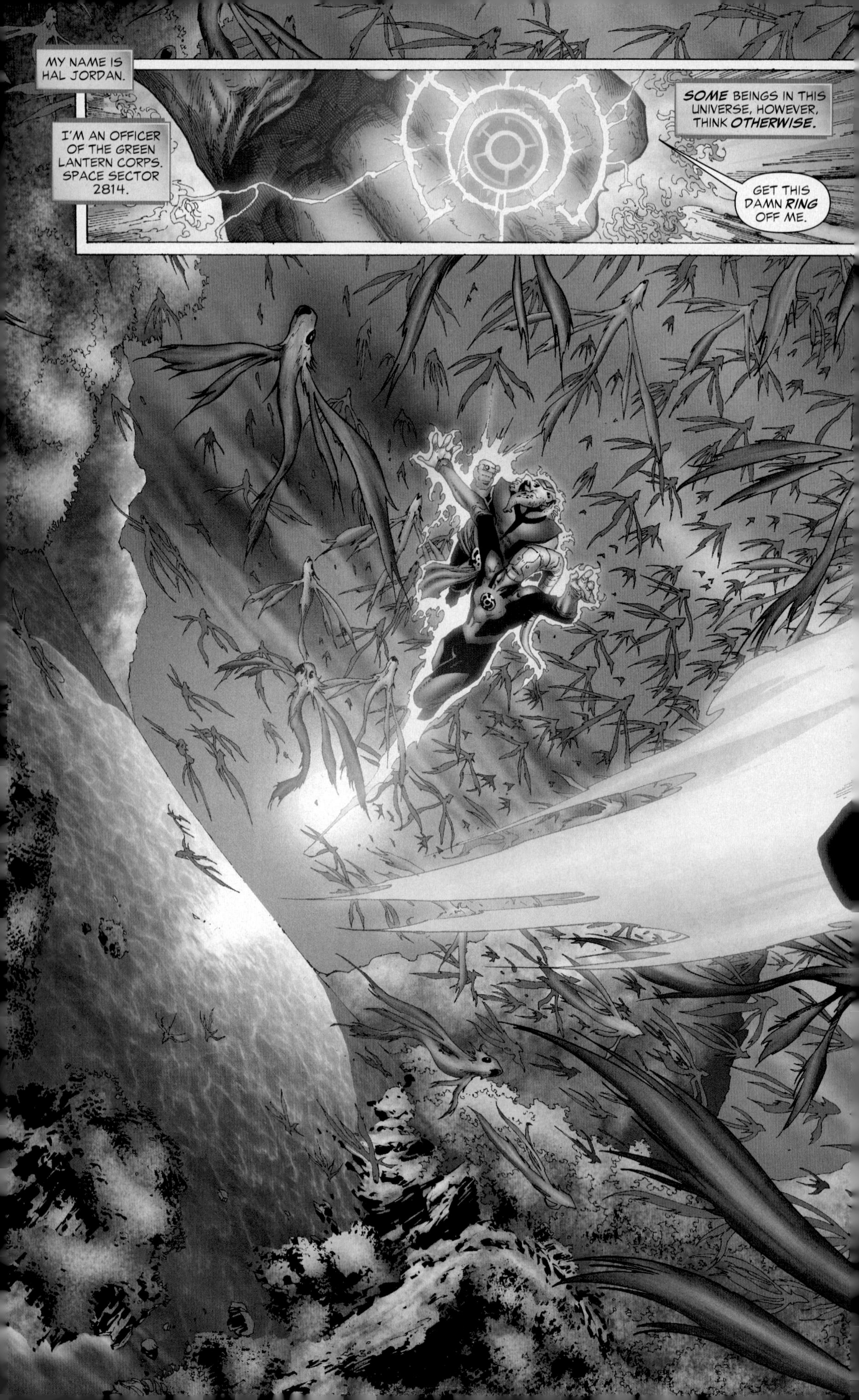
MY NAME IS HAL JORDAN.
I'M AN OFFICER OF THE GREEN LANTERN CORPS. SPACE SECTOR 2814.
SOME BEINGS IN THIS UNIVERSE, HOWEVER, THINK OTHERWISE.
GET THIS DAMN RING OFF ME.

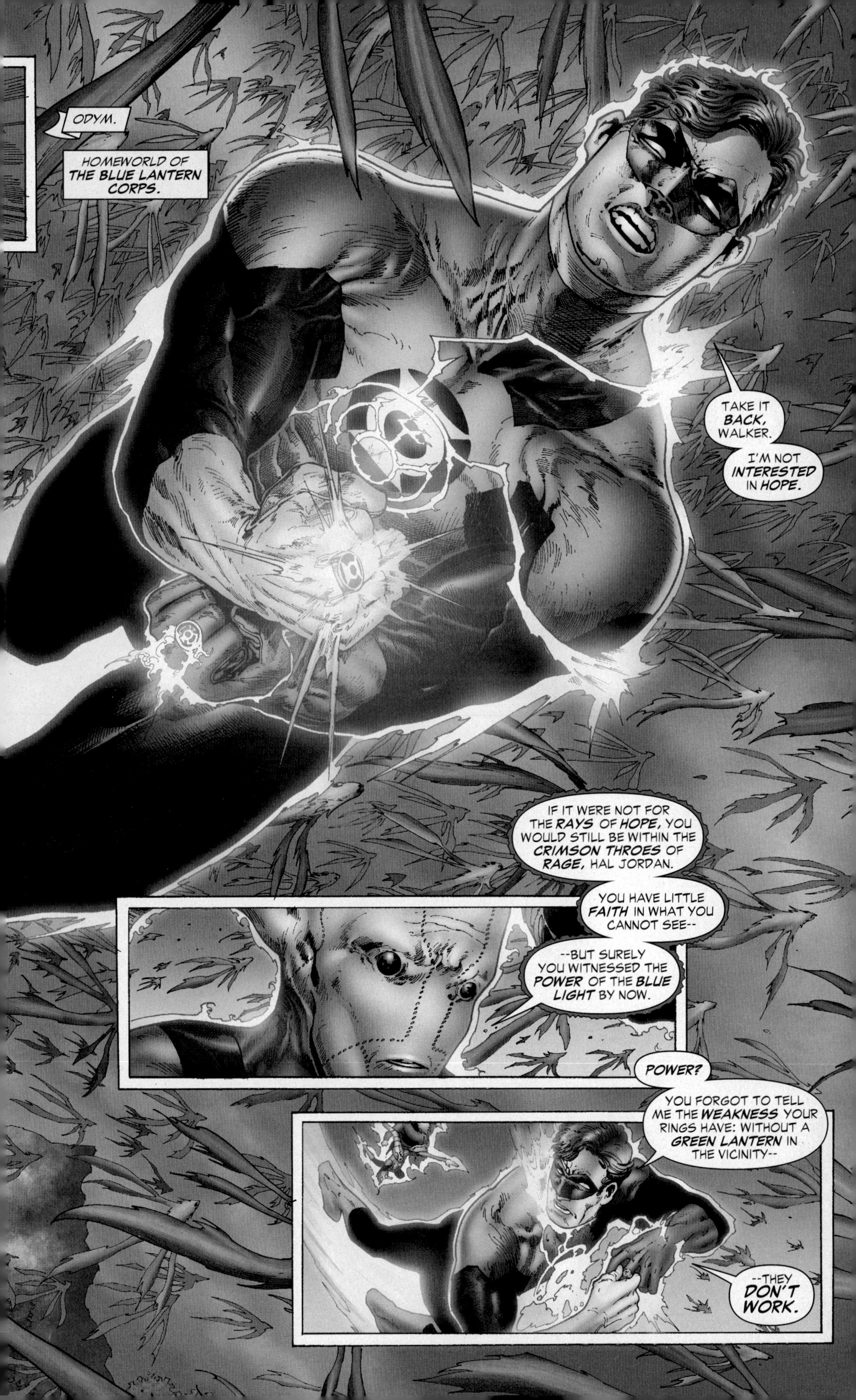
ODYM.
HOMEWORLD OF THE BLUE LANTERN CORPS.
TAKE IT BACK, WALKER.
I'M NOT INTERESTED IN HOPE.
IF IT WERE NOT FOR THE RAYS OF HOPE, YOU WOULD STILL BE WITHIN THE CRIMSON THROES OF RAGE, HAL JORDAN.
YOU HAVE LITTLE FAITH IN WHAT YOU CANNOT SEE--
--BUT SURELY YOU WITNESSED THE POWER OF THE BLUE LIGHT BY NOW.
POWER?
YOU FORGOT TO TELL ME THE WEAKNESS YOUR RINGS HAVE: WITHOUT A GREEN LANTERN IN THE VICINITY--
--THEY DON'T WORK.

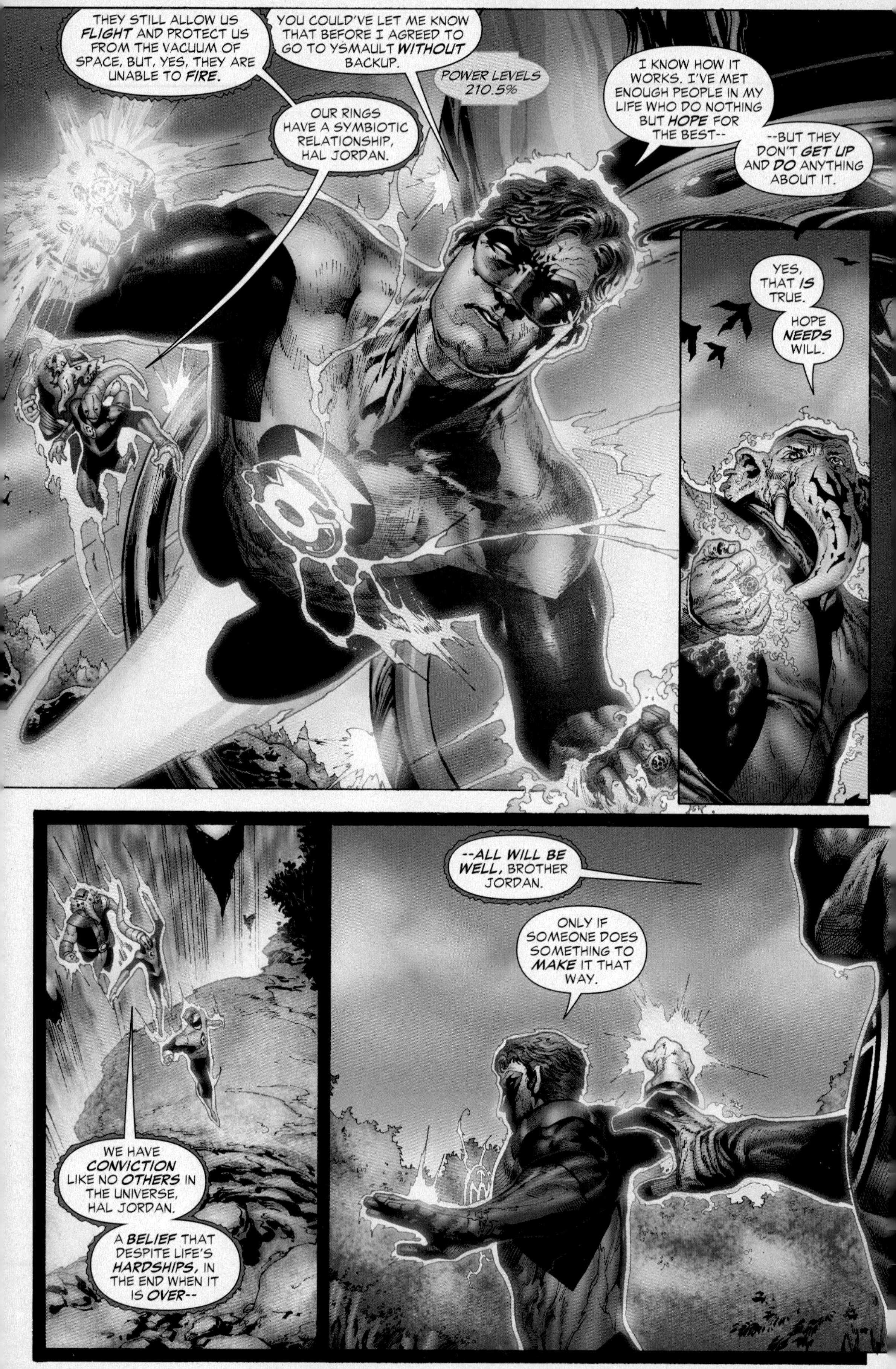
THEY STILL ALLOW US FLIGHT AND PROTECT US FROM THE VACUUM OF SPACE, BUT, YES, THEY ARE UNABLE TO FIRE.
OUR RINGS HAVE A SYMBIOTIC RELATIONSHIP, HAL JORDAN.
YOU COULD'VE LET ME KNOW THAT BEFORE I AGREED TO GO TO YSMAULT WITHOUT BACKUP.
POWER LEVELS 210.5%
I KNOW HOW IT WORKS. I'VE MET ENOUGH PEOPLE IN MY LIFE WHO DO NOTHING BUT HOPE FOR THE BEST--
--BUT THEY DON'T GET UP AND DO ANYTHING ABOUT IT.
YES, THAT IS TRUE.
HOPE NEEDS WILL.
WE HAVE CONVICTION LIKE NO OTHERS IN THE UNIVERSE, HAL JORDAN.
A BELIEF THAT DESPITE LIFE'S HARDSHIPS, IN THE END WHEN IT IS OVER--
--ALL WILL BE WELL, BROTHER JORDAN.
ONLY IF SOMEONE DOES SOMETHING TO MAKE IT THAT WAY.

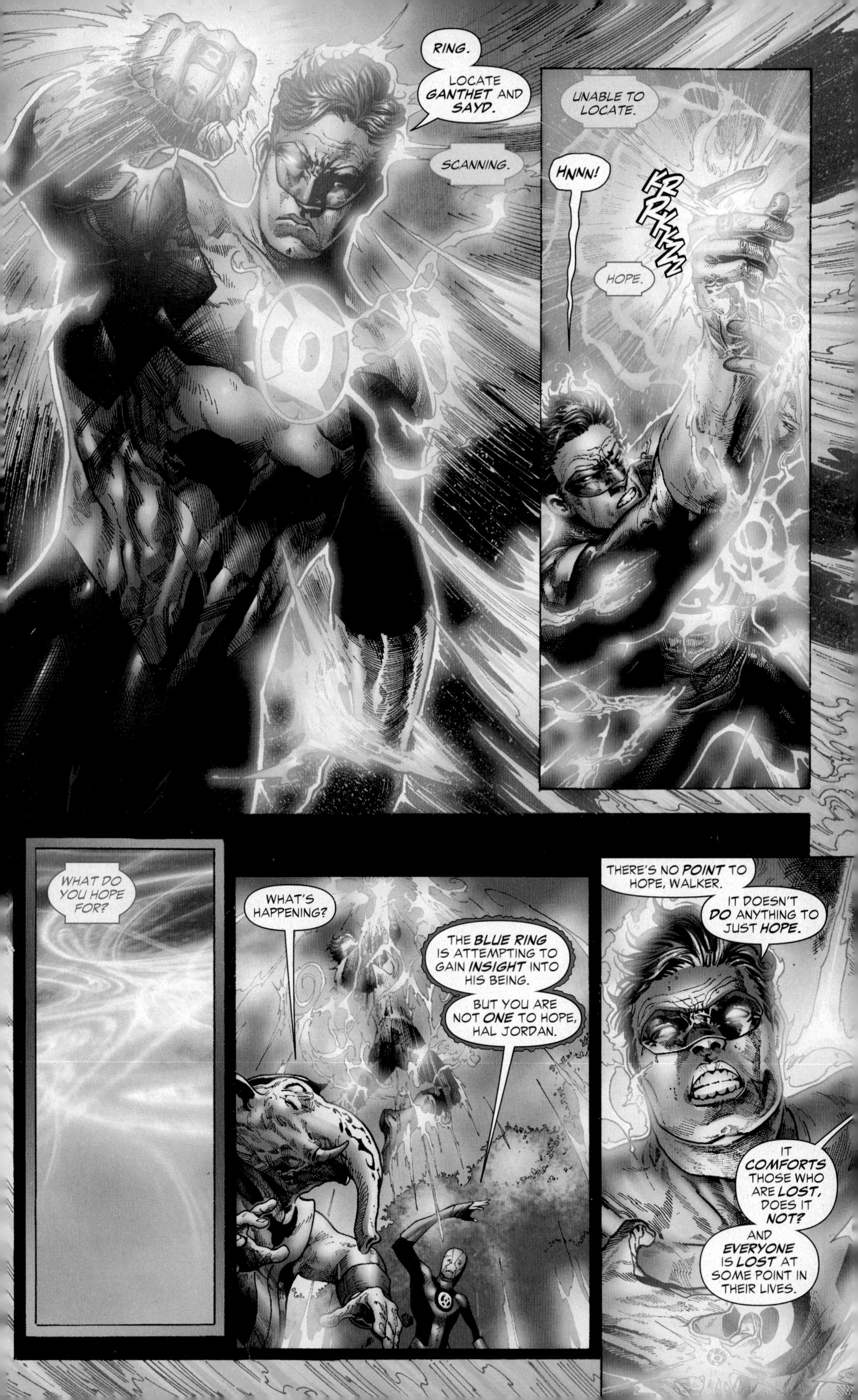
RING.
LOCATE GANTHET AND SAYD.
SCANNING.
UNABLE TO LOCATE.
HNNN!
KRRKKW
HOPE.
WHAT DO YOU HOPE FOR?
WHAT'S HAPPENING?
THE BLUE RING IS ATTEMPTING TO GAIN INSIGHT INTO HIS BEING.
BUT YOU ARE NOT ONE TO HOPE, HAL JORDAN.
THERE'S NO POINT TO HOPE, WALKER.
IT DOESN'T DO ANYTHING TO JUST HOPE.
IT COMFORTS THOSE WHO ARE LOST, DOES IT NOT?
AND EVERYONE IS LOST AT SOME POINT IN THEIR LIVES.

GANTHET, YOU'VE DONE MORE FOR ME THAN I CAN *EVER* REPAY, BUT I'M NOT GOING TO TURN MY BACK ON THE GREEN LANTERN CORPS.

YOU KNOW THAT AS MUCH AS *ANYONE*, HAL JORDAN.

WE DO NOT *EXPECT* YOU TO.

BUT, SAYD, YOU TOLD US HE WAS TO *LEAD* THE BLUE LANTERN CORPS.

AS A *GREEN LANTERN*, SAINT WALKER, NOT AS ONE OF YOU. *HIS* WILL CAN POWER OUR *ENTIRE* CORPS.

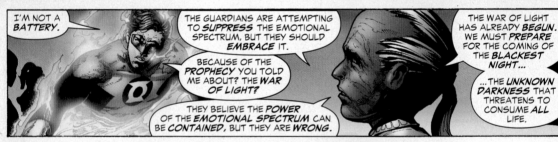

I'M NOT A *BATTERY*.

THE GUARDIANS ARE ATTEMPTING TO *SUPPRESS* THE EMOTIONAL SPECTRUM, BUT THEY SHOULD *EMBRACE* IT.

BECAUSE OF THE *PROPHECY* YOU TOLD ME ABOUT? THE *WAR OF LIGHT*?

THEY BELIEVE THE *POWER* OF THE *EMOTIONAL SPECTRUM* CAN BE *CONTAINED*, BUT THEY ARE *WRONG*.

THE WAR OF LIGHT HAS ALREADY *BEGUN*. WE MUST *PREPARE* FOR THE COMING OF THE *BLACKEST NIGHT*...

...THE *UNKNOWN DARKNESS* THAT THREATENS TO CONSUME *ALL* LIFE.

WE WILL HAVE TO PROVIDE YOU WITH A *NEW* RING, SAINT WALKER. WE ARE *UNABLE* TO REMOVE YOURS FROM THE GREEN LANTERN.

UNABLE? I'VE GOT *BLUE LIGHT* FLICKERING IN MY EYES. THE RING KEEPS SENDING *JOLTS* UP AND DOWN MY ARM.

I WANT IT *OFF*!

THEN YOU NEED TO *USE* IT.

YOU NEED TO FIND SOMETHING TO *HOPE* FOR, YOU NEED TO *SEE* IT IN YOUR *HEART* AND YOU NEED TO *UNLEASH* THE POWER OF THE RING.

ONLY WHEN IT IS *DRAINED* CAN IT BE REMOVED AND *PASSED ON* TO ONE WHO HAS *FAITH* IN THE *BRIGHTEST DAY*.

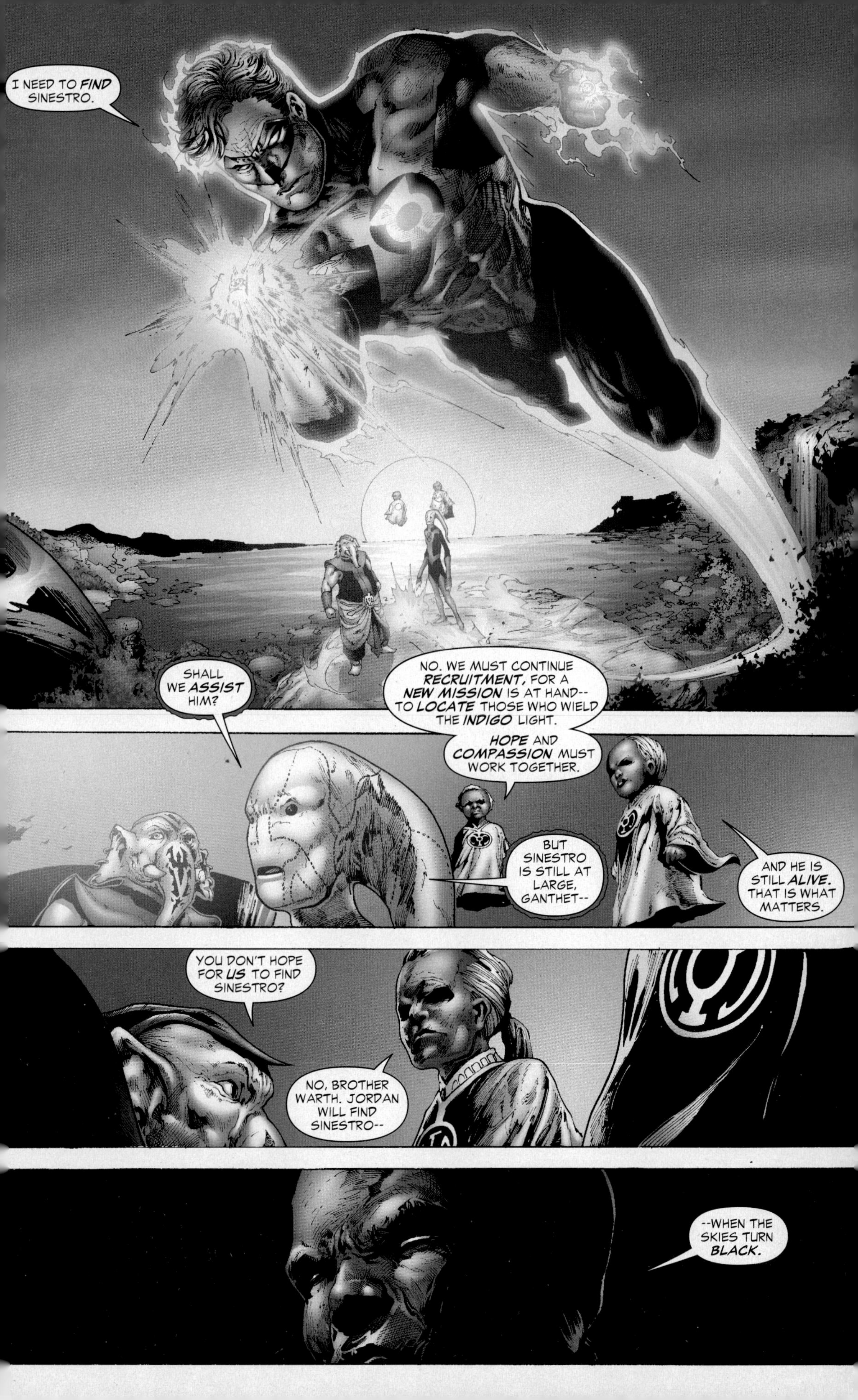
I NEED TO FIND SINESTRO.
SHALL WE ASSIST HIM?
NO. WE MUST CONTINUE RECRUITMENT, FOR A NEW MISSION IS AT HAND-- TO LOCATE THOSE WHO WIELD THE INDIGO LIGHT.
HOPE AND COMPASSION MUST WORK TOGETHER.
BUT SINESTRO IS STILL AT LARGE, GANTHET--
AND HE IS STILL ALIVE. THAT IS WHAT MATTERS.
YOU DON'T HOPE FOR US TO FIND SINESTRO?
NO, BROTHER WARTH. JORDAN WILL FIND SINESTRO--
--WHEN THE SKIES TURN BLACK.

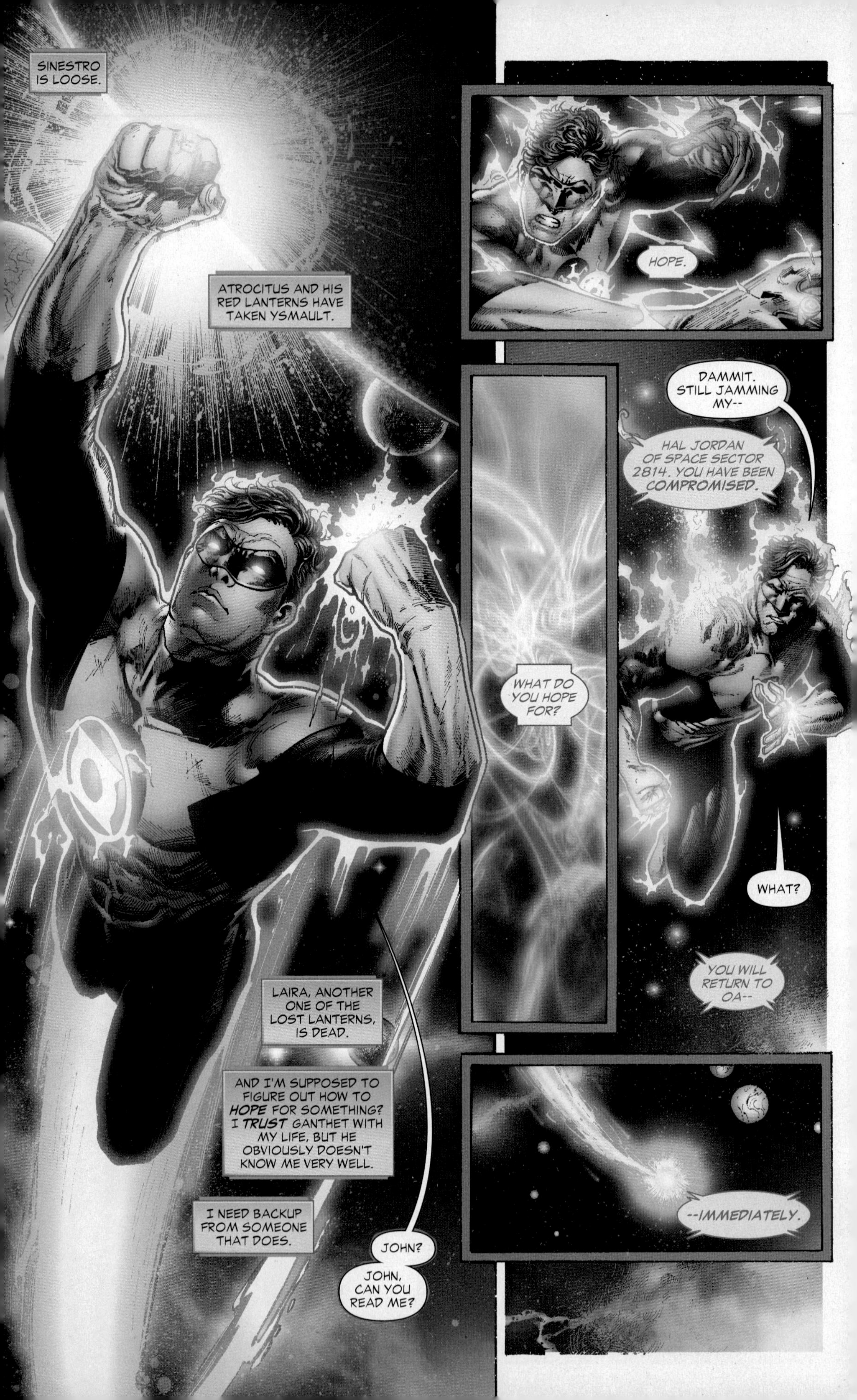
SINESTRO IS LOOSE.
ATROCITUS AND HIS RED LANTERNS HAVE TAKEN YSMAULT.
LAIRA, ANOTHER ONE OF THE LOST LANTERNS, IS DEAD.
AND I'M SUPPOSED TO FIGURE OUT HOW TO HOPE FOR SOMETHING? I TRUST GANTHET WITH MY LIFE, BUT HE OBVIOUSLY DOESN'T KNOW ME VERY WELL.
I NEED BACKUP FROM SOMEONE THAT DOES.
JOHN?
JOHN, CAN YOU READ ME?
HOPE.
WHAT DO YOU HOPE FOR?
DAMMIT. STILL JAMMING MY--
HAL JORDAN OF SPACE SECTOR 2814. YOU HAVE BEEN COMPROMISED.
WHAT?
YOU WILL RETURN TO OA--
--IMMEDIATELY.

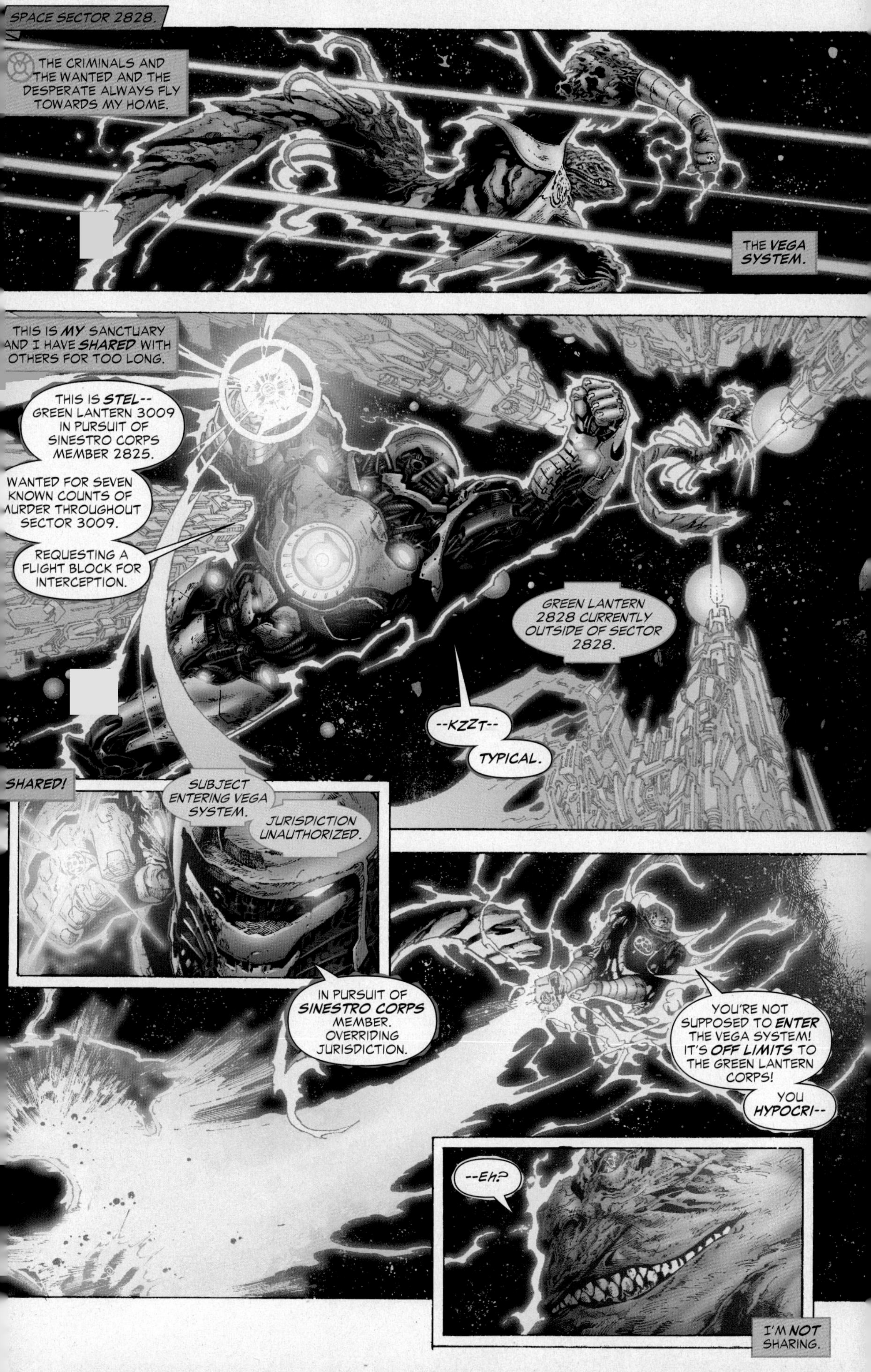
SPACE SECTOR 2828.
THE CRIMINALS AND THE WANTED AND THE DESPERATE ALWAYS FLY TOWARDS MY HOME.
THE VEGA SYSTEM.
THIS IS MY SANCTUARY AND I HAVE SHARED WITH OTHERS FOR TOO LONG.
THIS IS STEL-- GREEN LANTERN 3009 IN PURSUIT OF SINESTRO CORPS MEMBER 2825.
WANTED FOR SEVEN KNOWN COUNTS OF MURDER THROUGHOUT SECTOR 3009.
REQUESTING A FLIGHT BLOCK FOR INTERCEPTION.
GREEN LANTERN 2828 CURRENTLY OUTSIDE OF SECTOR 2828.
--KZZT--
TYPICAL.
SHARED!
SUBJECT ENTERING VEGA SYSTEM.
JURISDICTION UNAUTHORIZED.
IN PURSUIT OF SINESTRO CORPS MEMBER. OVERRIDING JURISDICTION.
YOU'RE NOT SUPPOSED TO ENTER THE VEGA SYSTEM! IT'S OFF LIMITS TO THE GREEN LANTERN CORPS!
YOU HYPOCRI--
--Eh?
I'M NOT SHARING.

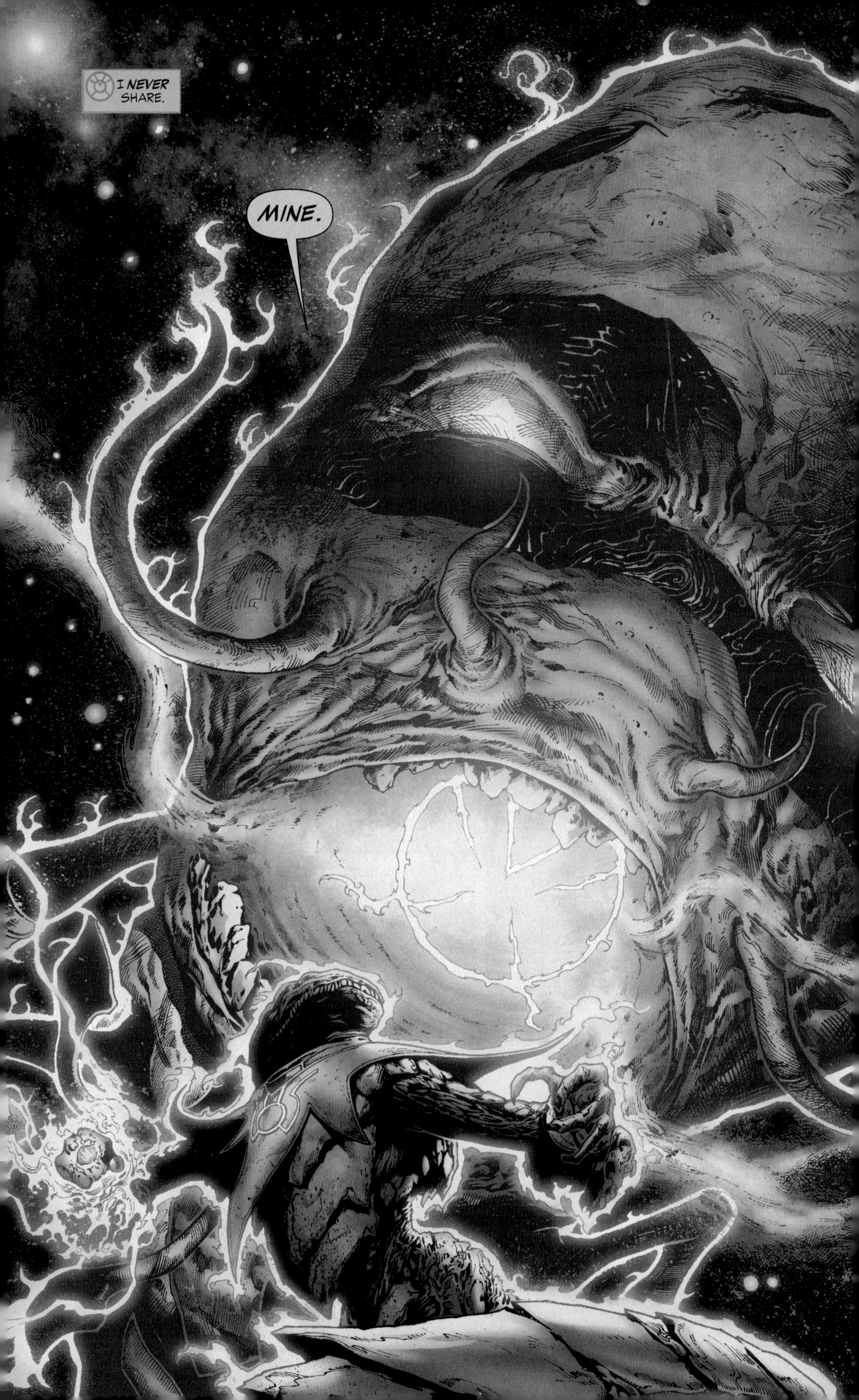
I NEVER SHARE.
MINE.

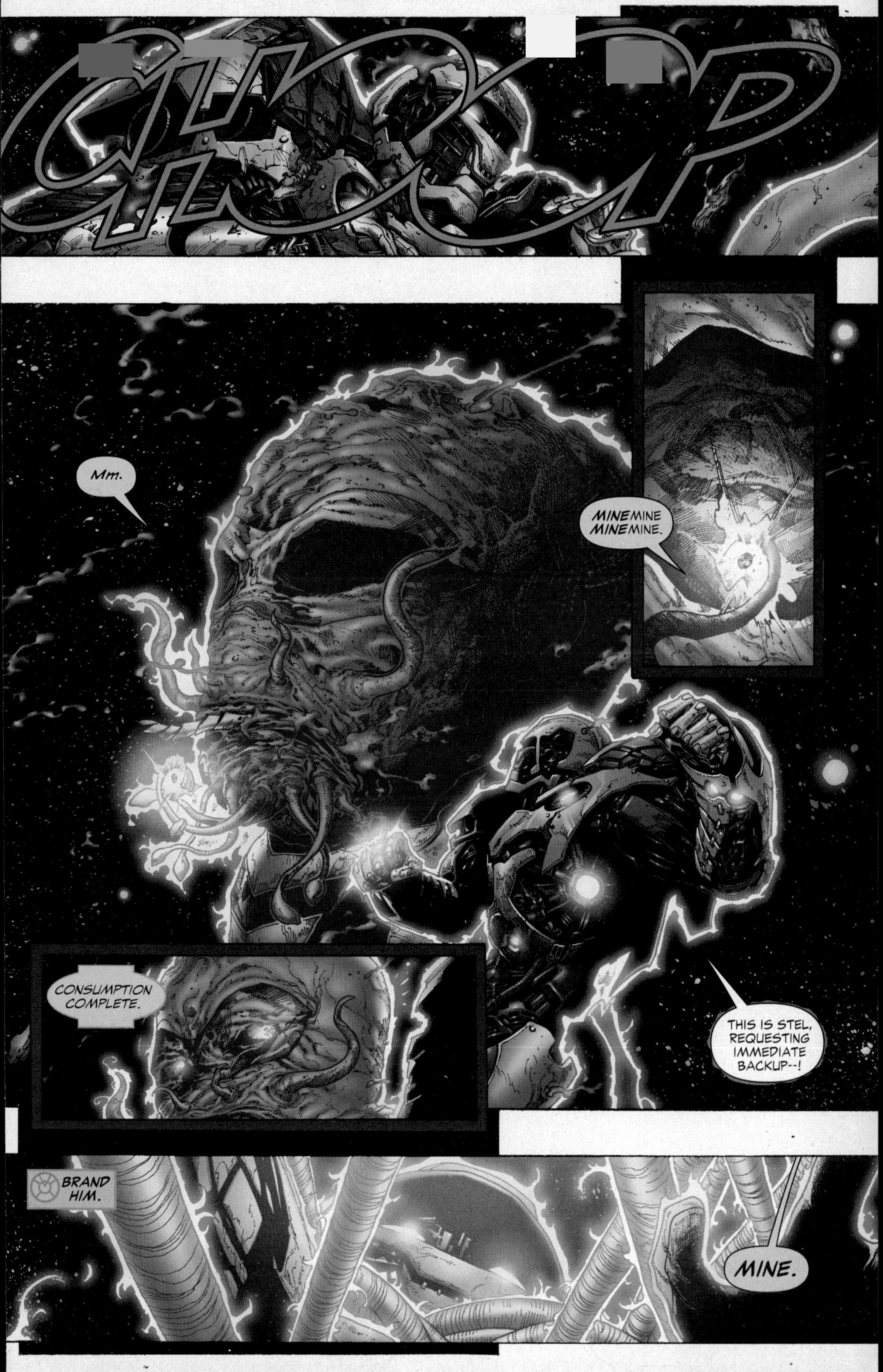
Mm.
MINEMINE MINEMINE.
CONSUMPTION COMPLETE.
THIS IS STEL, REQUESTING IMMEDIATE BACKUP--!
BRAND HIM.
MINE.

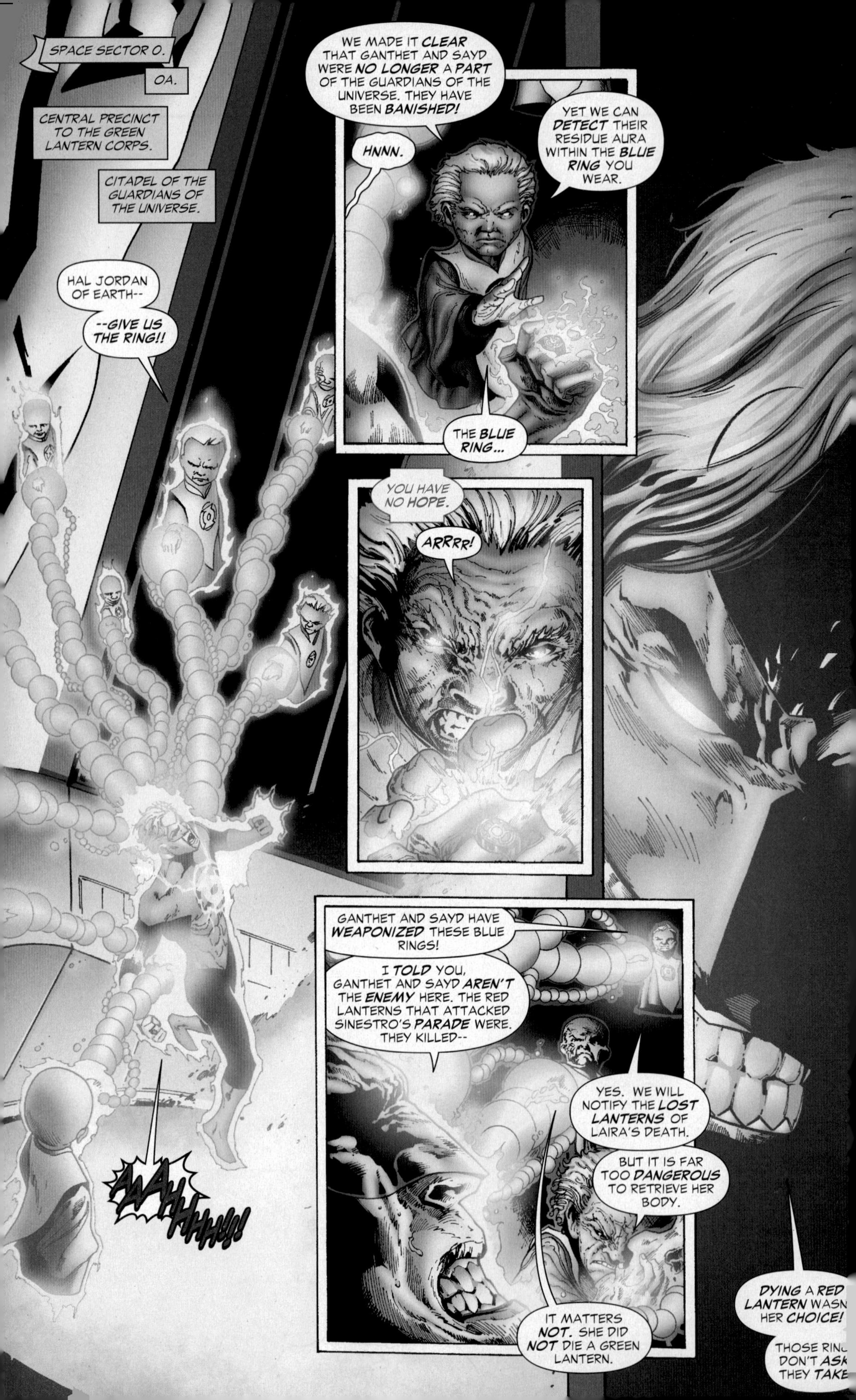
SPACE SECTOR 0.
OA.
CENTRAL PRECINCT TO THE GREEN LANTERN CORPS.
CITADEL OF THE GUARDIANS OF THE UNIVERSE.
HAL JORDAN OF EARTH--
--GIVE US THE RING!!
AAAHHHHH!!
WE MADE IT CLEAR THAT GANTHET AND SAYD WERE NO LONGER A PART OF THE GUARDIANS OF THE UNIVERSE. THEY HAVE BEEN BANISHED!
HNNN.
YET WE CAN DETECT THEIR RESIDUE AURA WITHIN THE BLUE RING YOU WEAR.
THE BLUE RING...
YOU HAVE NO HOPE.
ARRRR!
GANTHET AND SAYD HAVE WEAPONIZED THESE BLUE RINGS!
I TOLD YOU, GANTHET AND SAYD AREN'T THE ENEMY HERE. THE RED LANTERNS THAT ATTACKED SINESTRO'S PARADE WERE. THEY KILLED--
YES. WE WILL NOTIFY THE LOST LANTERNS OF LAIRA'S DEATH.
BUT IT IS FAR TOO DANGEROUS TO RETRIEVE HER BODY.
IT MATTERS NOT. SHE DID NOT DIE A GREEN LANTERN.
DYING A RED LANTERN WASN
HER CHOICE!
THOSE RIN
DON'T ASK
THEY TAKE

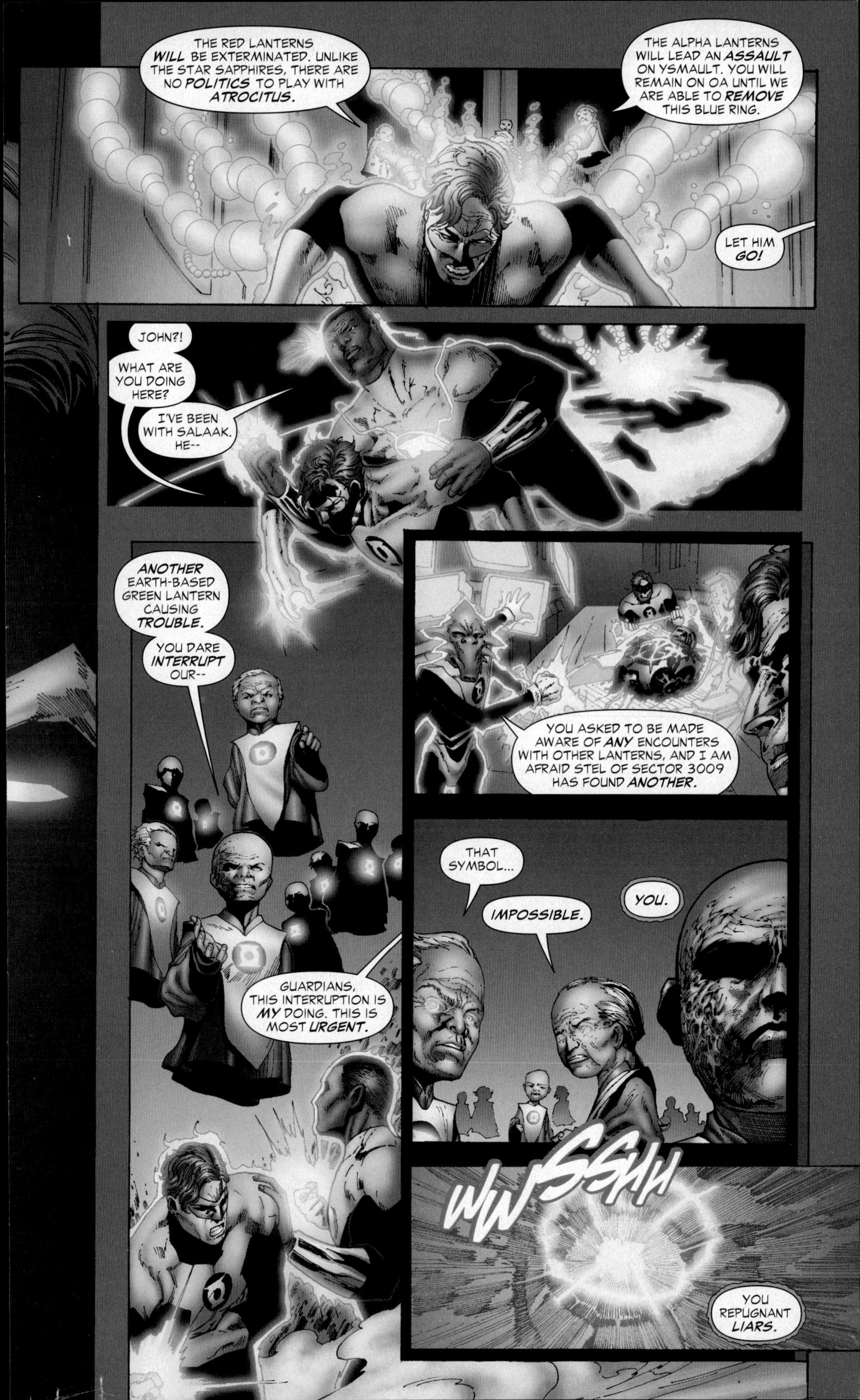
THE RED LANTERNS WILL BE EXTERMINATED. UNLIKE THE STAR SAPPHIRES, THERE ARE NO POLITICS TO PLAY WITH ATROCITUS.
THE ALPHA LANTERNS WILL LEAD AN ASSAULT ON YSMAULT. YOU WILL REMAIN ON OA UNTIL WE ARE ABLE TO REMOVE THIS BLUE RING.
LET HIM GO!
JOHN?!
WHAT ARE YOU DOING HERE?
I'VE BEEN WITH SALAAK. HE--
ANOTHER EARTH-BASED GREEN LANTERN CAUSING TROUBLE.
YOU DARE INTERRUPT OUR--
GUARDIANS, THIS INTERRUPTION IS MY DOING. THIS IS MOST URGENT.
YOU ASKED TO BE MADE AWARE OF ANY ENCOUNTERS WITH OTHER LANTERNS, AND I AM AFRAID STEL OF SECTOR 3009 HAS FOUND ANOTHER.
THAT SYMBOL...
IMPOSSIBLE.
YOU.
WWSSHH
YOU REPUGNANT LIARS.

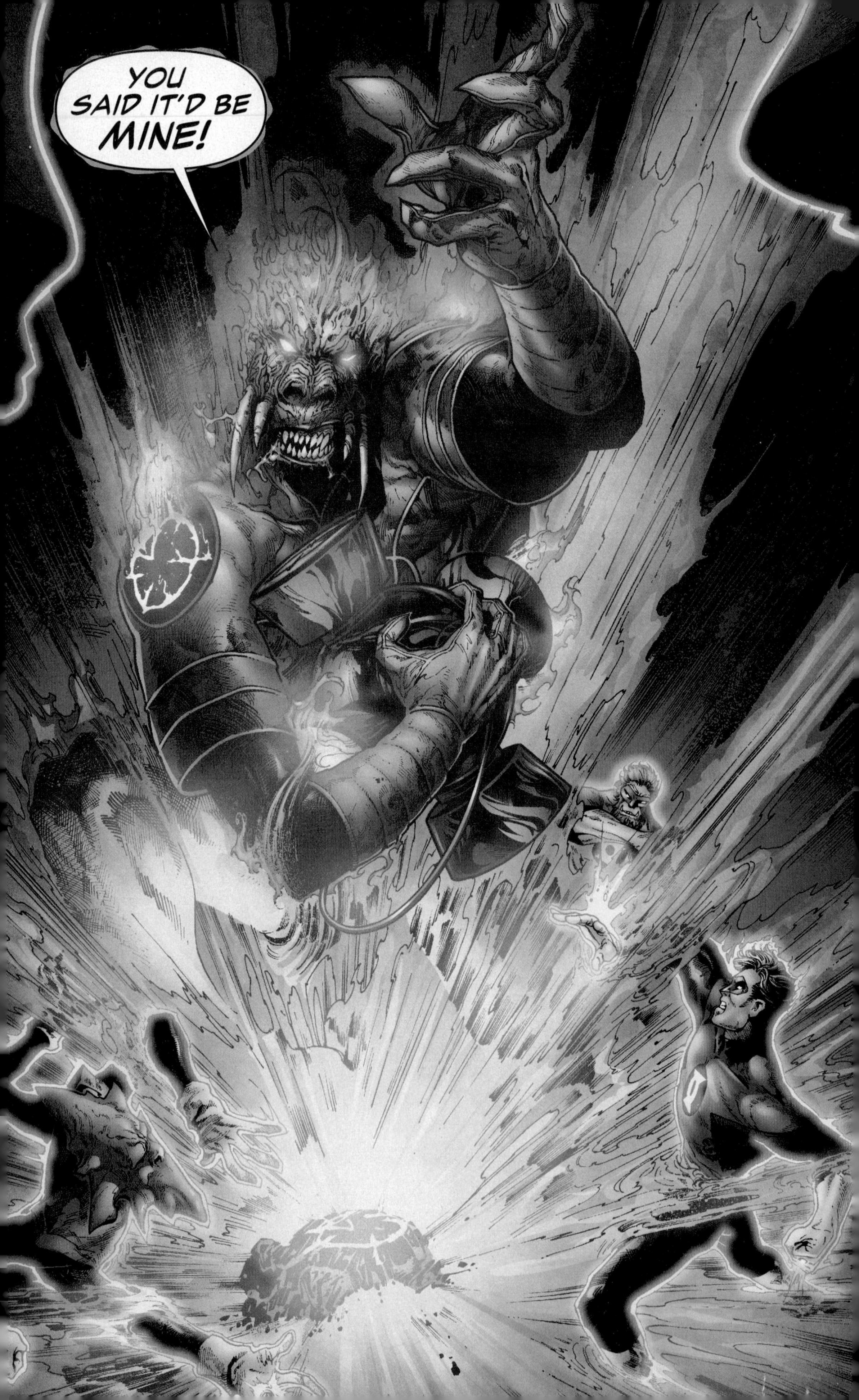
YOU SAID IT'D BE MINE!

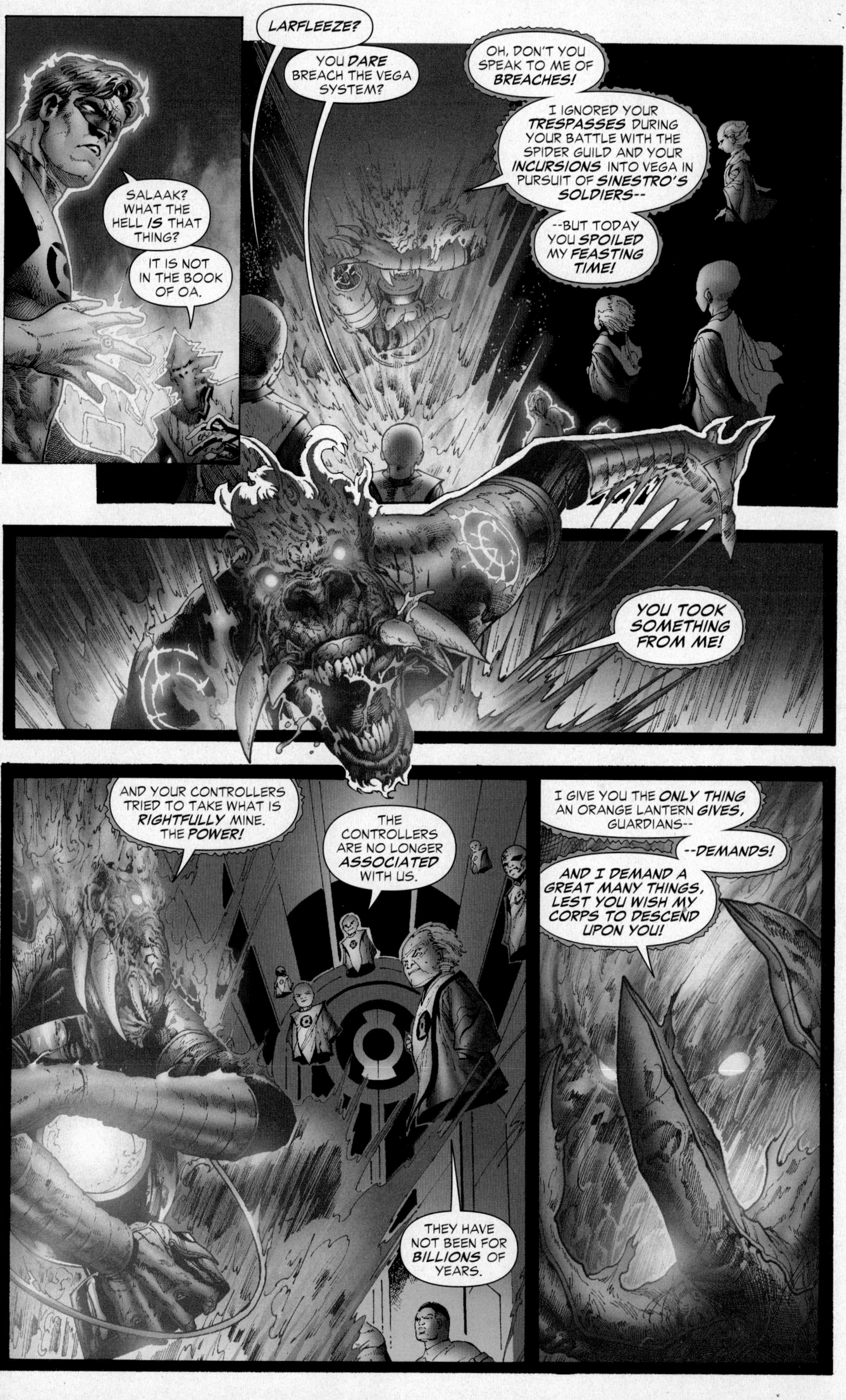
LARFLEEZE?
YOU DARE BREACH THE VEGA SYSTEM?
SALAAK? WHAT THE HELL IS THAT THING?
IT IS NOT IN THE BOOK OF OA.
OH, DON'T YOU SPEAK TO ME OF BREACHES!
I IGNORED YOUR TRESPASSES DURING YOUR BATTLE WITH THE SPIDER GUILD AND YOUR INCURSIONS INTO VEGA IN PURSUIT OF SINESTRO'S SOLDIERS--
--BUT TODAY YOU SPOILED MY FEASTING TIME!
YOU TOOK SOMETHING FROM ME!
AND YOUR CONTROLLERS TRIED TO TAKE WHAT IS RIGHTFULLY MINE. THE POWER!
THE CONTROLLERS ARE NO LONGER ASSOCIATED WITH US.
THEY HAVE NOT BEEN FOR BILLIONS OF YEARS.
I GIVE YOU THE ONLY THING AN ORANGE LANTERN GIVES, GUARDIANS--
--DEMANDS!
AND I DEMAND A GREAT MANY THINGS, LEST YOU WISH MY CORPS TO DESCEND UPON YOU!

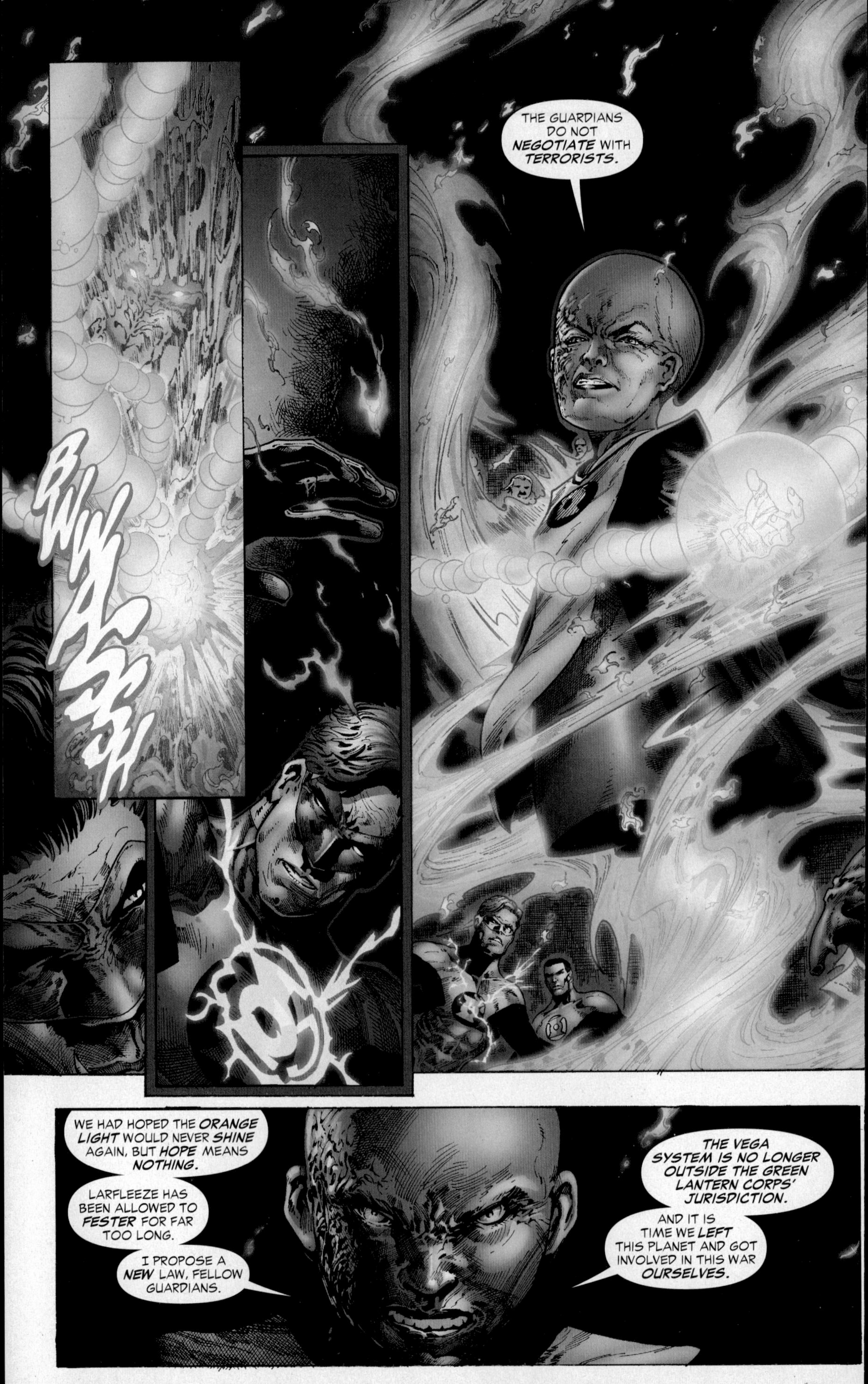
BWAAASCH
THE GUARDIANS DO NOT NEGOTIATE WITH TERRORISTS.
WE HAD HOPED THE ORANGE LIGHT WOULD NEVER SHINE AGAIN, BUT HOPE MEANS NOTHING.
LARFLEEZE HAS BEEN ALLOWED TO FESTER FOR FAR TOO LONG.
I PROPOSE A NEW LAW, FELLOW GUARDIANS.
THE VEGA SYSTEM IS NO LONGER OUTSIDE THE GREEN LANTERN CORPS' JURISDICTION.
AND IT IS TIME WE LEFT THIS PLANET AND GOT INVOLVED IN THIS WAR OURSELVES.

GREEN LANTERN 40 Cover by Philip Tan, Jonathan Glapion and Nei Ruffino

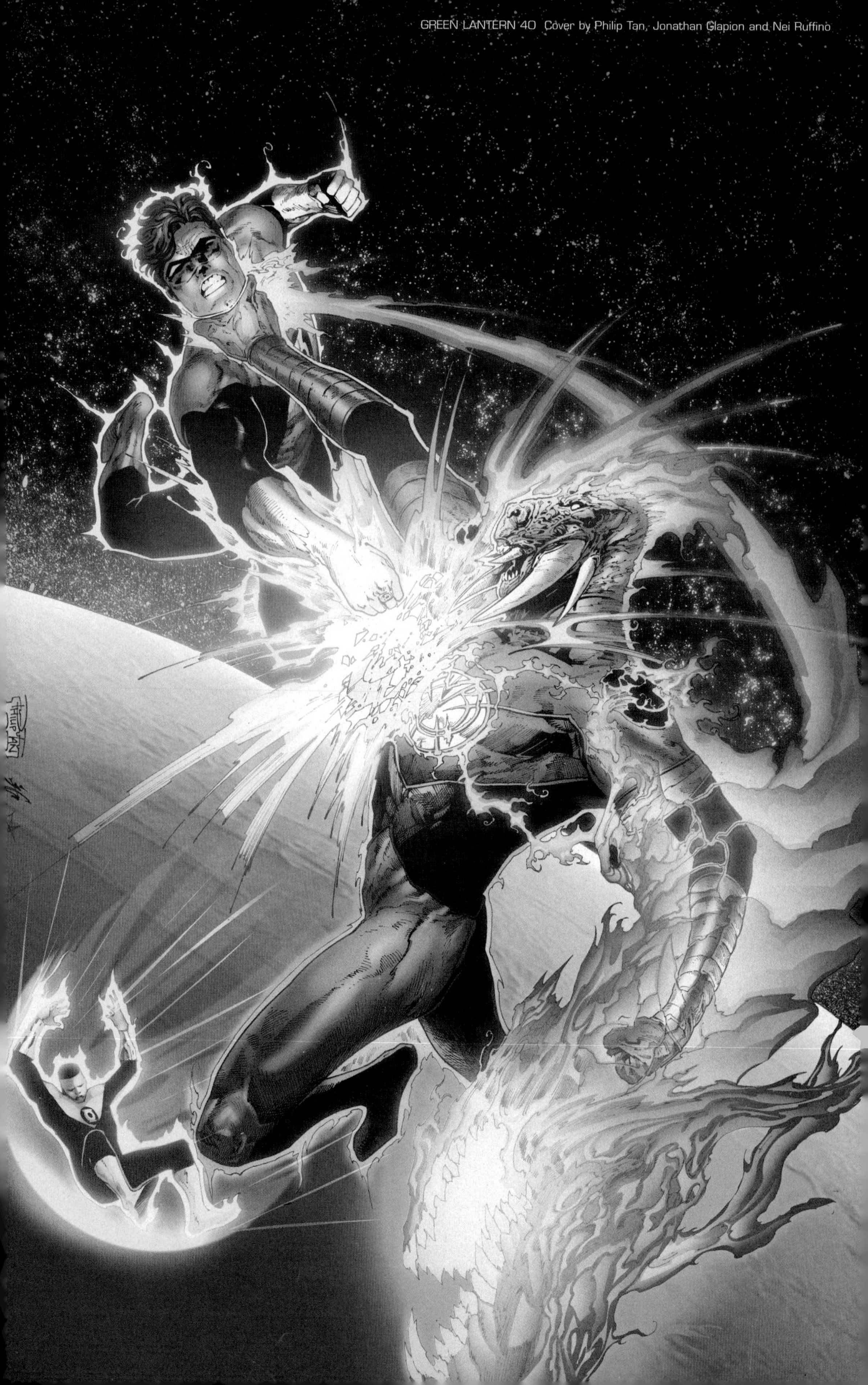

AGENT ORANGE
Part 2

Philip Tan Pencils
Jonathan Glapion Inks

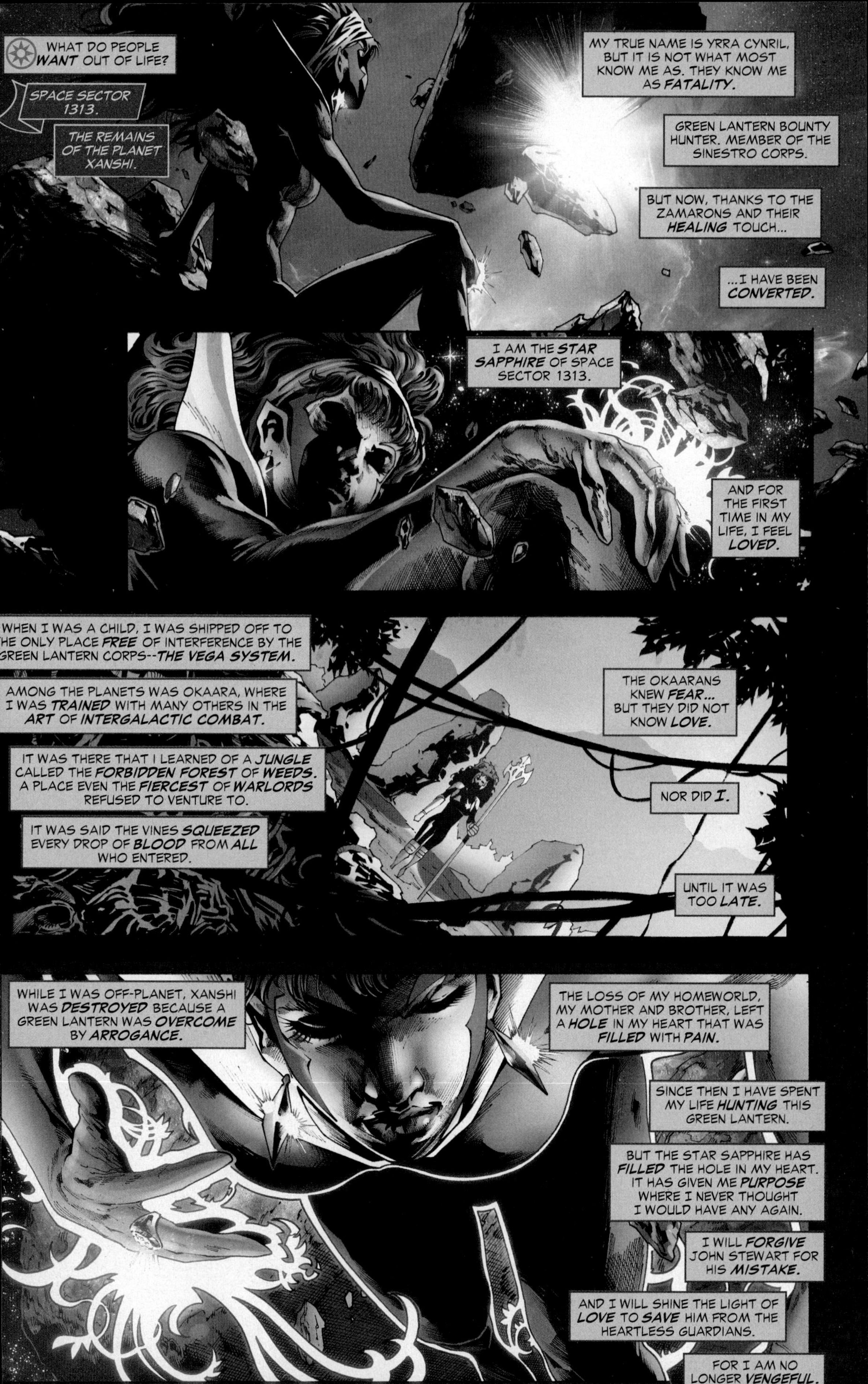
WHAT DO PEOPLE WANT OUT OF LIFE?
SPACE SECTOR 1313.
THE REMAINS OF THE PLANET XANSHI.
MY TRUE NAME IS YRRA CYNRIL, BUT IT IS NOT WHAT MOST KNOW ME AS. THEY KNOW ME AS FATALITY.
GREEN LANTERN BOUNTY HUNTER. MEMBER OF THE SINESTRO CORPS.
BUT NOW, THANKS TO THE ZAMARONS AND THEIR HEALING TOUCH...
...I HAVE BEEN CONVERTED.
I AM THE STAR SAPPHIRE OF SPACE SECTOR 1313.
AND FOR THE FIRST TIME IN MY LIFE, I FEEL LOVED.
WHEN I WAS A CHILD, I WAS SHIPPED OFF TO THE ONLY PLACE FREE OF INTERFERENCE BY THE GREEN LANTERN CORPS--THE VEGA SYSTEM.
AMONG THE PLANETS WAS OKAARA, WHERE I WAS TRAINED WITH MANY OTHERS IN THE ART OF INTERGALACTIC COMBAT.
IT WAS THERE THAT I LEARNED OF A JUNGLE CALLED THE FORBIDDEN FOREST OF WEEDS. A PLACE EVEN THE FIERCEST OF WARLORDS REFUSED TO VENTURE TO.
IT WAS SAID THE VINES SQUEEZED EVERY DROP OF BLOOD FROM ALL WHO ENTERED.
THE OKAARANS KNEW FEAR... BUT THEY DID NOT KNOW LOVE.
NOR DID I.
UNTIL IT WAS TOO LATE.
WHILE I WAS OFF-PLANET, XANSHI WAS DESTROYED BECAUSE A GREEN LANTERN WAS OVERCOME BY ARROGANCE.
THE LOSS OF MY HOMEWORLD, MY MOTHER AND BROTHER, LEFT A HOLE IN MY HEART THAT WAS FILLED WITH PAIN.
SINCE THEN I HAVE SPENT MY LIFE HUNTING THIS GREEN LANTERN.
BUT THE STAR SAPPHIRE HAS FILLED THE HOLE IN MY HEART. IT HAS GIVEN ME PURPOSE WHERE I NEVER THOUGHT I WOULD HAVE ANY AGAIN.
I WILL FORGIVE JOHN STEWART FOR HIS MISTAKE.
AND I WILL SHINE THE LIGHT OF LOVE TO SAVE HIM FROM THE HEARTLESS GUARDIANS.
FOR I AM NO LONGER VENGEFUL.

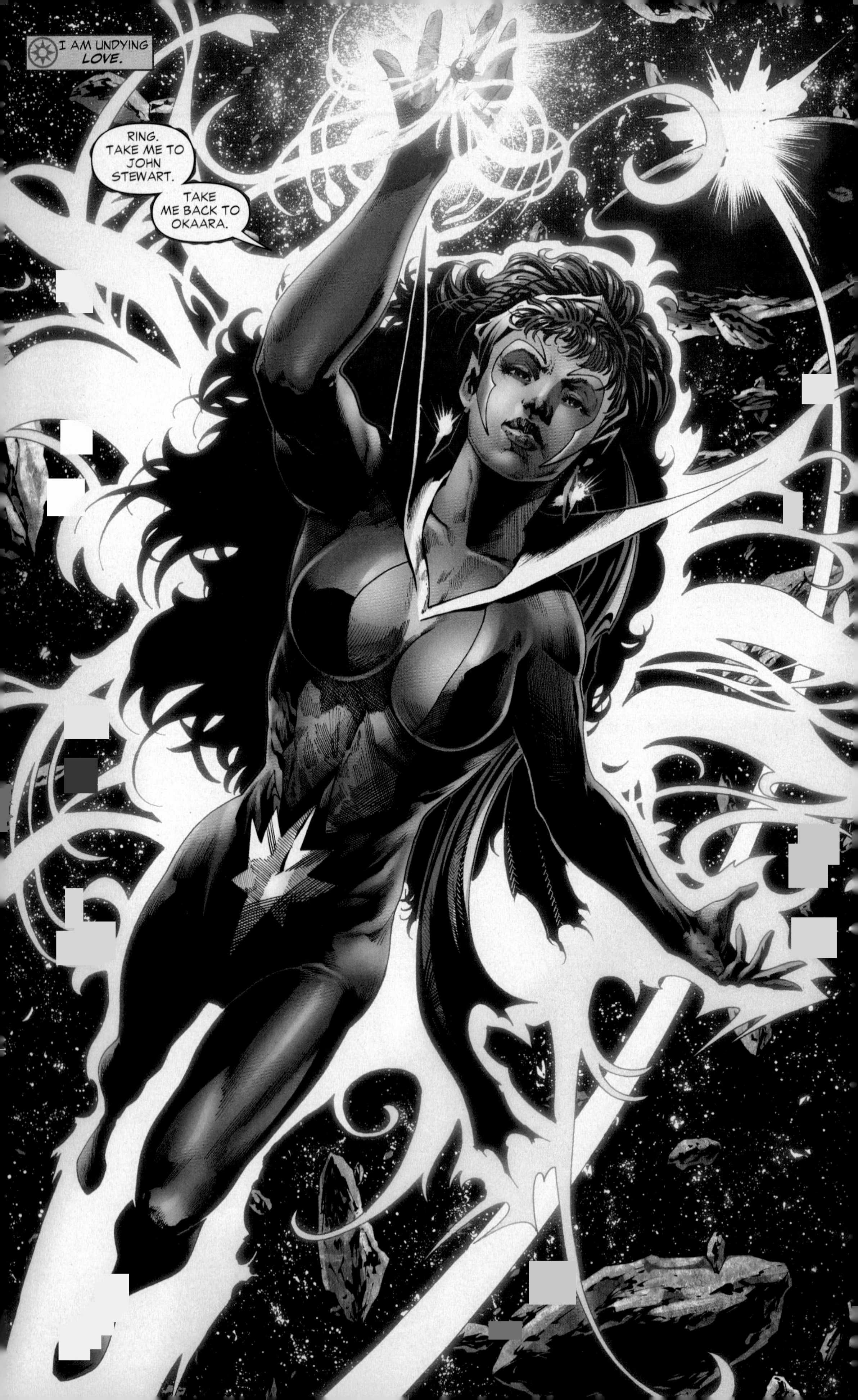
I AM UNDYING LOVE.
RING. TAKE ME TO JOHN STEWART.
TAKE ME BACK TO OKAARA.

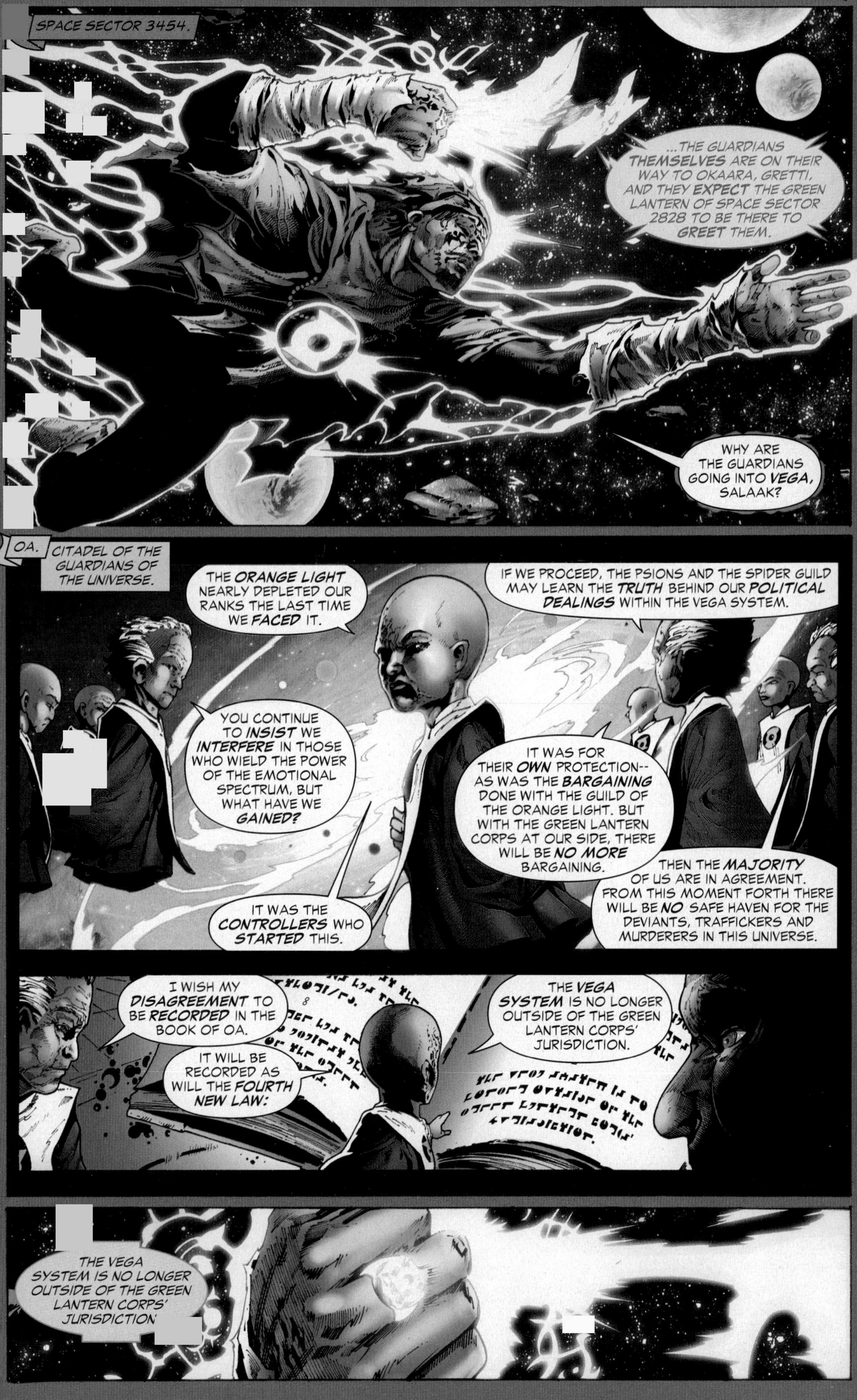

SPACE SECTOR 3454.
...THE GUARDIANS THEMSELVES ARE ON THEIR WAY TO OKAARA, GRETTI, AND THEY EXPECT THE GREEN LANTERN OF SPACE SECTOR 2828 TO BE THERE TO GREET THEM.
WHY ARE THE GUARDIANS GOING INTO VEGA, SALAAK?
OA.
CITADEL OF THE GUARDIANS OF THE UNIVERSE.
THE ORANGE LIGHT NEARLY DEPLETED OUR RANKS THE LAST TIME WE FACED IT.
IF WE PROCEED, THE PSIONS AND THE SPIDER GUILD MAY LEARN THE TRUTH BEHIND OUR POLITICAL DEALINGS WITHIN THE VEGA SYSTEM.
YOU CONTINUE TO INSIST WE INTERFERE IN THOSE WHO WIELD THE POWER OF THE EMOTIONAL SPECTRUM, BUT WHAT HAVE WE GAINED?
IT WAS THE CONTROLLERS WHO STARTED THIS.
IT WAS FOR THEIR OWN PROTECTION-- AS WAS THE BARGAINING DONE WITH THE GUILD OF THE ORANGE LIGHT. BUT WITH THE GREEN LANTERN CORPS AT OUR SIDE, THERE WILL BE NO MORE BARGAINING.
THEN THE MAJORITY OF US ARE IN AGREEMENT. FROM THIS MOMENT FORTH THERE WILL BE NO SAFE HAVEN FOR THE DEVIANTS, TRAFFICKERS AND MURDERERS IN THIS UNIVERSE.
I WISH MY DISAGREEMENT TO BE RECORDED IN THE BOOK OF OA.
IT WILL BE RECORDED AS WILL THE FOURTH NEW LAW:
THE VEGA SYSTEM IS NO LONGER OUTSIDE OF THE GREEN LANTERN CORPS' JURISDICTION.
THE VEGA SYSTEM IS NO LONGER OUTSIDE OF THE GREEN LANTERN CORPS' JURISDICTION

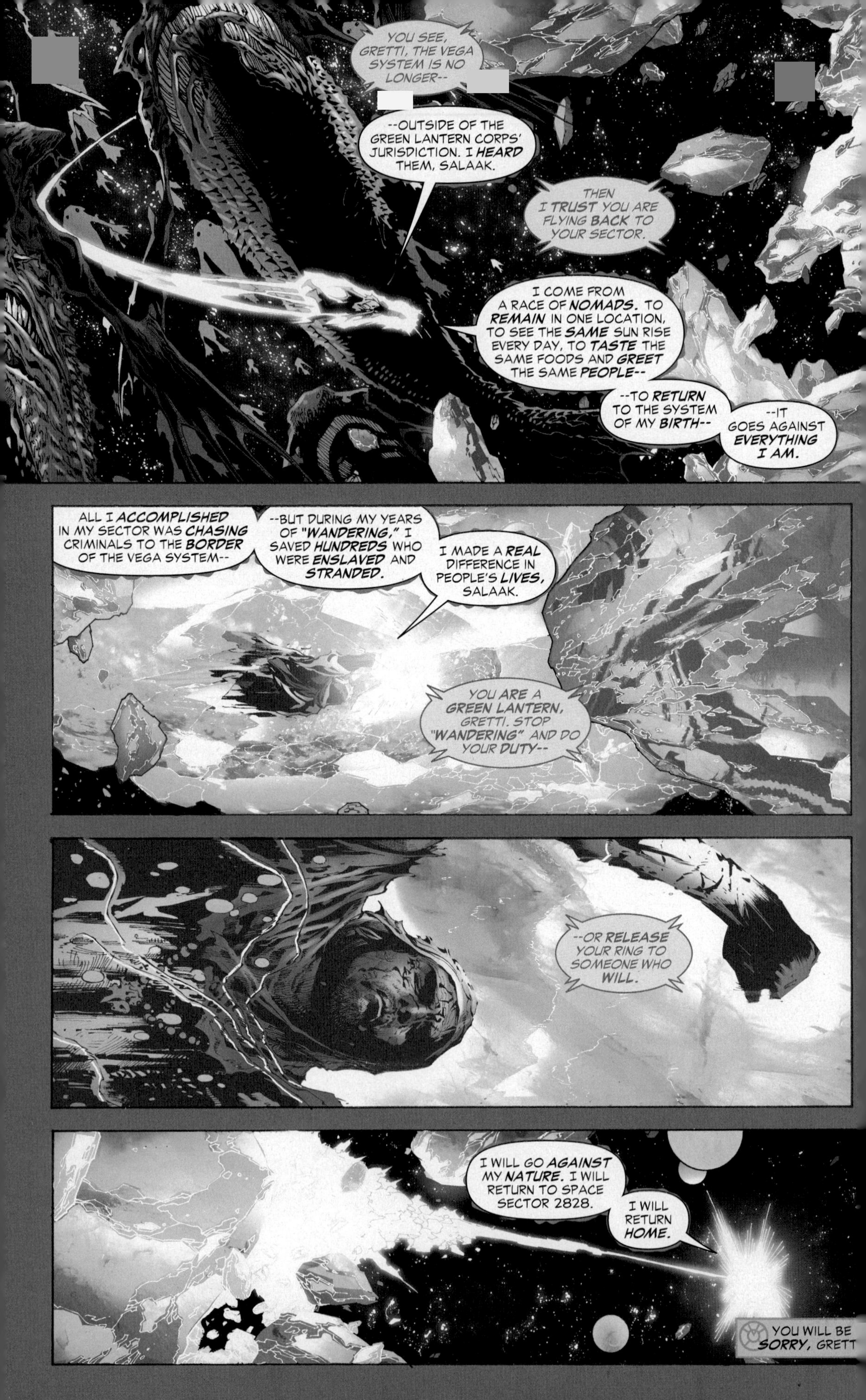

YOU SEE, GRETTI, THE VEGA SYSTEM IS NO LONGER--
--OUTSIDE OF THE GREEN LANTERN CORPS' JURISDICTION. I HEARD THEM, SALAAK.
THEN I TRUST YOU ARE FLYING BACK TO YOUR SECTOR.
I COME FROM A RACE OF NOMADS. TO REMAIN IN ONE LOCATION, TO SEE THE SAME SUN RISE EVERY DAY, TO TASTE THE SAME FOODS AND GREET THE SAME PEOPLE--
--TO RETURN TO THE SYSTEM OF MY BIRTH--
--IT GOES AGAINST EVERYTHING I AM.
ALL I ACCOMPLISHED IN MY SECTOR WAS CHASING CRIMINALS TO THE BORDER OF THE VEGA SYSTEM--
--BUT DURING MY YEARS OF "WANDERING," I SAVED HUNDREDS WHO WERE ENSLAVED AND STRANDED.
I MADE A REAL DIFFERENCE IN PEOPLE'S LIVES, SALAAK.
YOU ARE A GREEN LANTERN, GRETTI. STOP "WANDERING" AND DO YOUR DUTY--
--OR RELEASE YOUR RING TO SOMEONE WHO WILL.
I WILL GO AGAINST MY NATURE. I WILL RETURN TO SPACE SECTOR 2828.
I WILL RETURN HOME.
YOU WILL BE SORRY, GRETT

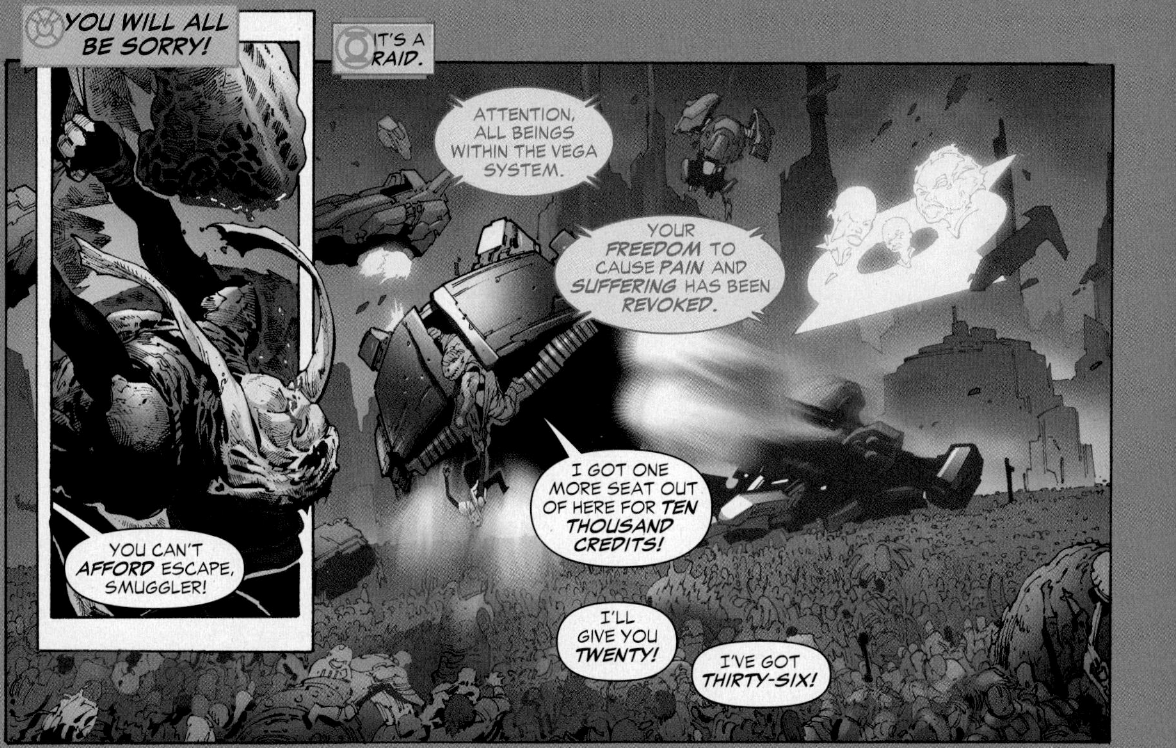
YOU WILL ALL BE SORRY!
IT'S A RAID.
ATTENTION, ALL BEINGS WITHIN THE VEGA SYSTEM.
YOUR FREEDOM TO CAUSE PAIN AND SUFFERING HAS BEEN REVOKED.
I GOT ONE MORE SEAT OUT OF HERE FOR TEN THOUSAND CREDITS!
YOU CAN'T AFFORD ESCAPE, SMUGGLER!
I'LL GIVE YOU TWENTY!
I'VE GOT THIRTY-SIX!

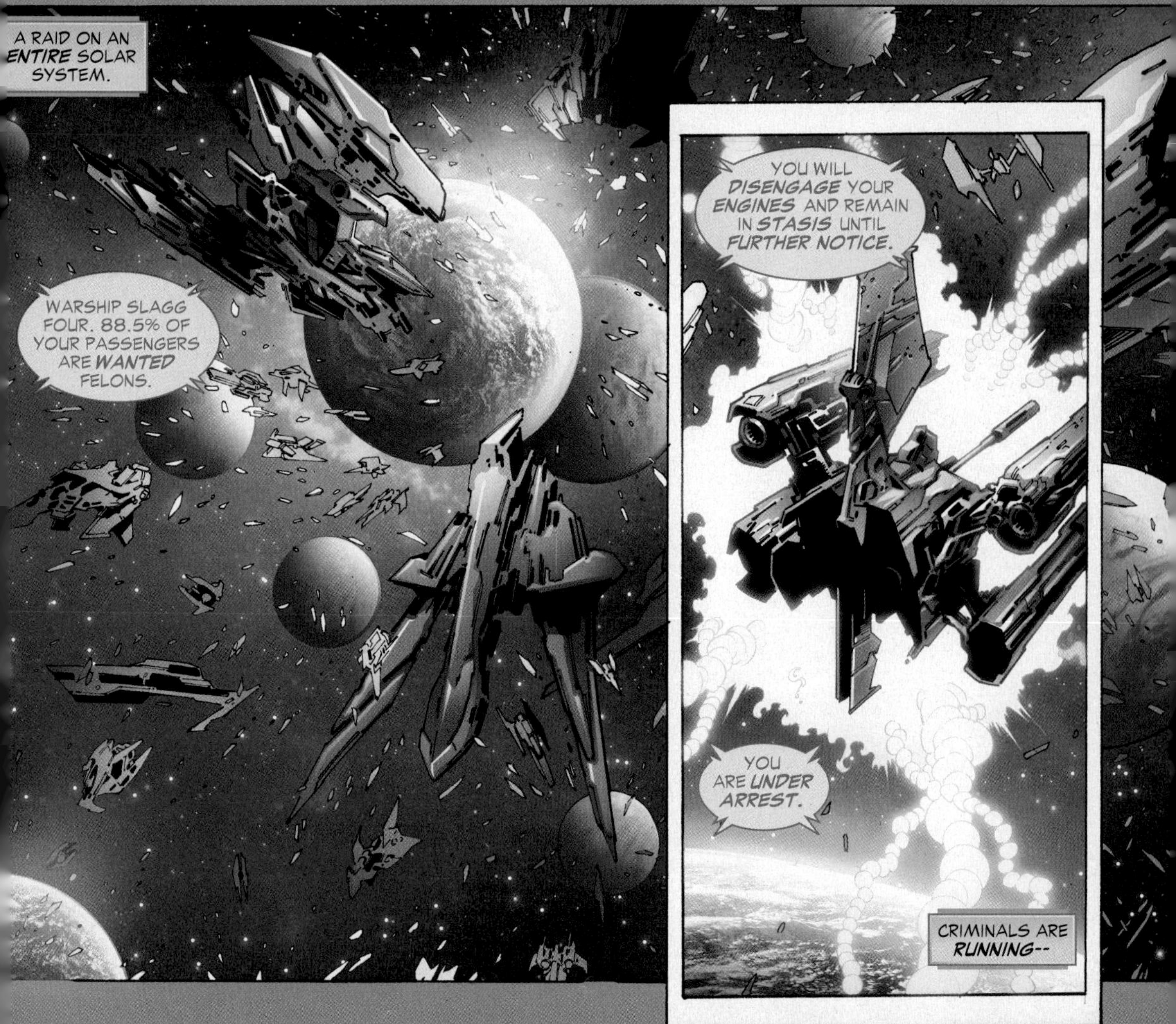
A RAID ON AN ENTIRE SOLAR SYSTEM.
WARSHIP SLAGG FOUR. 88.5% OF YOUR PASSENGERS ARE WANTED FELONS.
YOU WILL DISENGAGE YOUR ENGINES AND REMAIN IN STASIS UNTIL FURTHER NOTICE.
YOU ARE UNDER ARREST.
CRIMINALS ARE RUNNING--

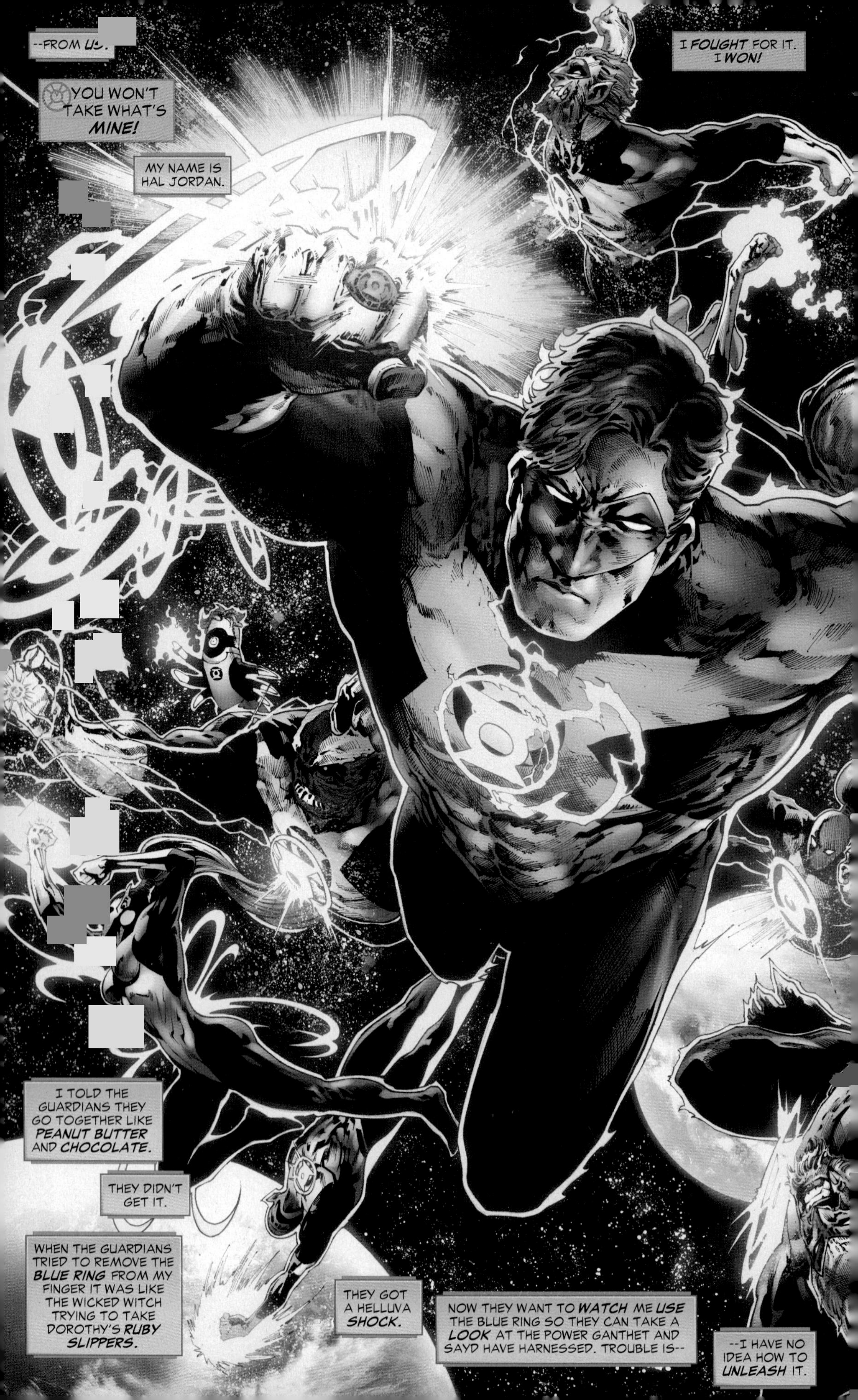
--FROM US.
YOU WON'T TAKE WHAT'S MINE!
I FOUGHT FOR IT. I WON!
MY NAME IS HAL JORDAN.
I TOLD THE GUARDIANS THEY GO TOGETHER LIKE PEANUT BUTTER AND CHOCOLATE.
THEY DIDN'T GET IT.
WHEN THE GUARDIANS TRIED TO REMOVE THE BLUE RING FROM MY FINGER IT WAS LIKE THE WICKED WITCH TRYING TO TAKE DOROTHY'S RUBY SLIPPERS.
THEY GOT A HELLUVA SHOCK.
NOW THEY WANT TO WATCH ME USE THE BLUE RING SO THEY CAN TAKE A LOOK AT THE POWER GANTHET AND SAYD HAVE HARNESSED. TROUBLE IS--
--I HAVE NO IDEA HOW TO UNLEASH IT.

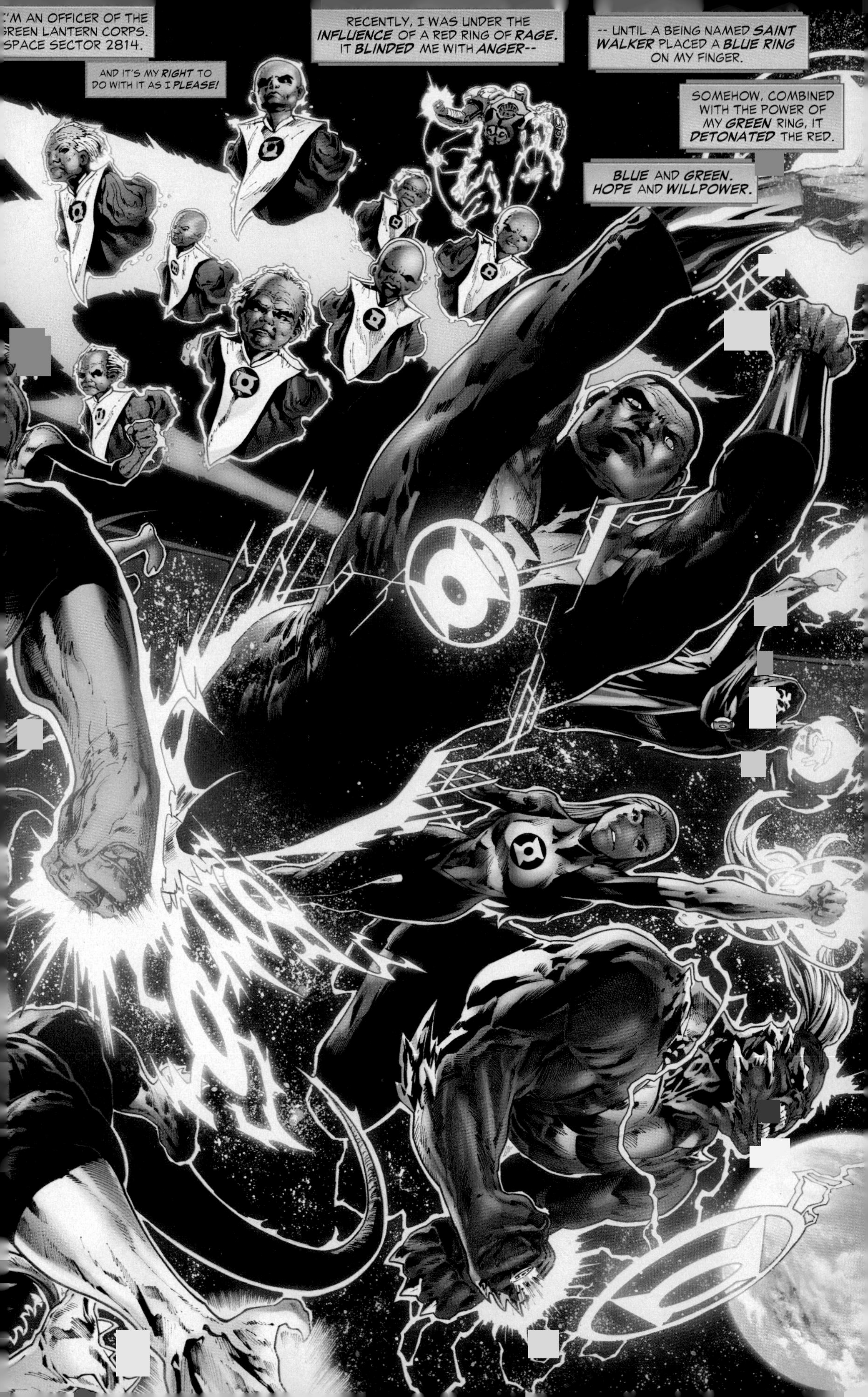
I'M AN OFFICER OF THE GREEN LANTERN CORPS. SPACE SECTOR 2814.
AND IT'S MY RIGHT TO DO WITH IT AS I PLEASE!
RECENTLY, I WAS UNDER THE INFLUENCE OF A RED RING OF RAGE. IT BLINDED ME WITH ANGER--
-- UNTIL A BEING NAMED SAINT WALKER PLACED A BLUE RING ON MY FINGER.
SOMEHOW, COMBINED WITH THE POWER OF MY GREEN RING, IT DETONATED THE RED.
BLUE AND GREEN. HOPE AND WILLPOWER.

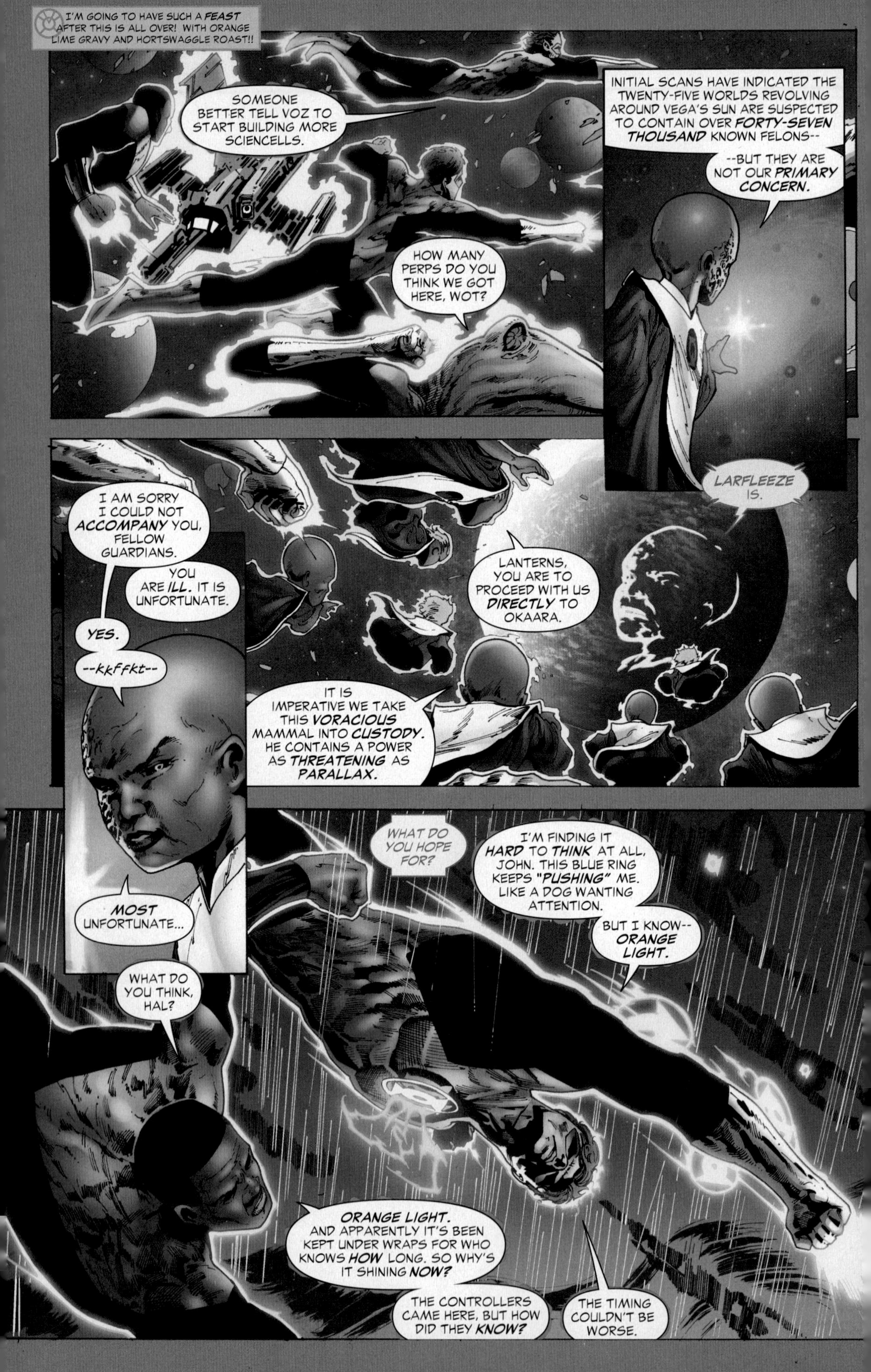
I'M GOING TO HAVE SUCH A FEAST AFTER THIS IS ALL OVER! WITH ORANGE LIME GRAVY AND HORTSWAGGLE ROAST!!
SOMEONE BETTER TELL VOZ TO START BUILDING MORE SCIENCELLS.
HOW MANY PERPS DO YOU THINK WE GOT HERE, WOT?
INITIAL SCANS HAVE INDICATED THE TWENTY-FIVE WORLDS REVOLVING AROUND VEGA'S SUN ARE SUSPECTED TO CONTAIN OVER FORTY-SEVEN THOUSAND KNOWN FELONS--
--BUT THEY ARE NOT OUR PRIMARY CONCERN.
LARFLEEZE IS.
LANTERNS, YOU ARE TO PROCEED WITH US DIRECTLY TO OKAARA.
IT IS IMPERATIVE WE TAKE THIS VORACIOUS MAMMAL INTO CUSTODY. HE CONTAINS A POWER AS THREATENING AS PARALLAX.
I AM SORRY I COULD NOT ACCOMPANY YOU, FELLOW GUARDIANS.
YOU ARE ILL. IT IS UNFORTUNATE.
YES.
--kkffkt--
MOST UNFORTUNATE...
WHAT DO YOU THINK, HAL?
WHAT DO YOU HOPE FOR?
I'M FINDING IT HARD TO THINK AT ALL, JOHN. THIS BLUE RING KEEPS "PUSHING" ME. LIKE A DOG WANTING ATTENTION.
BUT I KNOW-- ORANGE LIGHT.
ORANGE LIGHT. AND APPARENTLY IT'S BEEN KEPT UNDER WRAPS FOR WHO KNOWS HOW LONG. SO WHY'S IT SHINING NOW?
THE CONTROLLERS CAME HERE, BUT HOW DID THEY KNOW?
THE TIMING COULDN'T BE WORSE.

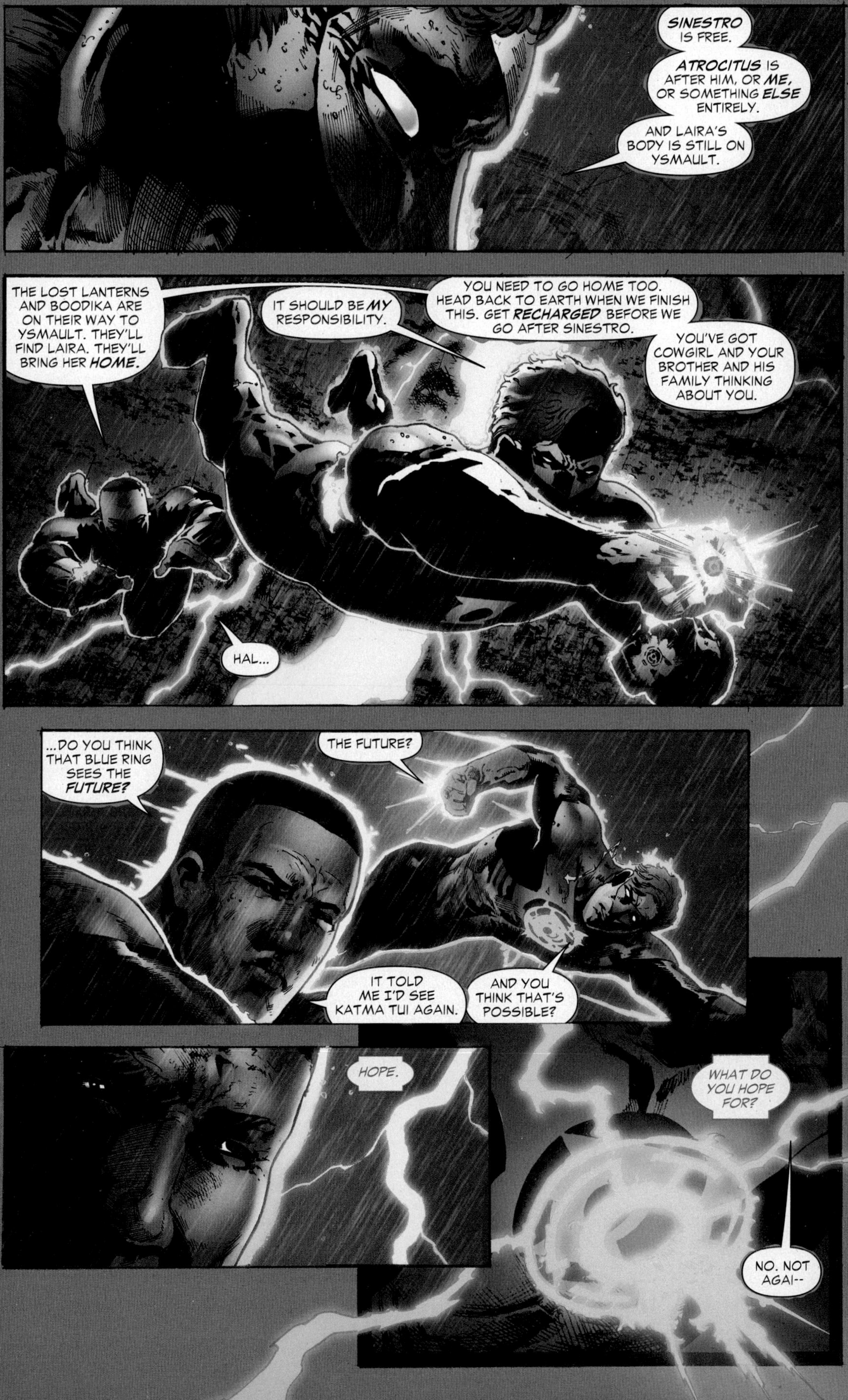
SINESTRO IS FREE.
ATROCITUS IS AFTER HIM, OR ME, OR SOMETHING ELSE ENTIRELY.
AND LAIRA'S BODY IS STILL ON YSMAULT.
THE LOST LANTERNS AND BOODIKA ARE ON THEIR WAY TO YSMAULT. THEY'LL FIND LAIRA. THEY'LL BRING HER HOME.
IT SHOULD BE MY RESPONSIBILITY.
YOU NEED TO GO HOME TOO. HEAD BACK TO EARTH WHEN WE FINISH THIS. GET RECHARGED BEFORE WE GO AFTER SINESTRO.
YOU'VE GOT COWGIRL AND YOUR BROTHER AND HIS FAMILY THINKING ABOUT YOU.
HAL...
...DO YOU THINK THAT BLUE RING SEES THE FUTURE?
THE FUTURE?
IT TOLD ME I'D SEE KATMA TUI AGAIN.
AND YOU THINK THAT'S POSSIBLE?
HOPE.
WHAT DO YOU HOPE FOR?
NO. NOT AGAI--

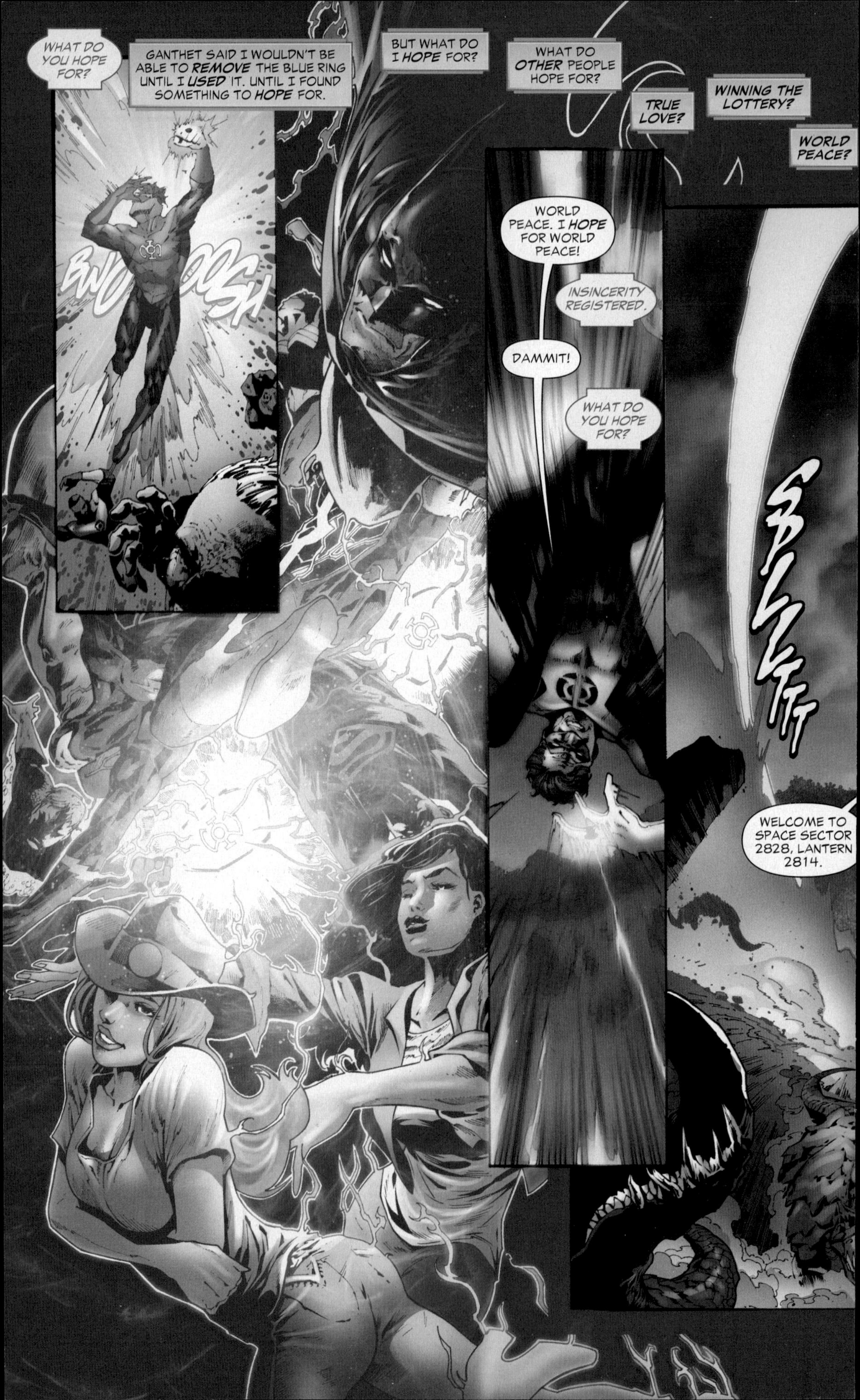
WHAT DO YOU HOPE FOR?
GANTHET SAID I WOULDN'T BE ABLE TO REMOVE THE BLUE RING UNTIL I USED IT. UNTIL I FOUND SOMETHING TO HOPE FOR.
BWOOOOSH
BUT WHAT DO I HOPE FOR?
WHAT DO OTHER PEOPLE HOPE FOR?
TRUE LOVE?
WINNING THE LOTTERY?
WORLD PEACE?
WORLD PEACE. I HOPE FOR WORLD PEACE!
INSINCERITY REGISTERED.
DAMMIT!
WHAT DO YOU HOPE FOR?
SPLLTTT
WELCOME TO SPACE SECTOR 2828, LANTERN 2814.

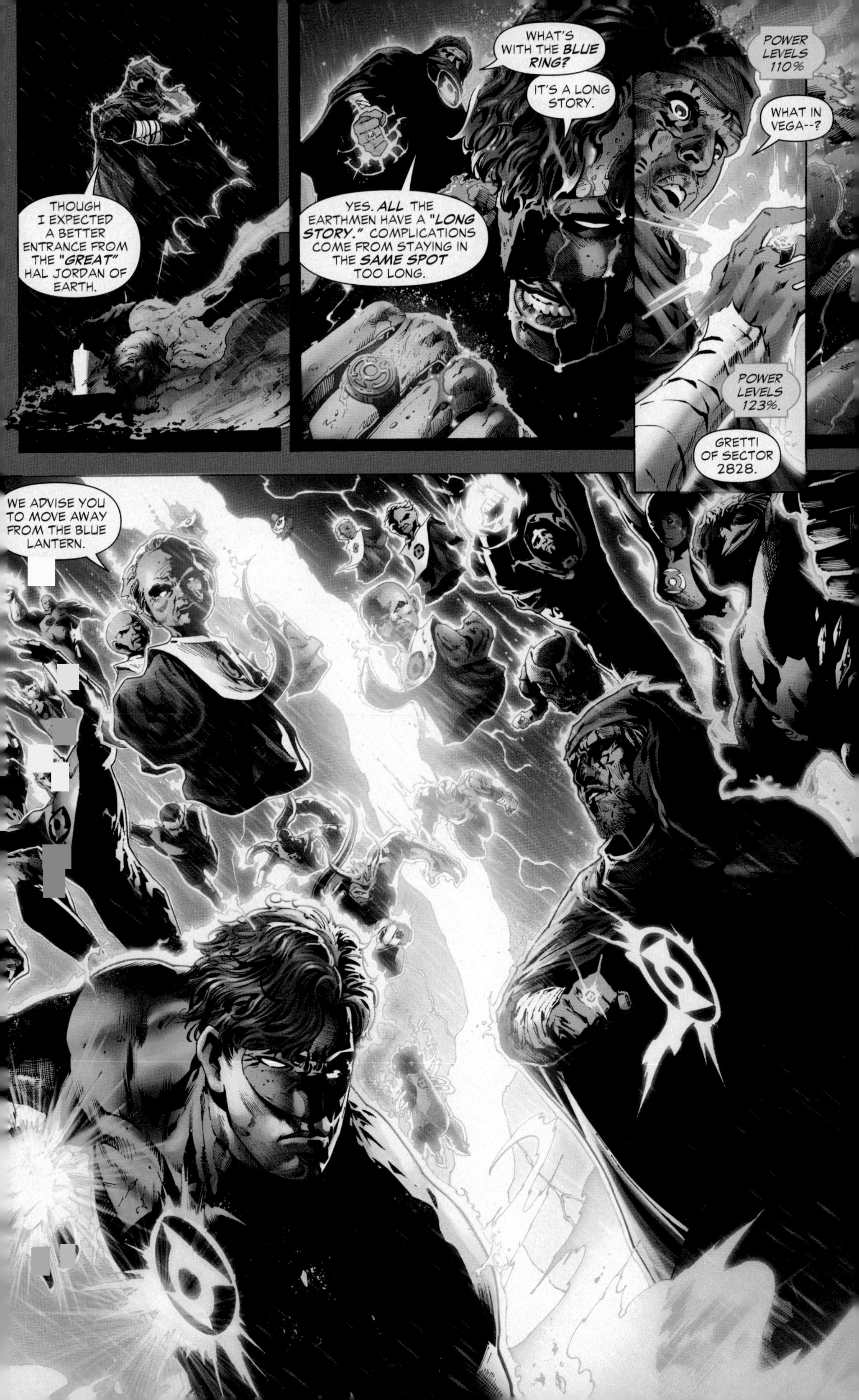

THOUGH I EXPECTED A BETTER ENTRANCE FROM THE "GREAT" HAL JORDAN OF EARTH.
WHAT'S WITH THE BLUE RING?
IT'S A LONG STORY.
YES. ALL THE EARTHMEN HAVE A "LONG STORY." COMPLICATIONS COME FROM STAYING IN THE SAME SPOT TOO LONG.
POWER LEVELS 110%
WHAT IN VEGA--?
POWER LEVELS 123%.
GRETTI OF SECTOR 2828.
WE ADVISE YOU TO MOVE AWAY FROM THE BLUE LANTERN.

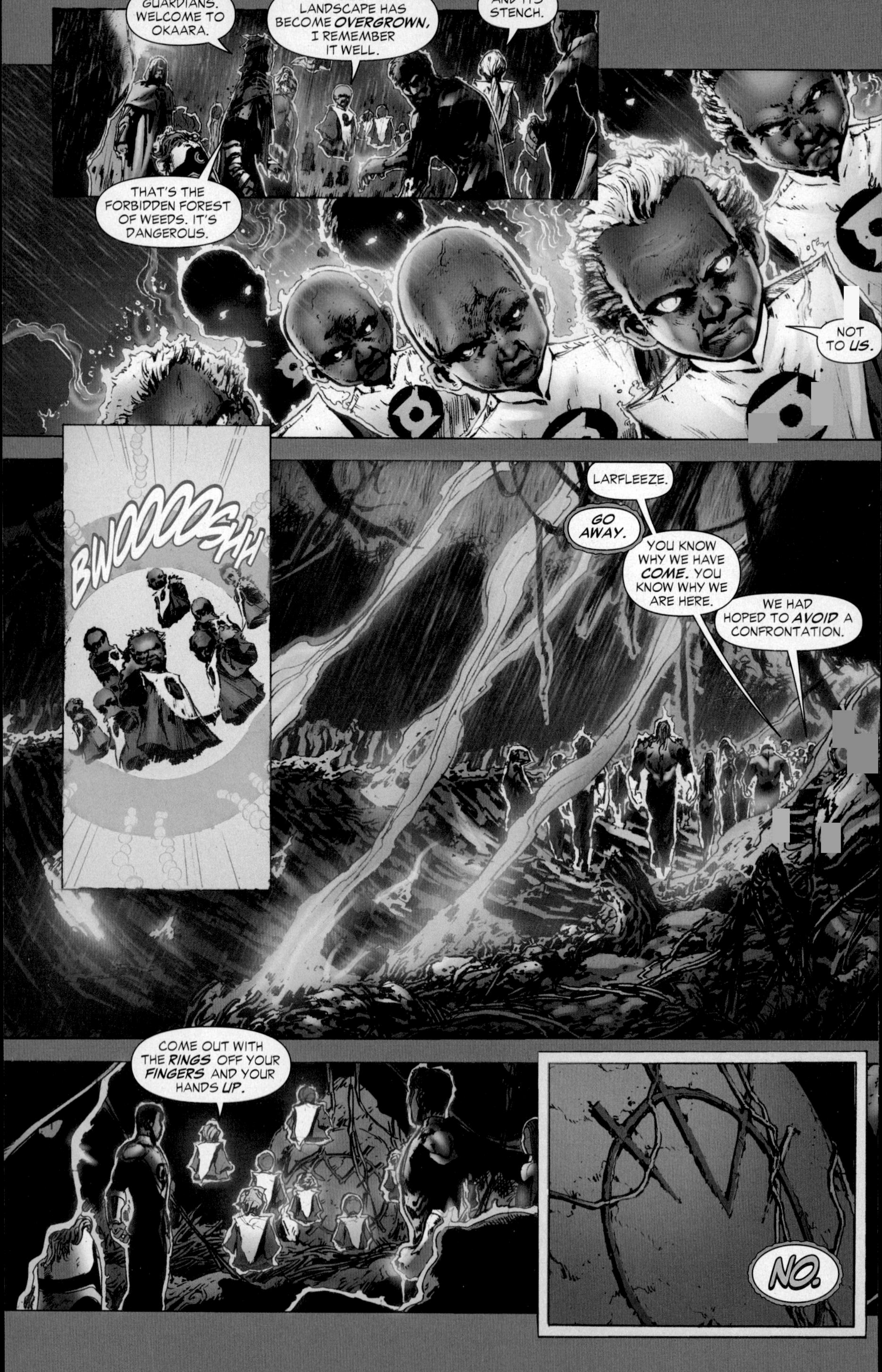
GUARDIANS. WELCOME TO OKAARA.
ALTHOUGH THE LANDSCAPE HAS BECOME OVERGROWN, I REMEMBER IT WELL.
AND ITS STENCH.
THAT'S THE FORBIDDEN FOREST OF WEEDS. IT'S DANGEROUS.
NOT TO US.
BWOOOOSHH
LARFLEEZE.
GO AWAY.
YOU KNOW WHY WE HAVE COME. YOU KNOW WHY WE ARE HERE.
WE HAD HOPED TO AVOID A CONFRONTATION.
COME OUT WITH THE RINGS OFF YOUR FINGERS AND YOUR HANDS UP.
NO.

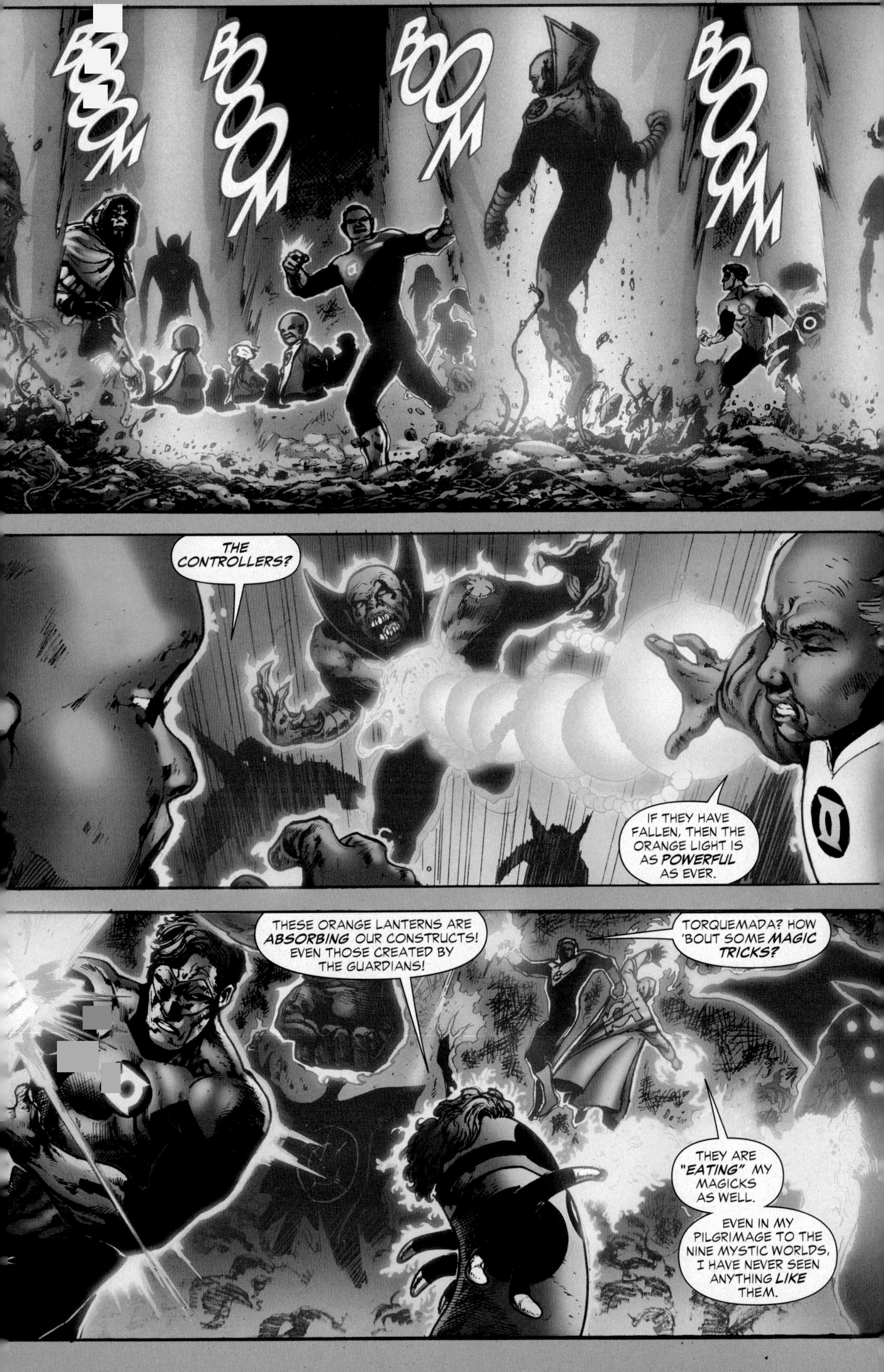
BOOM
BOOOM
BOOM
BOOOMM
THE CONTROLLERS?
IF THEY HAVE FALLEN, THEN THE ORANGE LIGHT IS AS POWERFUL AS EVER.
THESE ORANGE LANTERNS ARE ABSORBING OUR CONSTRUCTS! EVEN THOSE CREATED BY THE GUARDIANS!
TORQUEMADA? HOW 'BOUT SOME MAGIC TRICKS?
THEY ARE "EATING" MY MAGICKS AS WELL.
EVEN IN MY PILGRIMAGE TO THE NINE MYSTIC WORLDS, I HAVE NEVER SEEN ANYTHING LIKE THEM.

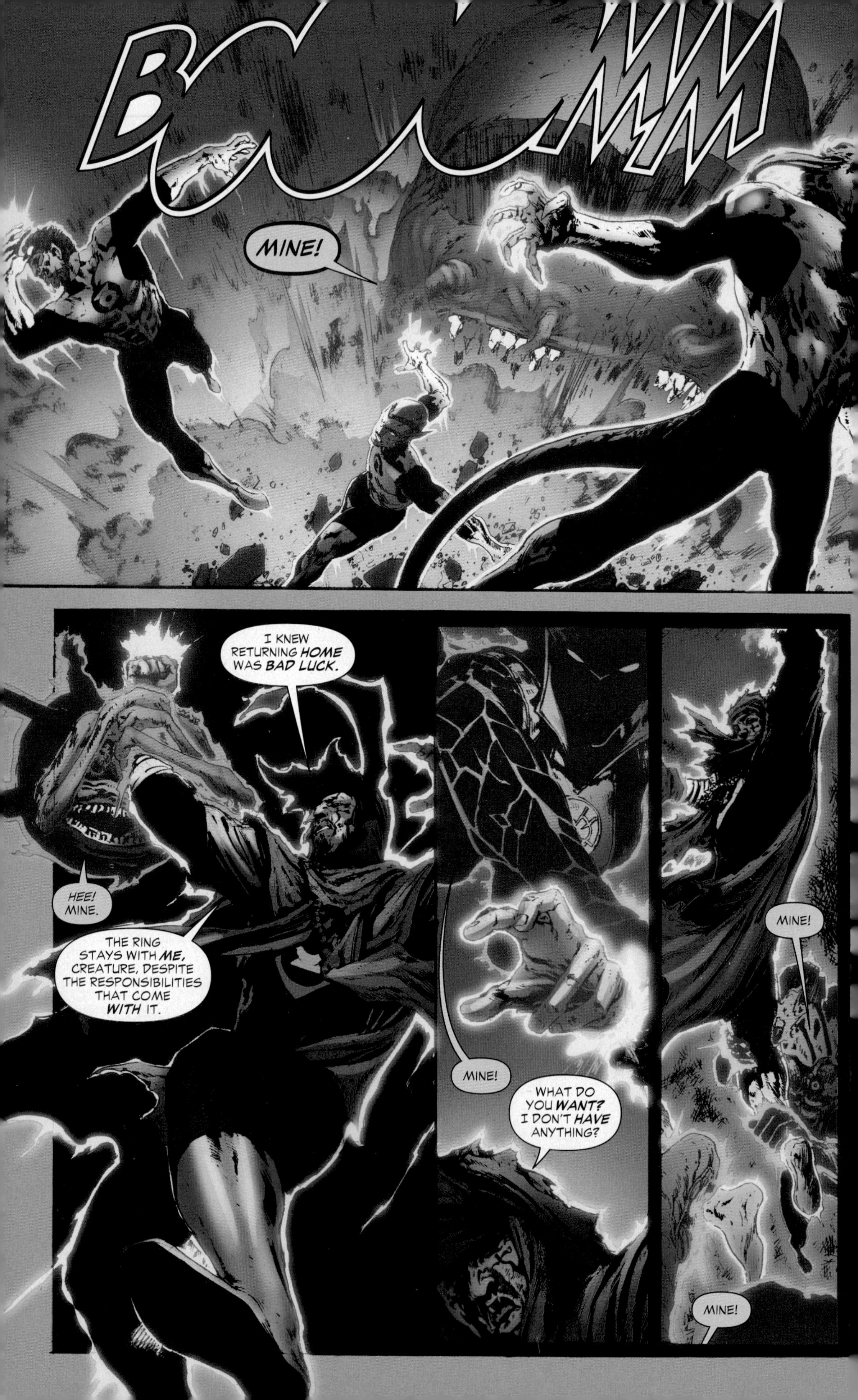
BOOMM
MINE!
I KNEW RETURNING HOME WAS BAD LUCK.
HEE! MINE.
THE RING STAYS WITH ME, CREATURE, DESPITE THE RESPONSIBILITIES THAT COME WITH IT.
MINE!
WHAT DO YOU WANT? I DON'T HAVE ANYTHING?
MINE!
MINE!

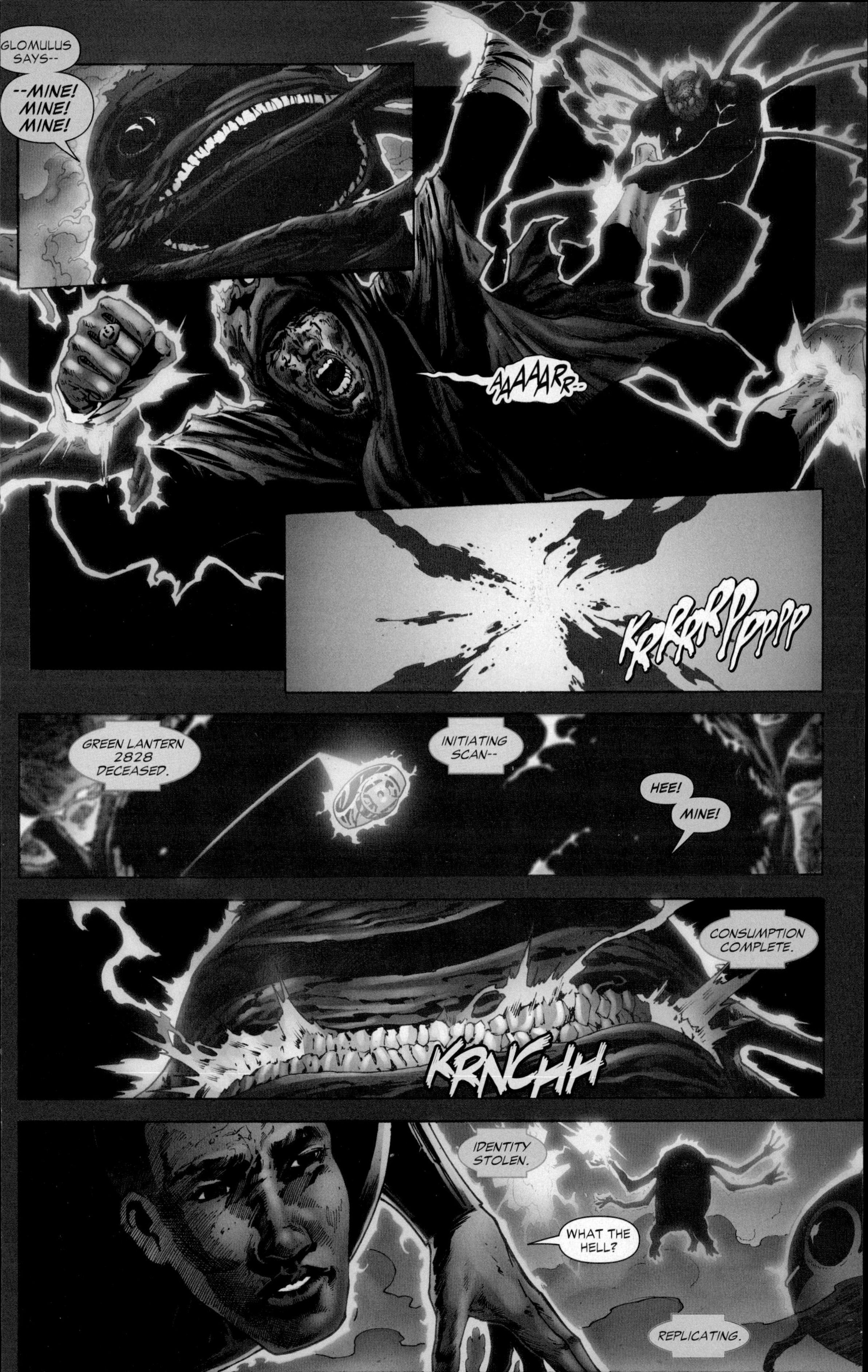
GLOMULUS SAYS--
--MINE! MINE! MINE!
AAAAARR--
KRRRRPPPPP
GREEN LANTERN 2828 DECEASED.
INITIATING SCAN--
HEE!
MINE!
CONSUMPTION COMPLETE.
KRNCHH
IDENTITY STOLEN.
WHAT THE HELL?
REPLICATING.

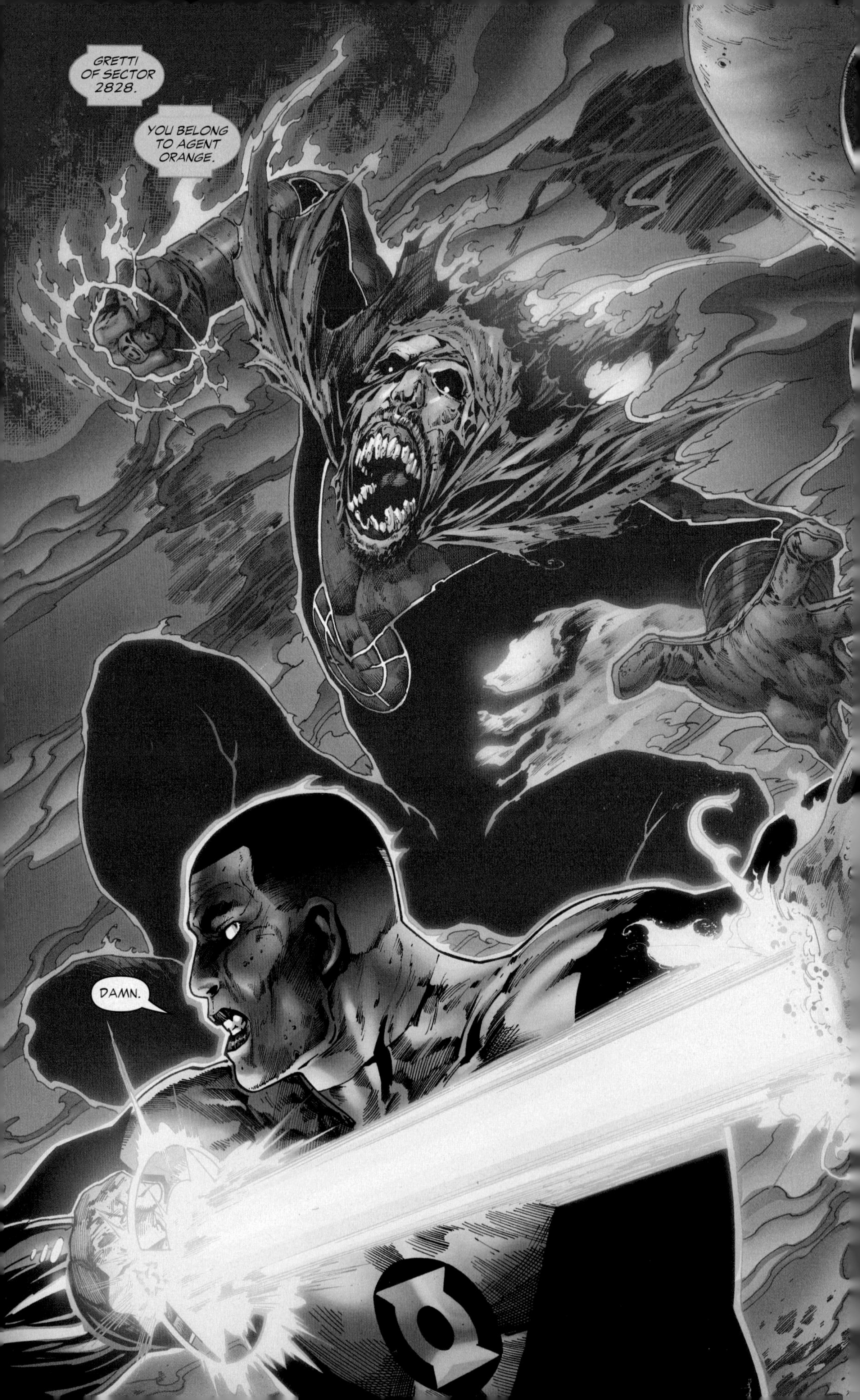
GRETTI OF SECTOR 2828.
YOU BELONG TO AGENT ORANGE.
DAMN.

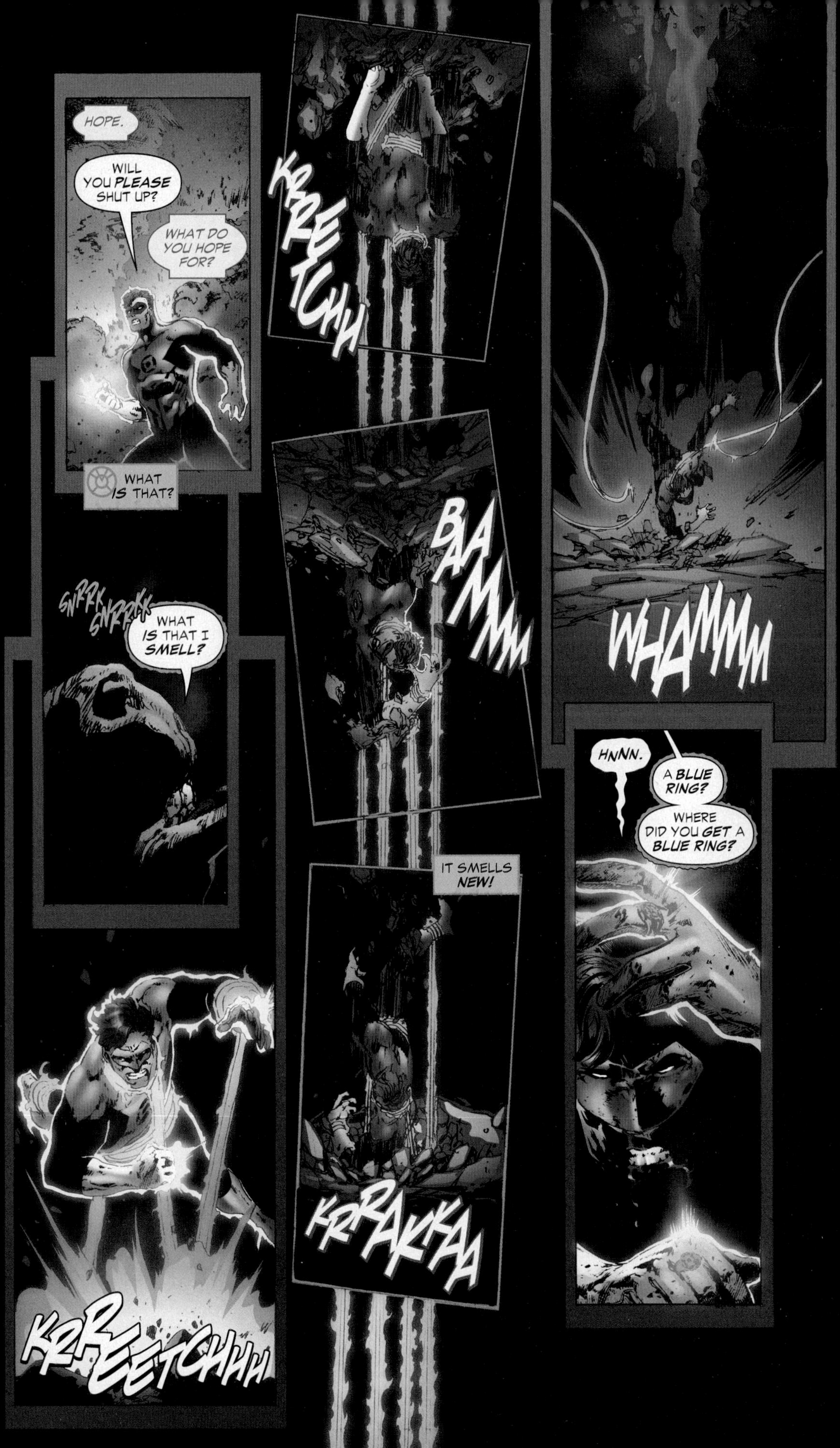
HOPE.
WILL YOU PLEASE SHUT UP?
WHAT DO YOU HOPE FOR?
WHAT IS THAT?
SNRRK SNRRKK
WHAT IS THAT I SMELL?
KRREETCHHH
KRRETCHHH
BAMMMM
IT SMELLS NEW!
KRRAKKAA
WHAMMM
HNNN.
A BLUE RING?
WHERE DID YOU GET A BLUE RING?

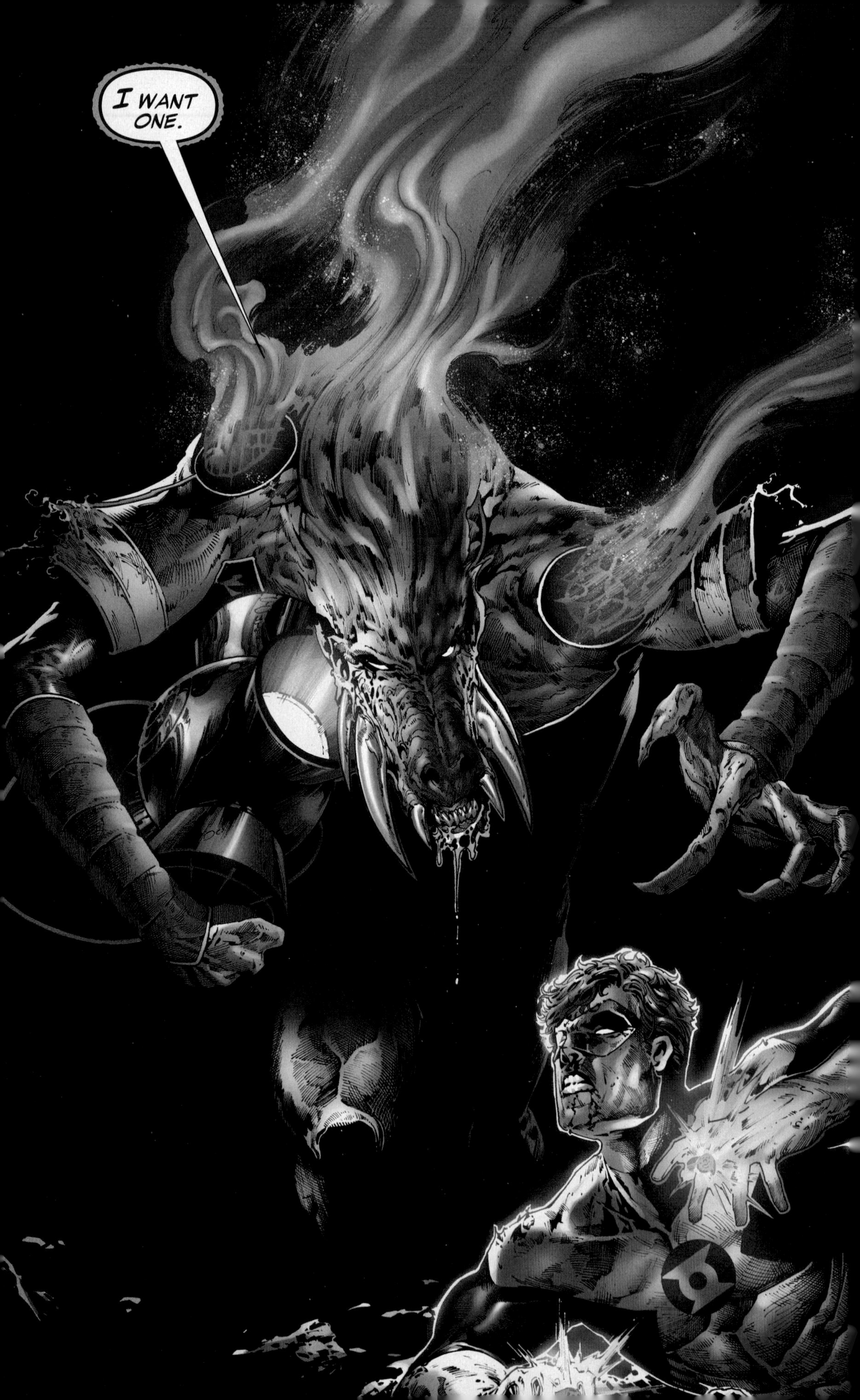
I WANT ONE.

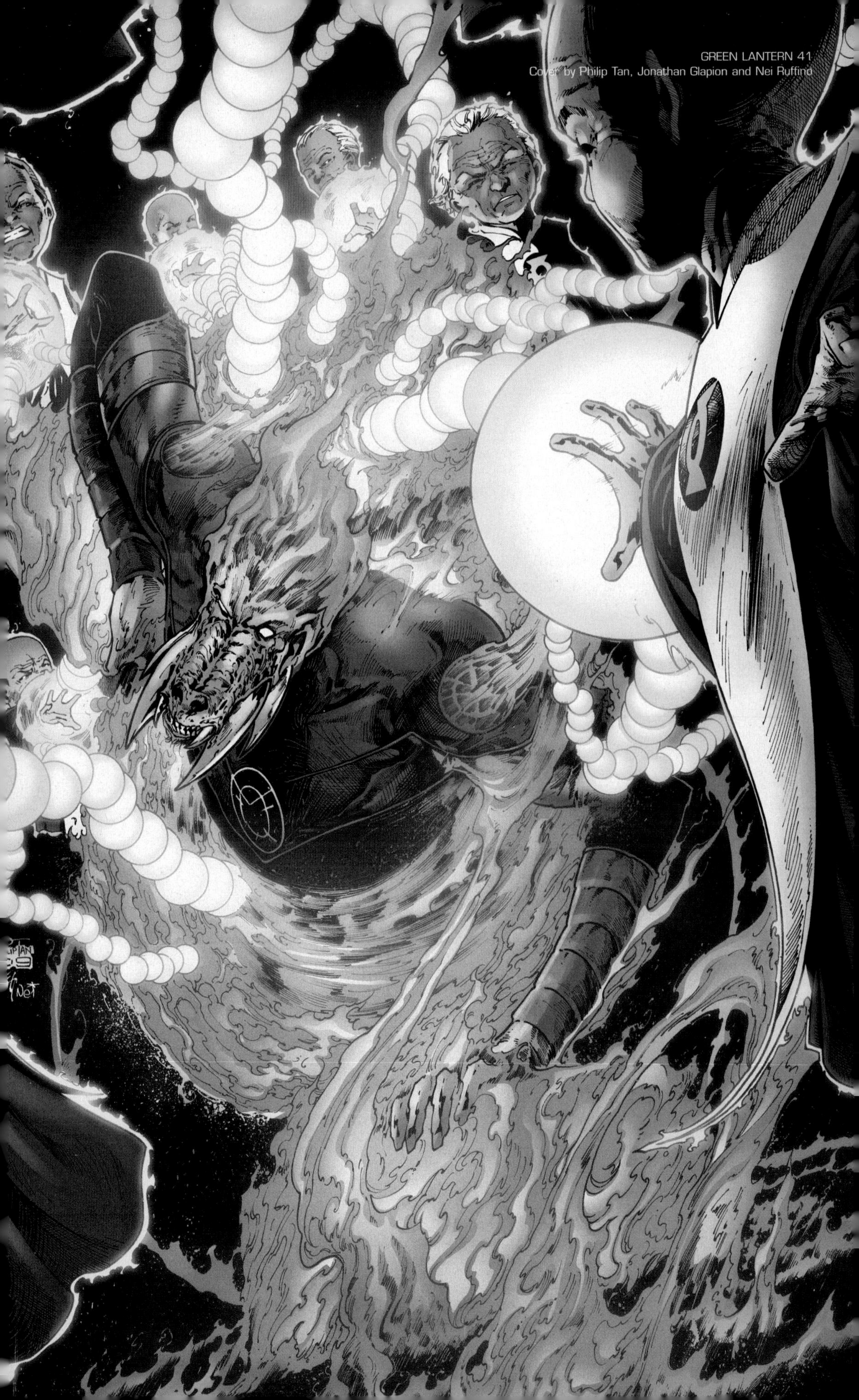

GREEN LANTERN 41
Cover by Philip Tan, Jonathan Glapion and Nei Ruffino

AGENT ORANGE
Part 3

Philip Tan   **Eddy Barrows** Pencils
Jonathan Glapion   **Ruy José**   **Julio Ferreira** Inks

SNRKK

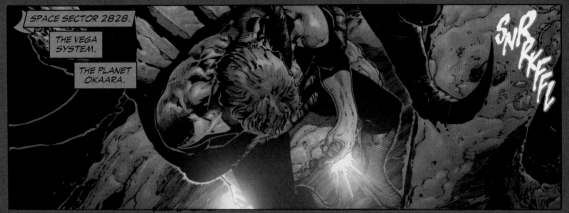

SPACE SECTOR 2828.

THE VEGA SYSTEM.

THE PLANET OKAARA.

SNRRKFFL

SNRKK SNURKK

SNORK

ARE YOU *HUNGRY,* GREEN LANTERN?

I CAN *SMELL* HIM, BUT I CAN'T--

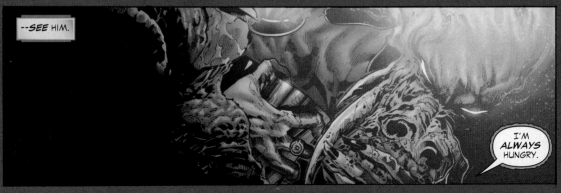

--SEE HIM.

I'M *ALWAYS* HUNGRY.

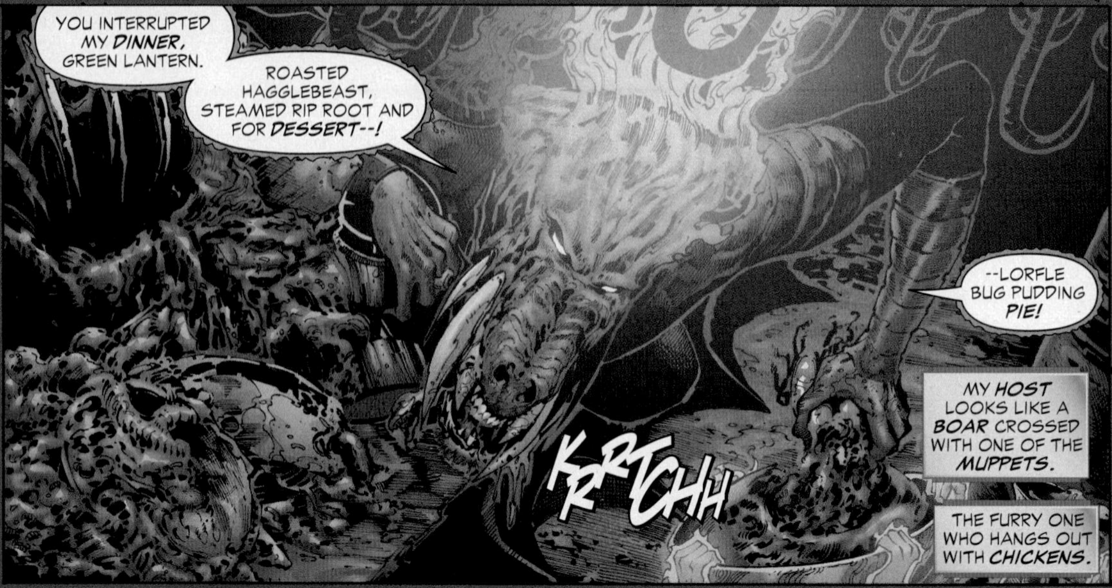
YOU INTERRUPTED MY DINNER, GREEN LANTERN.
ROASTED HAGGLEBEAST, STEAMED RIP ROOT AND FOR DESSERT--!
--LORFLE BUG PUDDING PIE!
KRRRTCHH
MY HOST LOOKS LIKE A BOAR CROSSED WITH ONE OF THE MUPPETS.
THE FURRY ONE WHO HANGS OUT WITH CHICKENS.

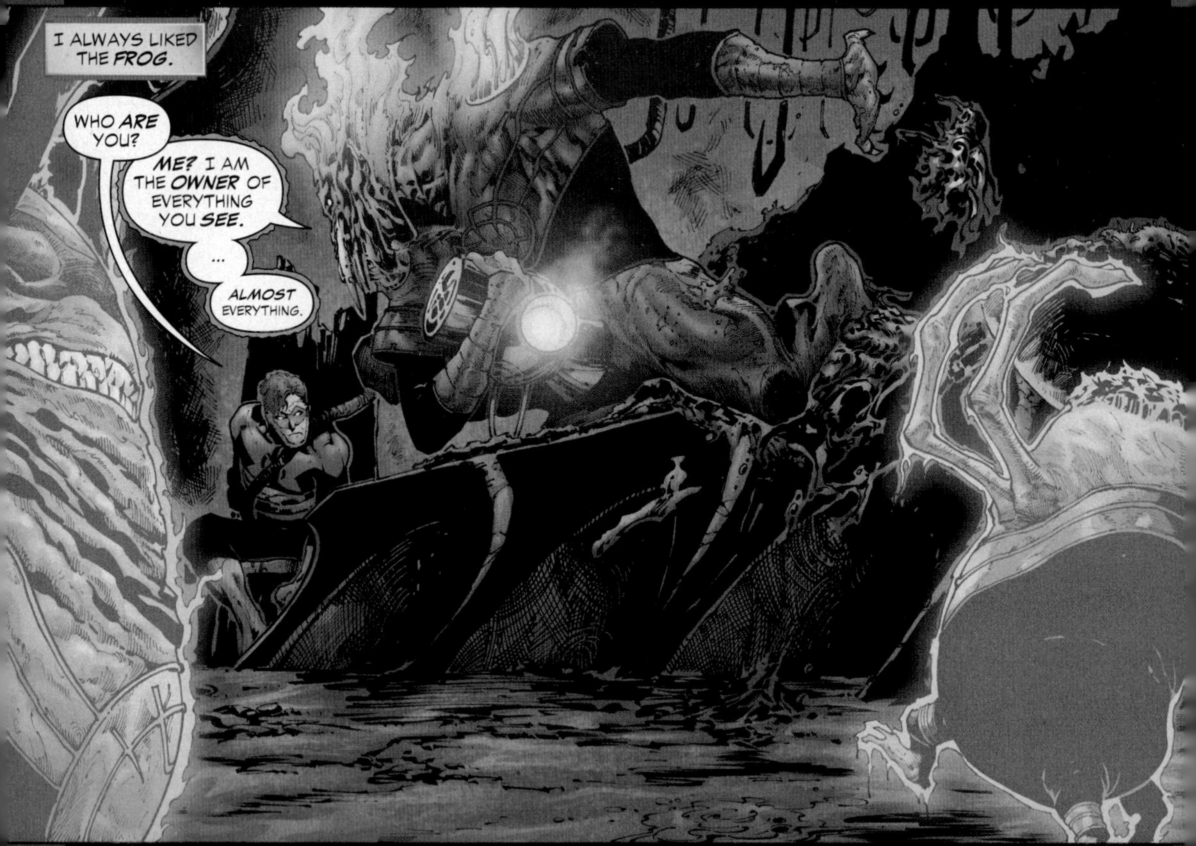
I ALWAYS LIKED THE FROG.
WHO ARE YOU?
ME? I AM THE OWNER OF EVERYTHING YOU SEE.
...
ALMOST EVERYTHING.

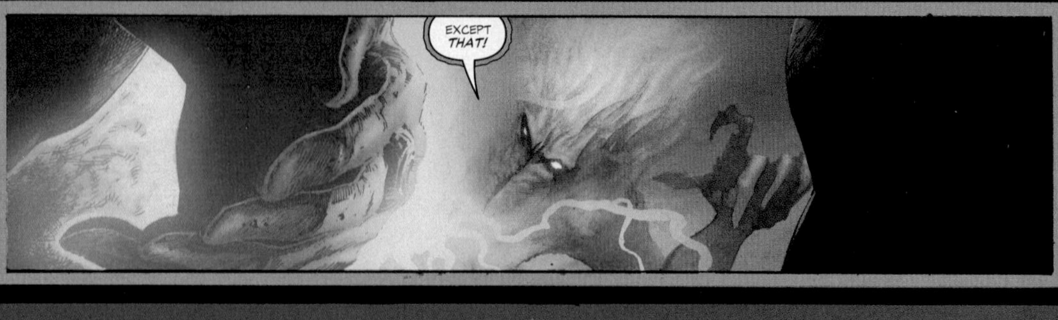
EXCEPT THAT!

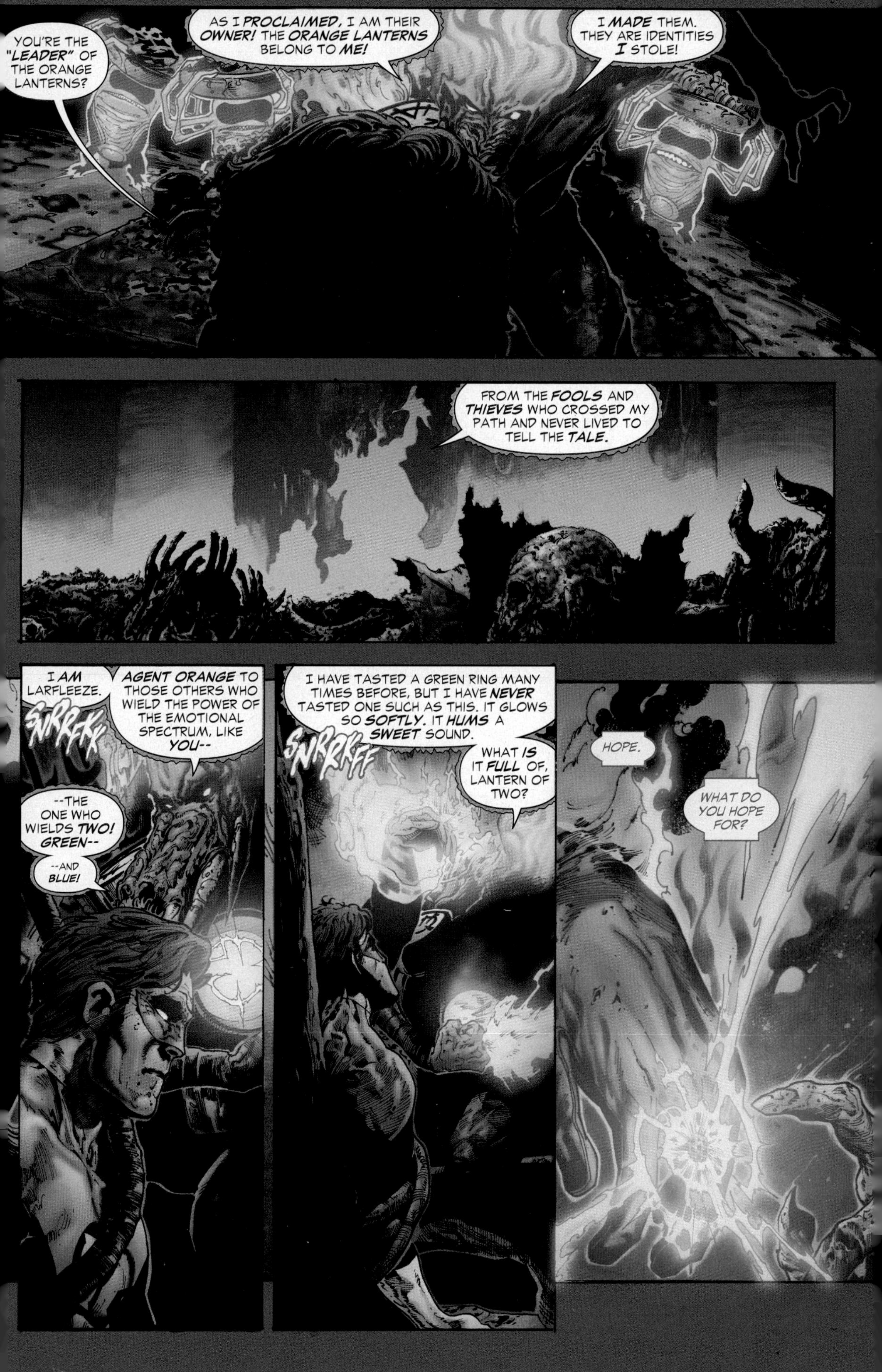
YOU'RE THE "LEADER" OF THE ORANGE LANTERNS?
AS I PROCLAIMED, I AM THEIR OWNER! THE ORANGE LANTERNS BELONG TO ME!
I MADE THEM. THEY ARE IDENTITIES I STOLE!
FROM THE FOOLS AND THIEVES WHO CROSSED MY PATH AND NEVER LIVED TO TELL THE TALE.
I AM LARFLEEZE.
SNRRFKK
AGENT ORANGE TO THOSE OTHERS WHO WIELD THE POWER OF THE EMOTIONAL SPECTRUM, LIKE YOU--
--THE ONE WHO WIELDS TWO! GREEN--
--AND BLUE!
I HAVE TASTED A GREEN RING MANY TIMES BEFORE, BUT I HAVE NEVER TASTED ONE SUCH AS THIS. IT GLOWS SO SOFTLY. IT HUMS A SWEET SOUND.
SNRRKFF
WHAT IS IT FULL OF, LANTERN OF TWO?
HOPE.
WHAT DO YOU HOPE FOR?

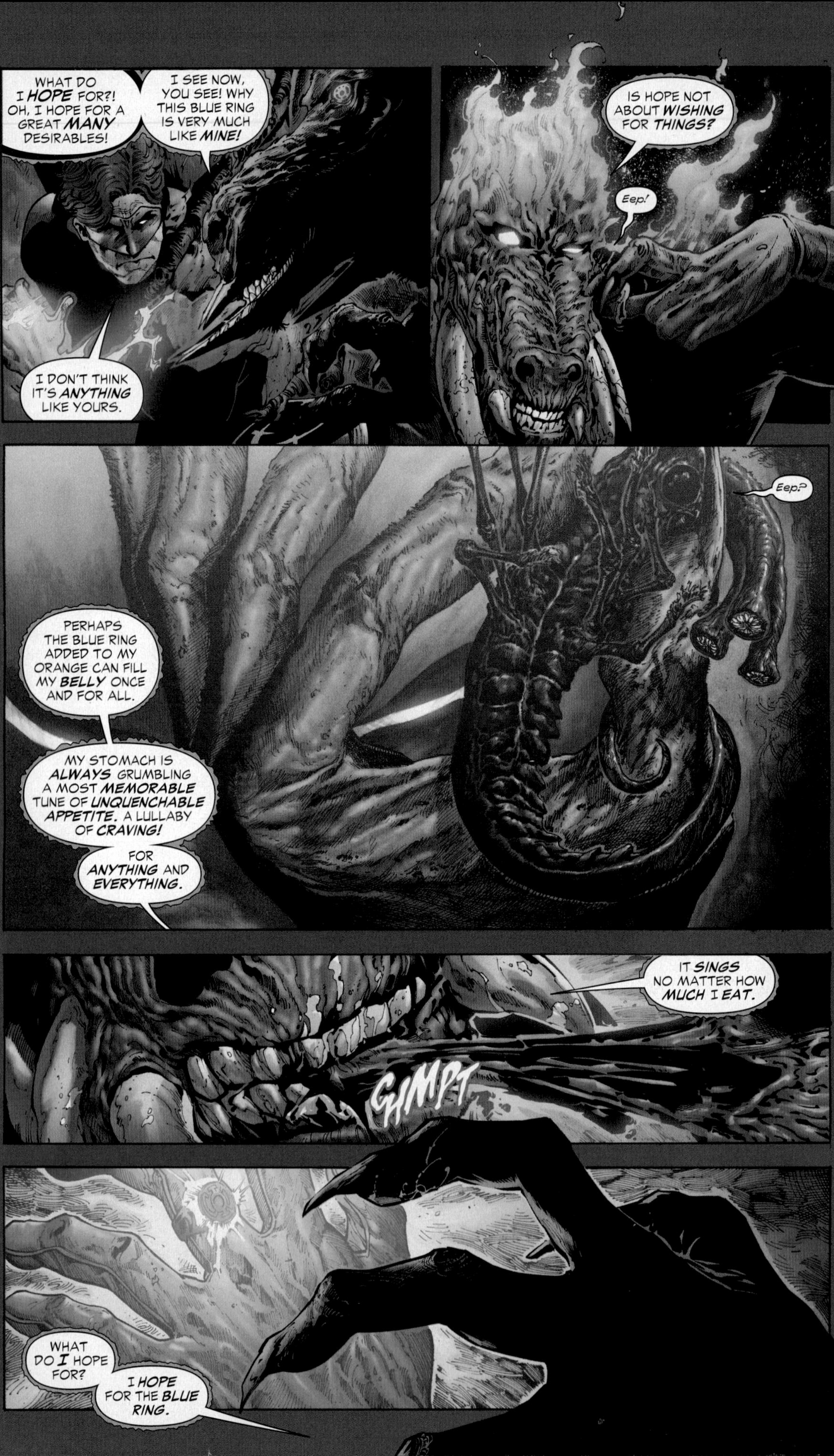
WHAT DO I HOPE FOR?! OH, I HOPE FOR A GREAT MANY DESIRABLES!
I SEE NOW, YOU SEE! WHY THIS BLUE RING IS VERY MUCH LIKE MINE!
I DON'T THINK IT'S ANYTHING LIKE YOURS.
IS HOPE NOT ABOUT WISHING FOR THINGS?
Eep!
Eep?
PERHAPS THE BLUE RING ADDED TO MY ORANGE CAN FILL MY BELLY ONCE AND FOR ALL.
MY STOMACH IS ALWAYS GRUMBLING A MOST MEMORABLE TUNE OF UNQUENCHABLE APPETITE. A LULLABY OF CRAVING!
FOR ANYTHING AND EVERYTHING.
IT SINGS NO MATTER HOW MUCH I EAT.
GHMPT
WHAT DO I HOPE FOR?
I HOPE FOR THE BLUE RING.

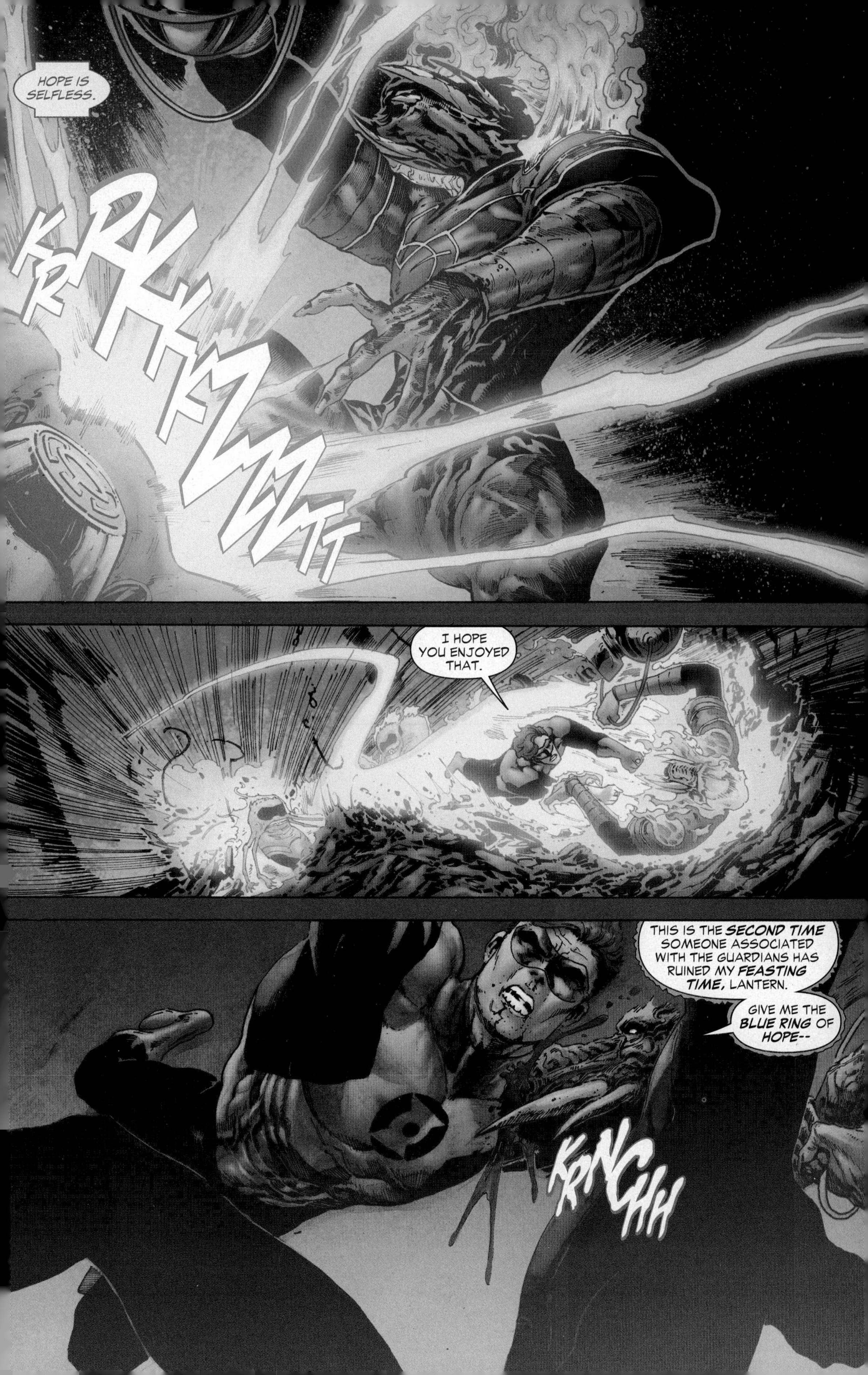
HOPE IS SELFLESS.
KRRKKZZZTT
I HOPE YOU ENJOYED THAT.
THIS IS THE SECOND TIME SOMEONE ASSOCIATED WITH THE GUARDIANS HAS RUINED MY FEASTING TIME, LANTERN.
GIVE ME THE BLUE RING OF HOPE--
KRNCHH

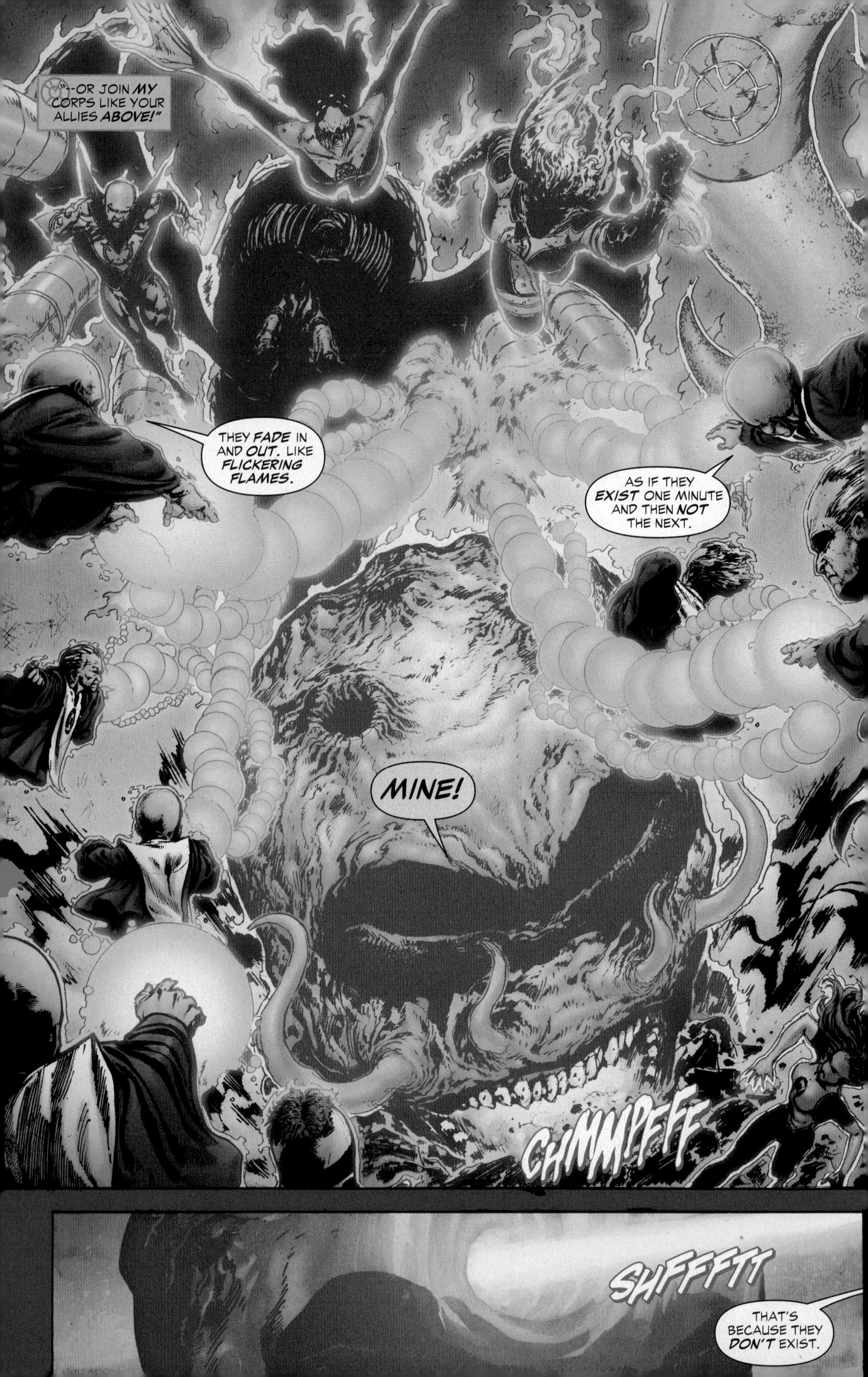
"--OR JOIN MY CORPS LIKE YOUR ALLIES ABOVE!"
THEY FADE IN AND OUT. LIKE FLICKERING FLAMES.
AS IF THEY EXIST ONE MINUTE AND THEN NOT THE NEXT.
MINE!
CHMMPFFF
SHFFFTT
THAT'S BECAUSE THEY DON'T EXIST.

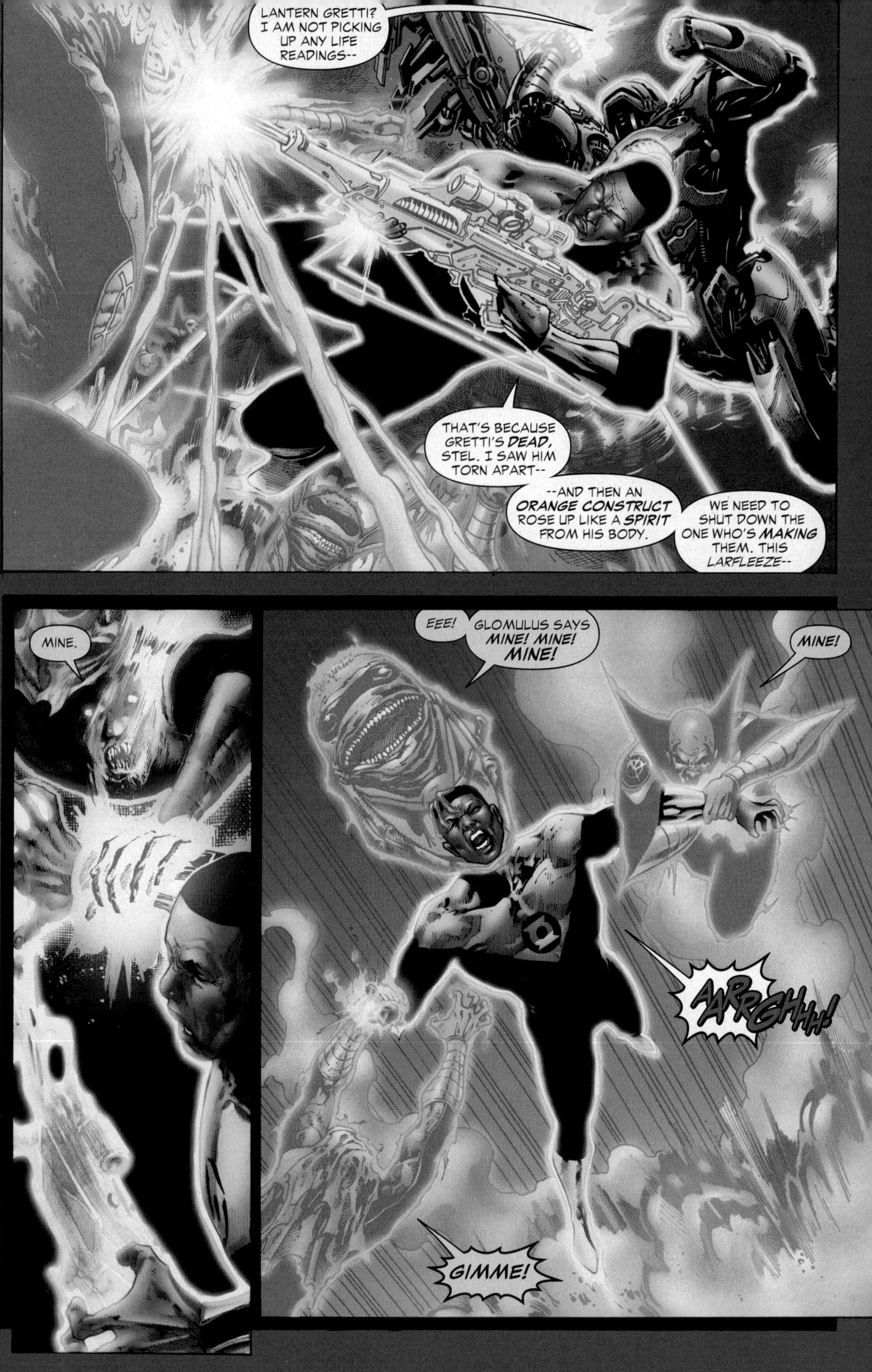
LANTERN GRETTI? I AM NOT PICKING UP ANY LIFE READINGS--
THAT'S BECAUSE GRETTI'S DEAD, STEL. I SAW HIM TORN APART--
--AND THEN AN ORANGE CONSTRUCT ROSE UP LIKE A SPIRIT FROM HIS BODY.
WE NEED TO SHUT DOWN THE ONE WHO'S MAKING THEM. THIS LARFLEEZE--
MINE.
EEE!
GLOMULUS SAYS MINE! MINE! MINE!
MINE!
AARRGHHH!
GIMME!

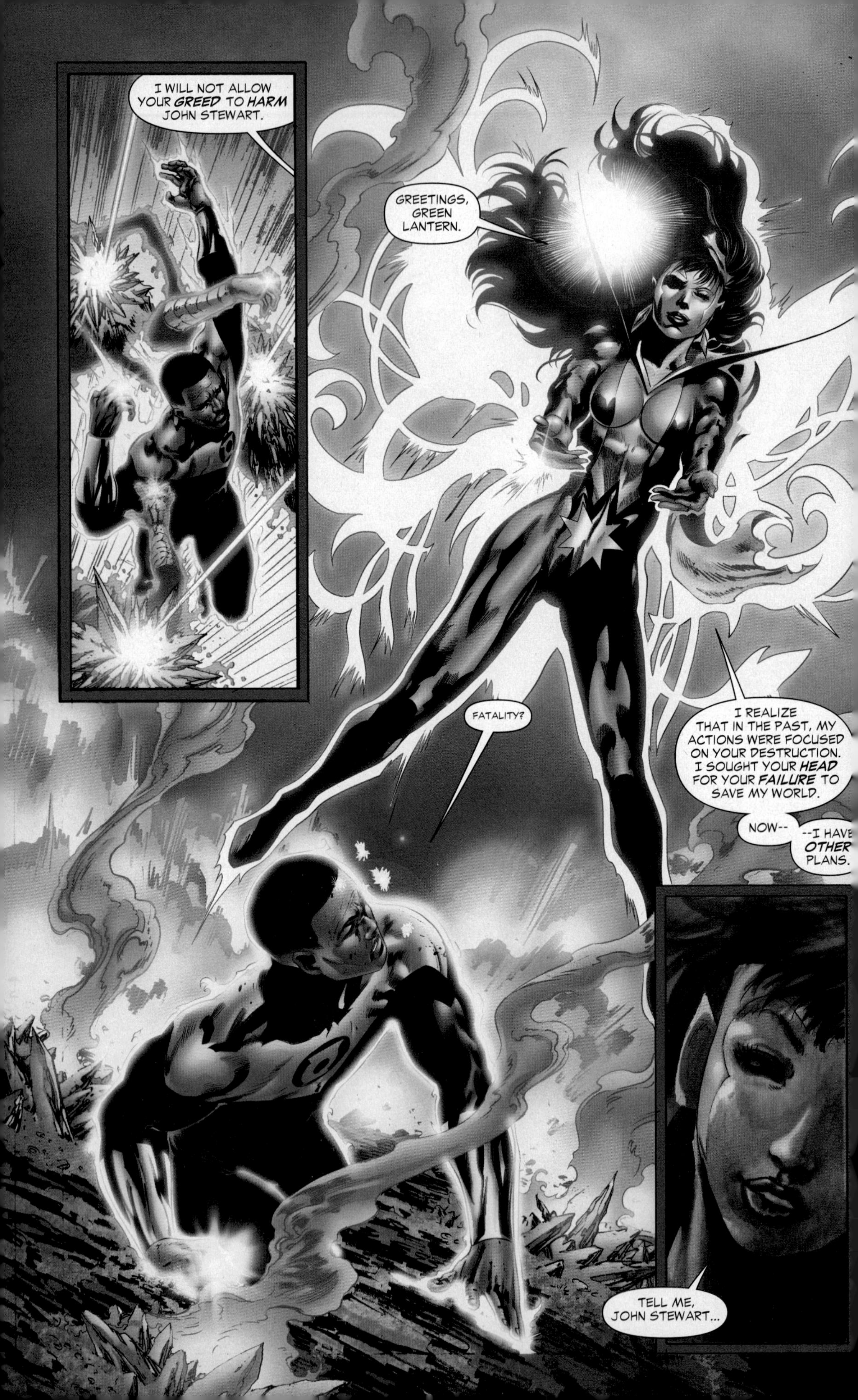
I WILL NOT ALLOW YOUR GREED TO HARM JOHN STEWART.
GREETINGS, GREEN LANTERN.
FATALITY?
I REALIZE THAT IN THE PAST, MY ACTIONS WERE FOCUSED ON YOUR DESTRUCTION. I SOUGHT YOUR HEAD FOR YOUR FAILURE TO SAVE MY WORLD.
NOW--
--I HAVE OTHER PLANS.
TELL ME, JOHN STEWART...

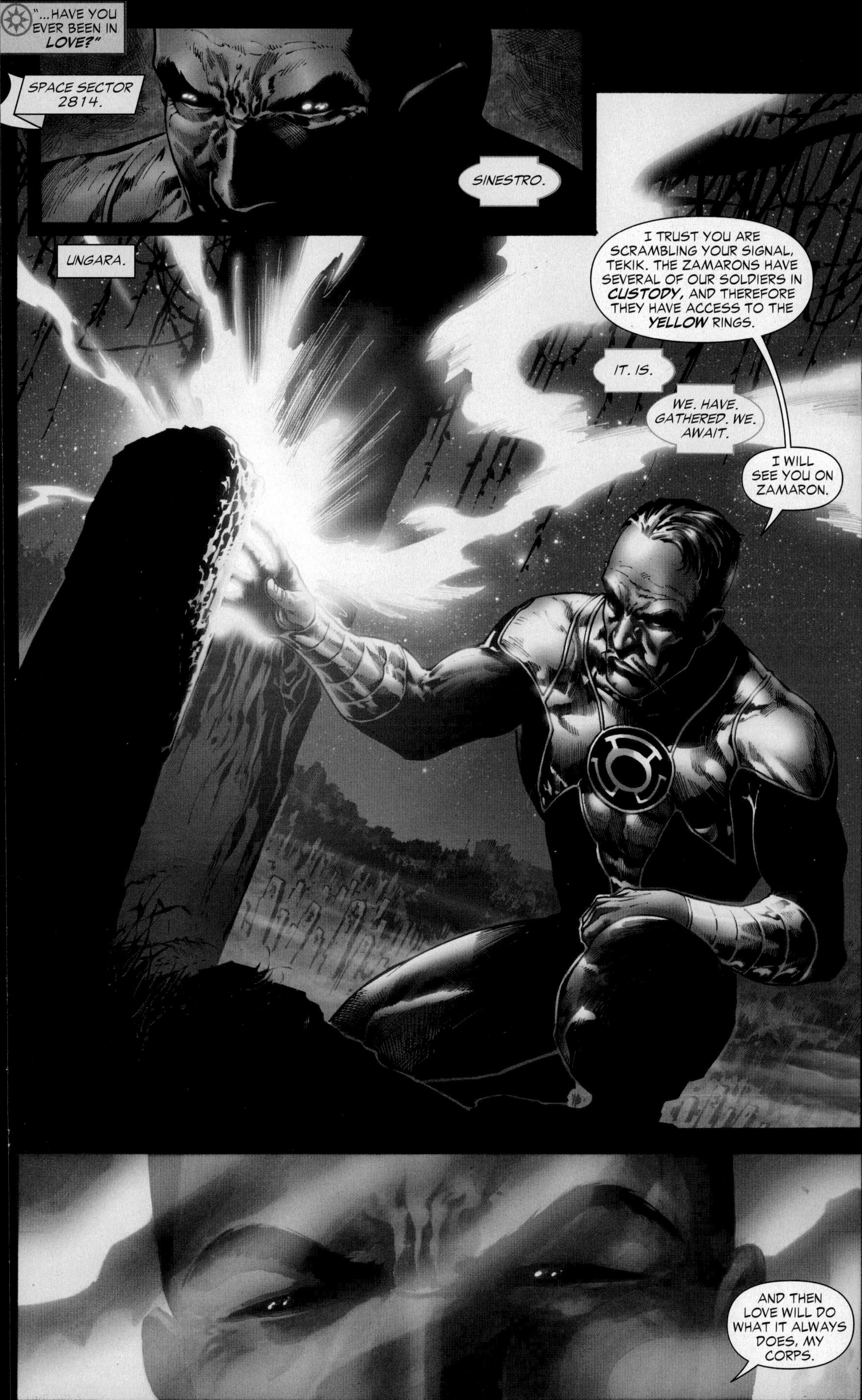
"...HAVE YOU EVER BEEN IN LOVE?"
SPACE SECTOR 2814.
SINESTRO.
UNGARA.
I TRUST YOU ARE SCRAMBLING YOUR SIGNAL, TEKIK. THE ZAMARONS HAVE SEVERAL OF OUR SOLDIERS IN CUSTODY, AND THEREFORE THEY HAVE ACCESS TO THE YELLOW RINGS.
IT. IS.
WE. HAVE. GATHERED. WE. AWAIT.
I WILL SEE YOU ON ZAMARON.
AND THEN LOVE WILL DO WHAT IT ALWAYS DOES, MY CORPS.

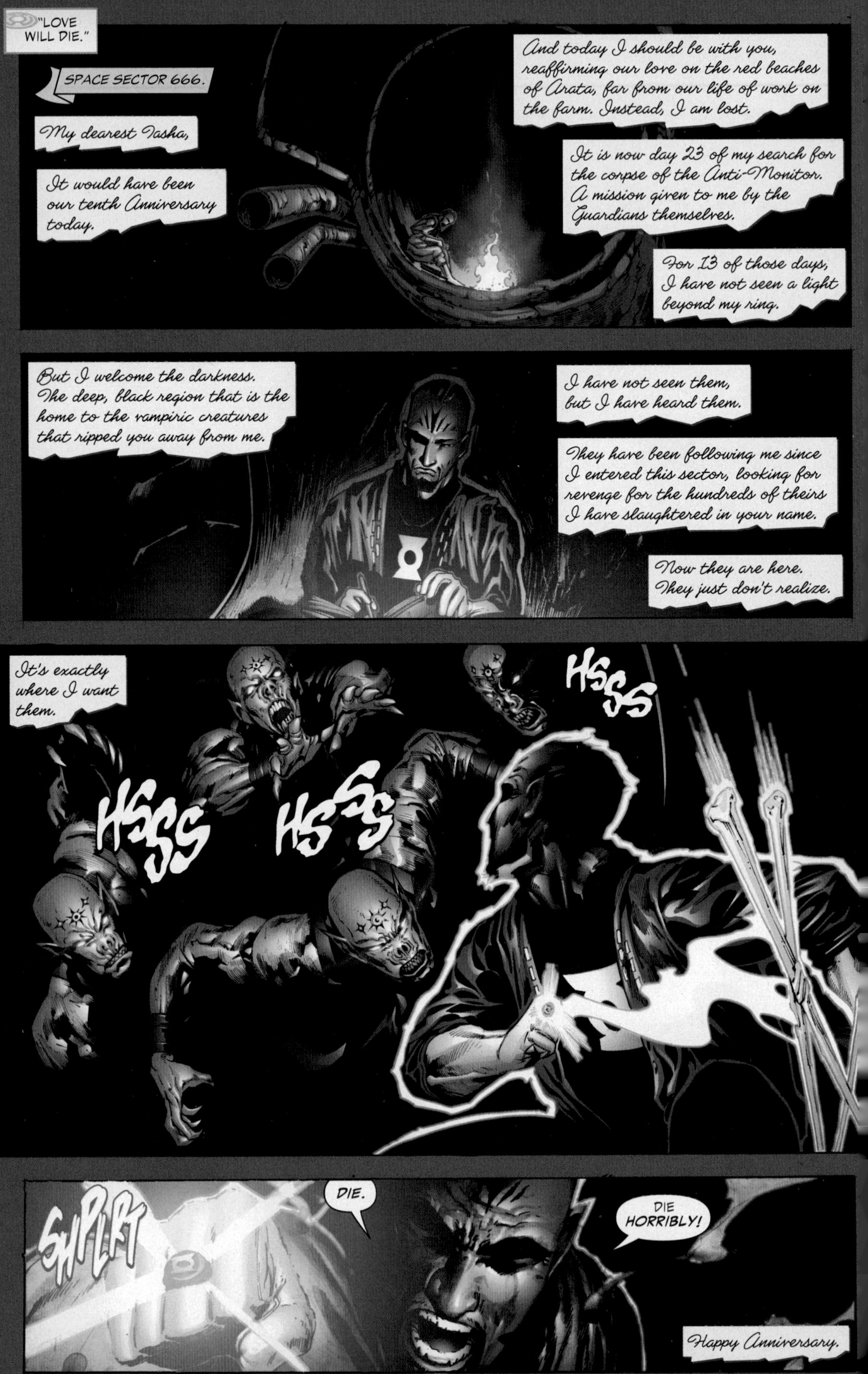
"LOVE WILL DIE."
SPACE SECTOR 666.
My dearest Tasha,
It would have been our tenth Anniversary today.
And today I should be with you, reaffirming our love on the red beaches of Arata, far from our life of work on the farm. Instead, I am lost.
It is now day 23 of my search for the corpse of the Anti-Monitor. A mission given to me by the Guardians themselves.
For 13 of those days, I have not seen a light beyond my ring.
But I welcome the darkness. The deep, black region that is the home to the vampiric creatures that ripped you away from me.
I have not seen them, but I have heard them.
They have been following me since I entered this sector, looking for revenge for the hundreds of theirs I have slaughtered in your name.
Now they are here. They just don't realize.
It's exactly where I want them.
HSSS
HSSS
HSSS
SHPLRT
DIE.
DIE HORRIBLY!
Happy Anniversary.

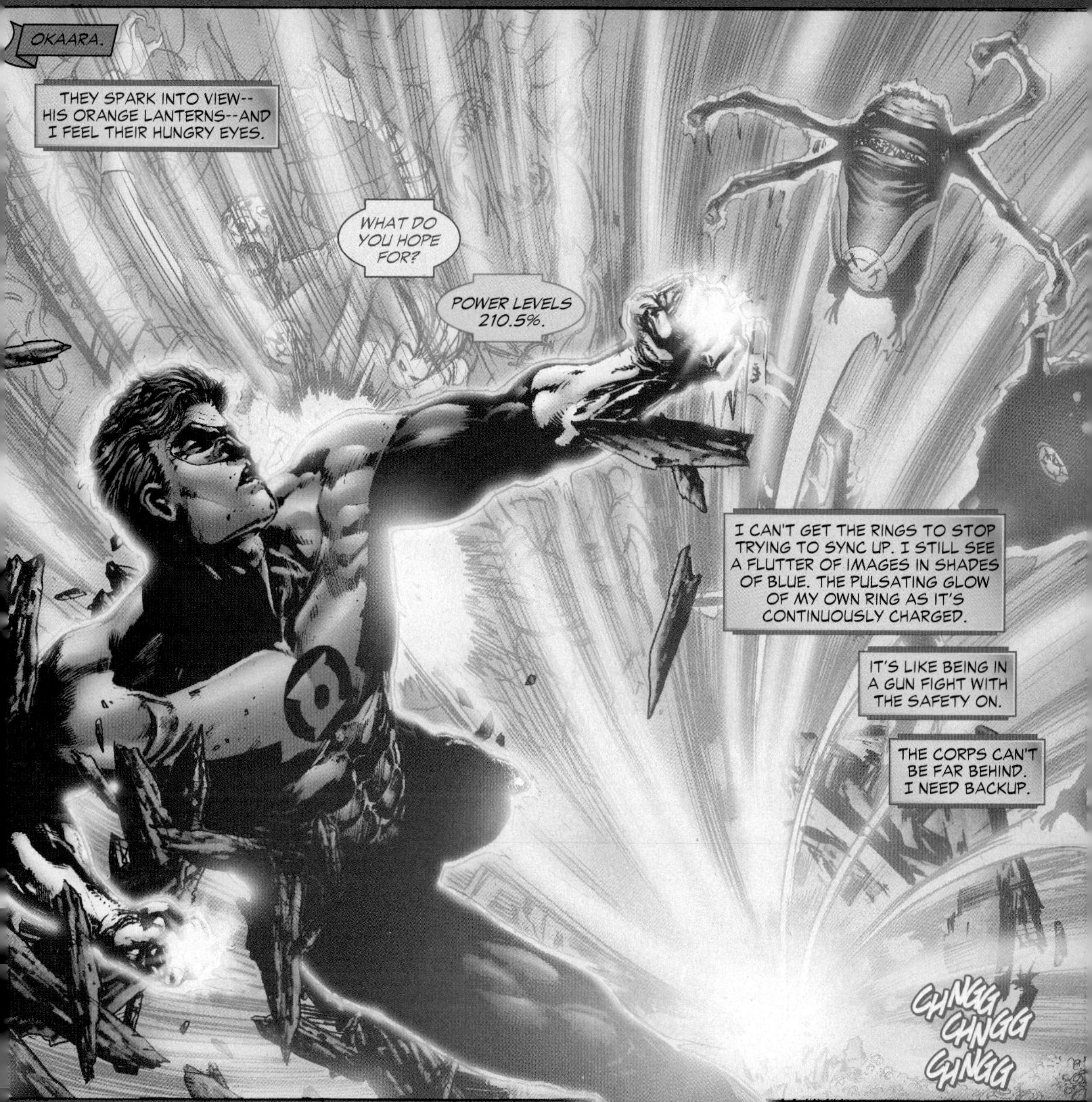
OKAARA.
THEY SPARK INTO VIEW-- HIS ORANGE LANTERNS--AND I FEEL THEIR HUNGRY EYES.
WHAT DO YOU HOPE FOR?
POWER LEVELS 210.5%.
I CAN'T GET THE RINGS TO STOP TRYING TO SYNC UP. I STILL SEE A FLUTTER OF IMAGES IN SHADES OF BLUE. THE PULSATING GLOW OF MY OWN RING AS IT'S CONTINUOUSLY CHARGED.
IT'S LIKE BEING IN A GUN FIGHT WITH THE SAFETY ON.
THE CORPS CAN'T BE FAR BEHIND. I NEED BACKUP.
CHNGG CHNGG CHNGG

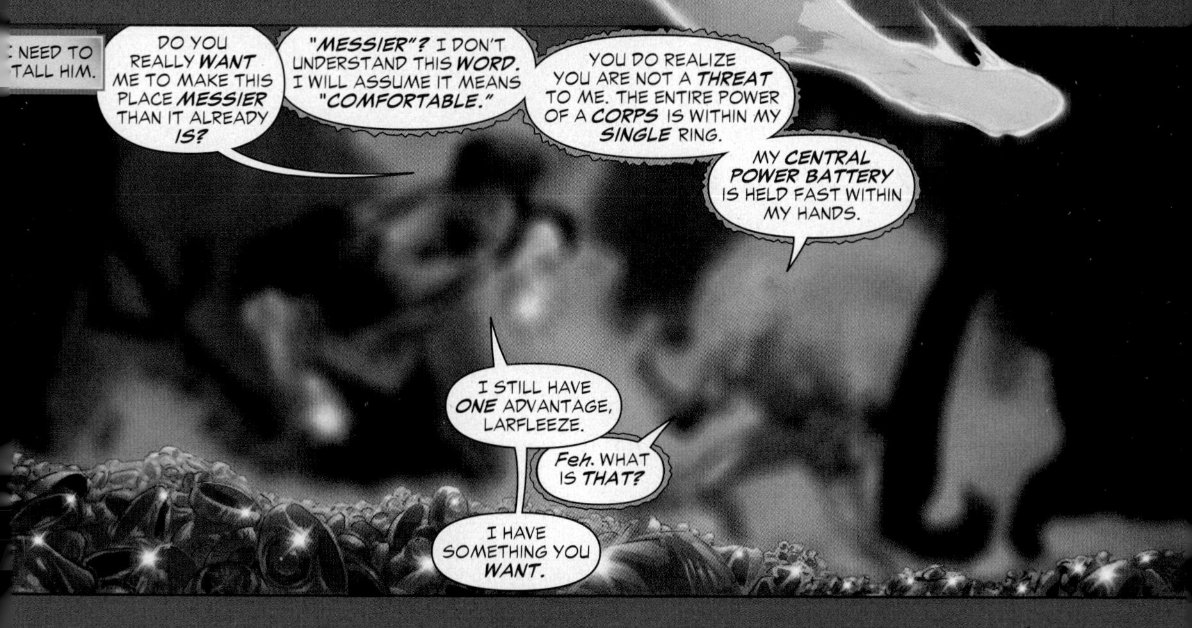
NEED TO TALL HIM.
DO YOU REALLY WANT ME TO MAKE THIS PLACE MESSIER THAN IT ALREADY IS?
"MESSIER"? I DON'T UNDERSTAND THIS WORD. I WILL ASSUME IT MEANS "COMFORTABLE."
YOU DO REALIZE YOU ARE NOT A THREAT TO ME. THE ENTIRE POWER OF A CORPS IS WITHIN MY SINGLE RING.
MY CENTRAL POWER BATTERY IS HELD FAST WITHIN MY HANDS.
I STILL HAVE ONE ADVANTAGE, LARFLEEZE.
Feh. WHAT IS THAT?
I HAVE SOMETHING YOU WANT.

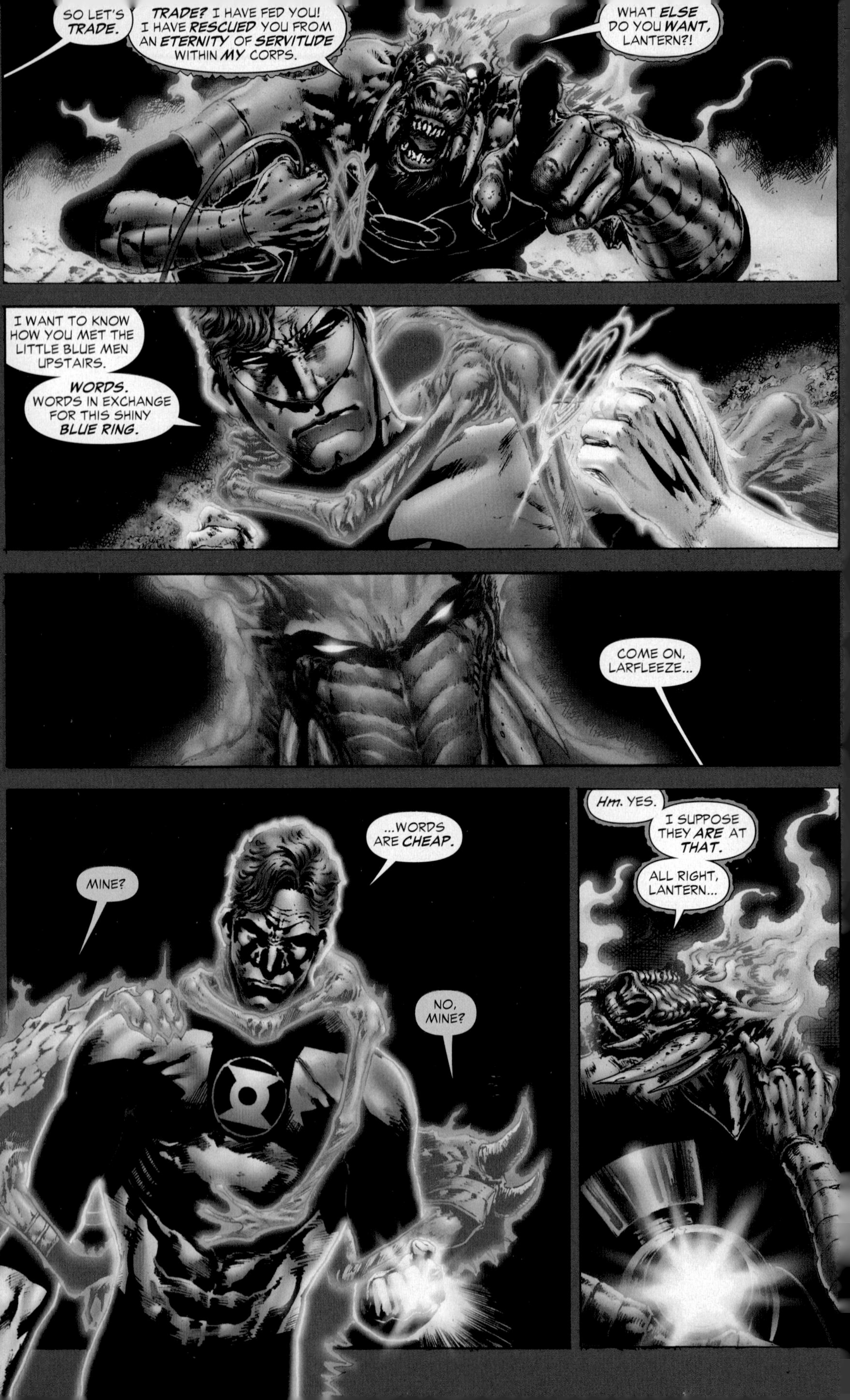
SO LET'S TRADE.
TRADE? I HAVE FED YOU! I HAVE RESCUED YOU FROM AN ETERNITY OF SERVITUDE WITHIN MY CORPS.
WHAT ELSE DO YOU WANT, LANTERN?!
I WANT TO KNOW HOW YOU MET THE LITTLE BLUE MEN UPSTAIRS.
WORDS. WORDS IN EXCHANGE FOR THIS SHINY BLUE RING.
COME ON, LARFLEEZE...
...WORDS ARE CHEAP.
MINE?
NO, MINE?
Hm. YES.
I SUPPOSE THEY ARE AT THAT.
ALL RIGHT, LANTERN...

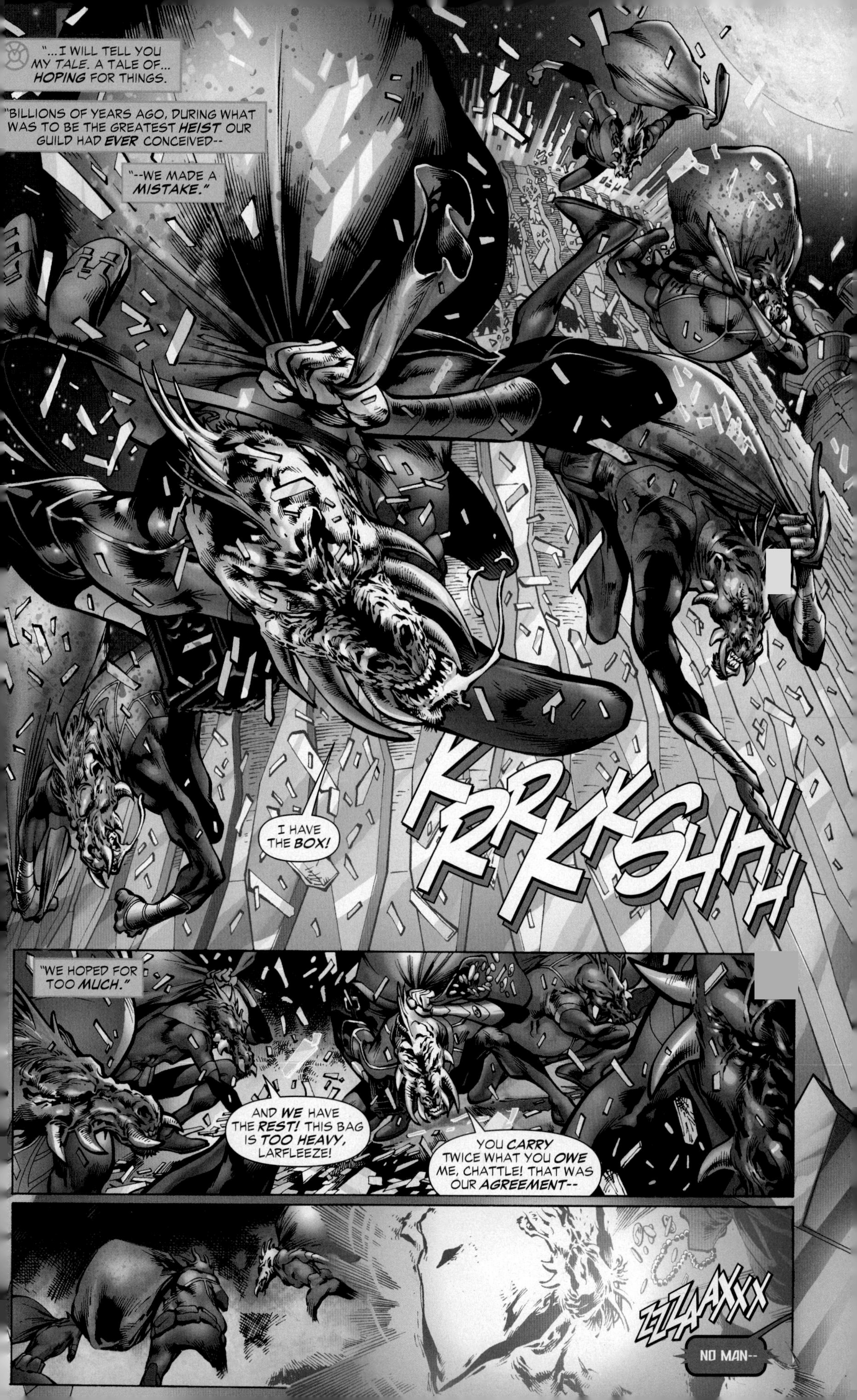
"...I WILL TELL YOU MY TALE. A TALE OF... HOPING FOR THINGS.
"BILLIONS OF YEARS AGO, DURING WHAT WAS TO BE THE GREATEST HEIST OUR GUILD HAD EVER CONCEIVED--
"--WE MADE A MISTAKE."
I HAVE THE BOX!
KRRKSHH
"WE HOPED FOR TOO MUCH."
AND WE HAVE THE REST! THIS BAG IS TOO HEAVY, LARFLEEZE!
YOU CARRY TWICE WHAT YOU OWE ME, CHATTLE! THAT WAS OUR AGREEMENT--
ZZZAAXXX
NO MAN--

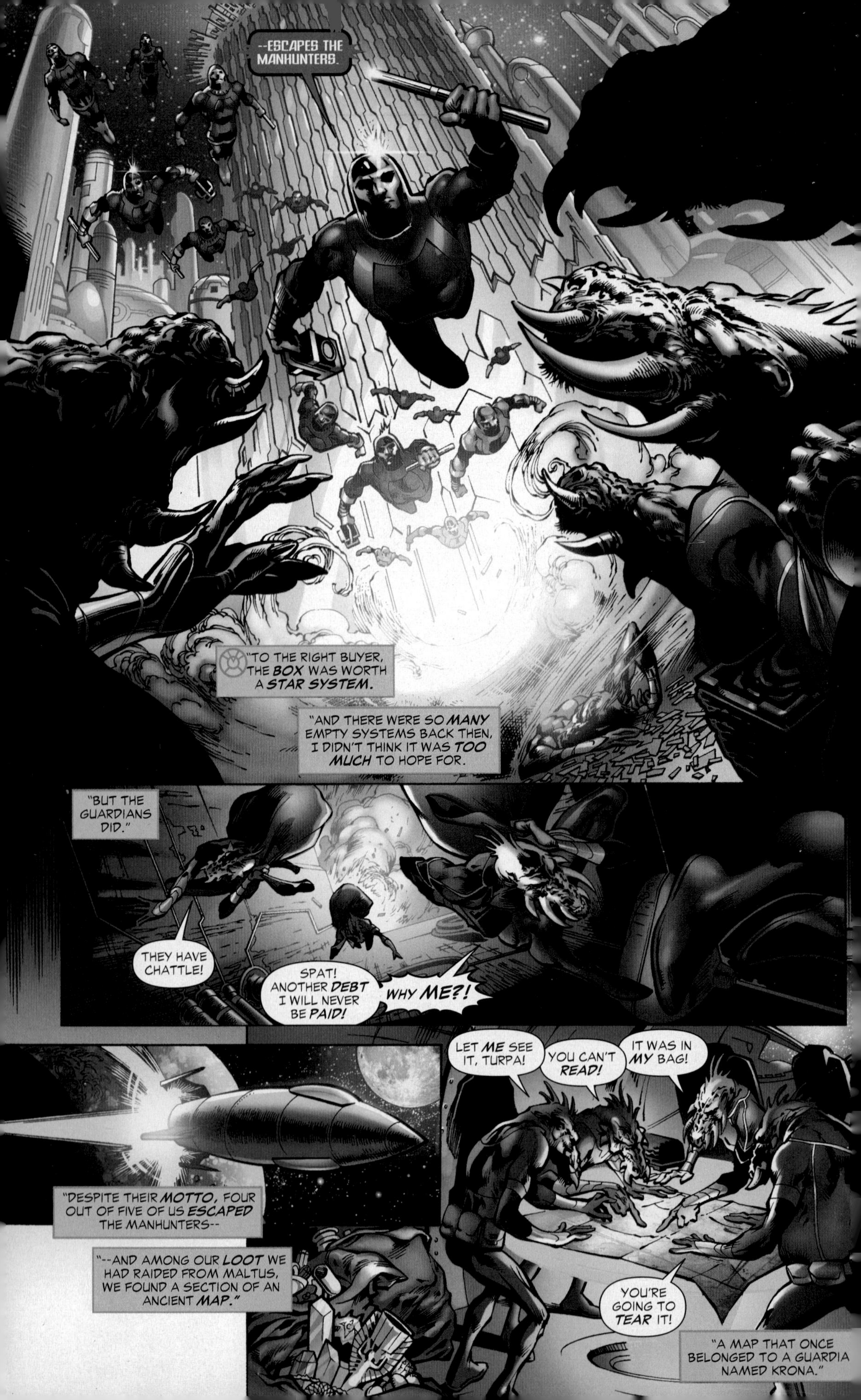
--ESCAPES THE MANHUNTERS.
"TO THE RIGHT BUYER, THE BOX WAS WORTH A STAR SYSTEM.
"AND THERE WERE SO MANY EMPTY SYSTEMS BACK THEN, I DIDN'T THINK IT WAS TOO MUCH TO HOPE FOR.
"BUT THE GUARDIANS DID."
THEY HAVE CHATTLE!
SPAT! ANOTHER DEBT I WILL NEVER BE PAID!
WHY ME?!
"DESPITE THEIR MOTTO, FOUR OUT OF FIVE OF US ESCAPED THE MANHUNTERS--
"--AND AMONG OUR LOOT WE HAD RAIDED FROM MALTUS, WE FOUND A SECTION OF AN ANCIENT MAP."
LET ME SEE IT, TURPA!
YOU CAN'T READ!
IT WAS IN MY BAG!
YOU'RE GOING TO TEAR IT!
"A MAP THAT ONCE BELONGED TO A GUARDIA NAMED KRONA."

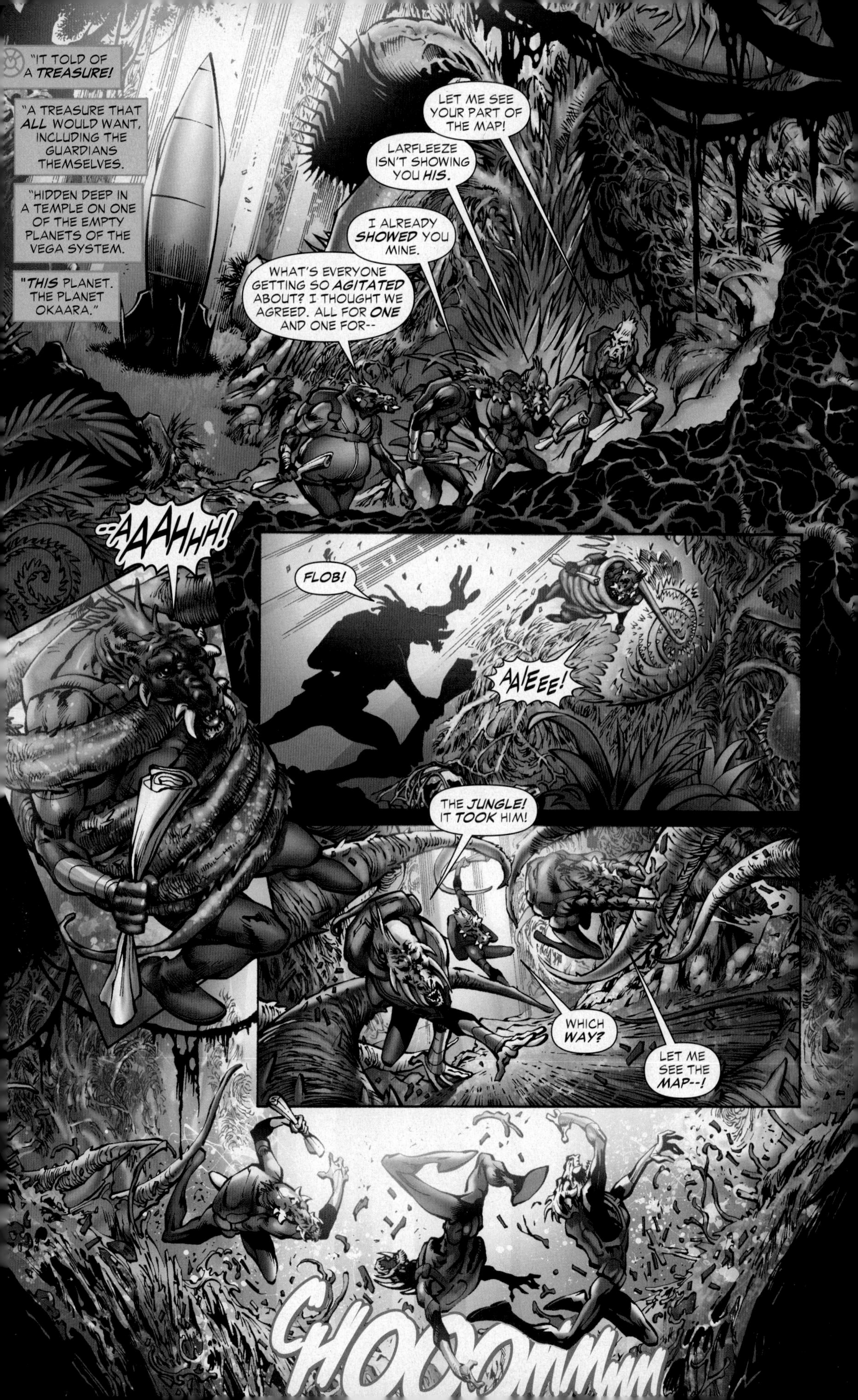
"IT TOLD OF A TREASURE!
"A TREASURE THAT ALL WOULD WANT, INCLUDING THE GUARDIANS THEMSELVES.
"HIDDEN DEEP IN A TEMPLE ON ONE OF THE EMPTY PLANETS OF THE VEGA SYSTEM.
"THIS PLANET. THE PLANET OKAARA."
LET ME SEE YOUR PART OF THE MAP!
LARFLEEZE ISN'T SHOWING YOU HIS.
I ALREADY SHOWED YOU MINE.
WHAT'S EVERYONE GETTING SO AGITATED ABOUT? I THOUGHT WE AGREED. ALL FOR ONE AND ONE FOR--
--AAAHHH!
FLOB!
AAIEEE!
THE JUNGLE! IT TOOK HIM!
WHICH WAY?
LET ME SEE THE MAP--!
CHOOOMMMM

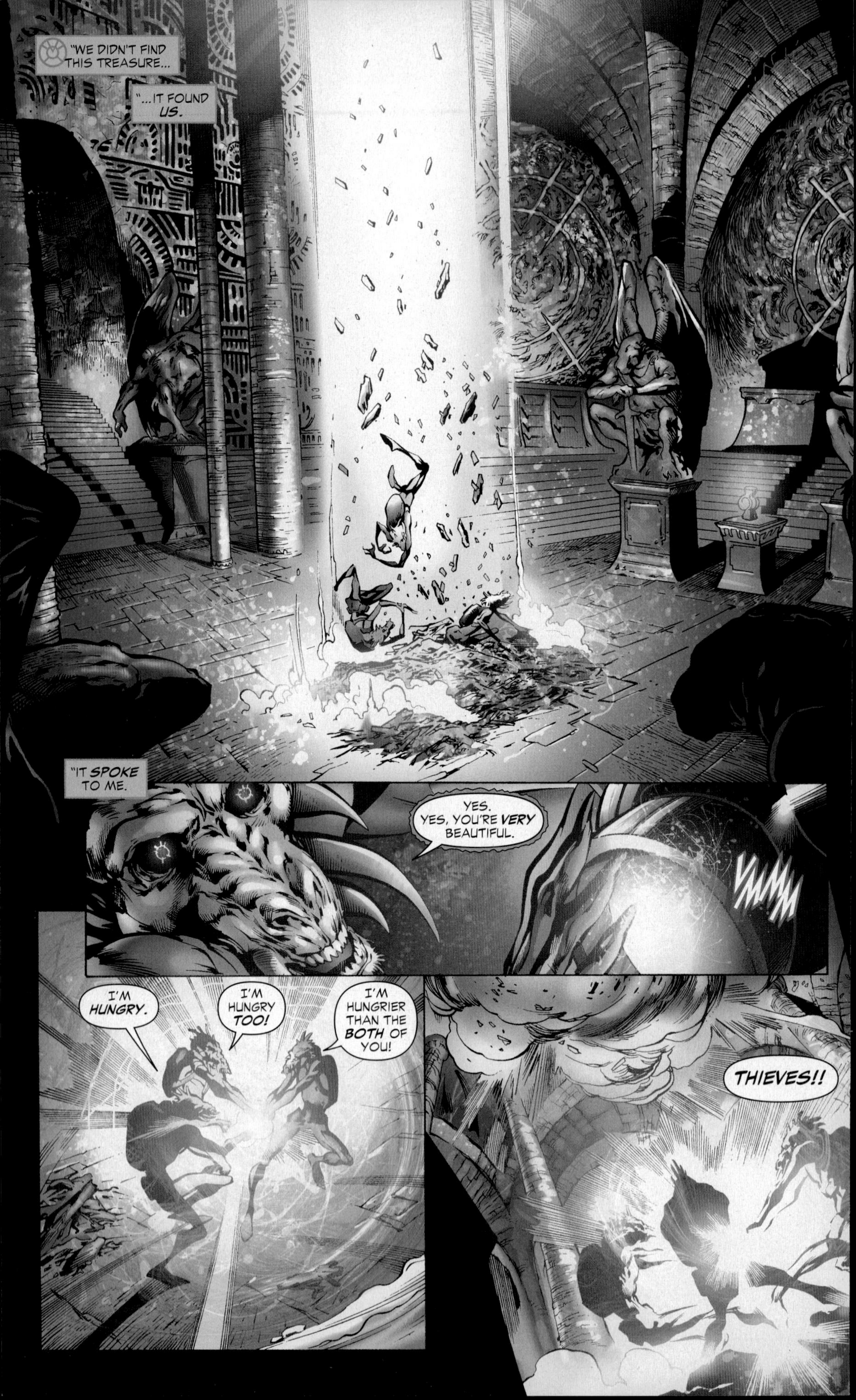
"WE DIDN'T FIND THIS TREASURE...
"...IT FOUND US.
"IT SPOKE TO ME.
YES. YES, YOU'RE VERY BEAUTIFUL.
VMMM
I'M HUNGRY.
I'M HUNGRY TOO!
I'M HUNGRIER THAN THE BOTH OF YOU!
THIEVES!!

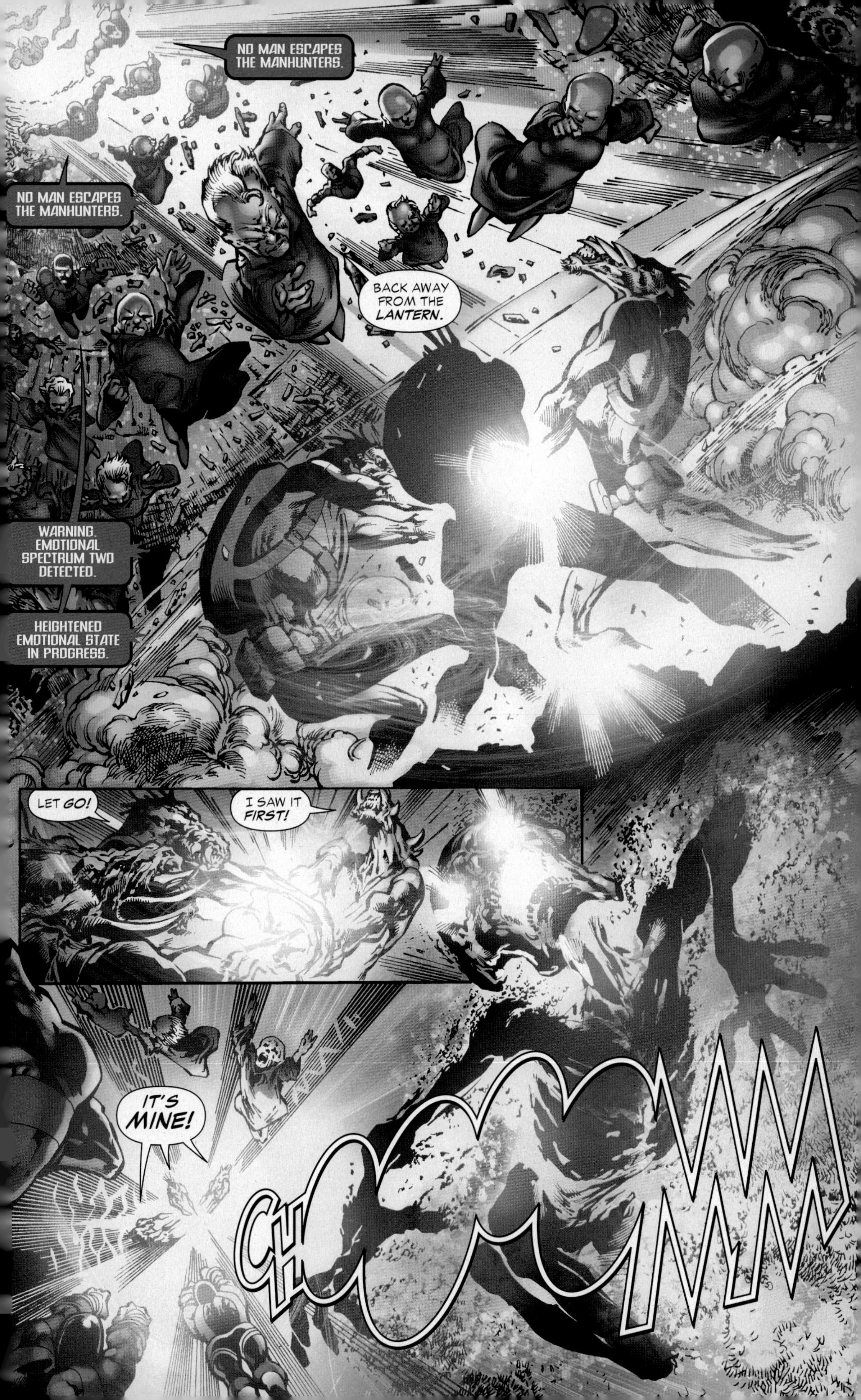
NO MAN ESCAPES THE MANHUNTERS.
NO MAN ESCAPES THE MANHUNTERS.
BACK AWAY FROM THE LANTERN.
WARNING. EMOTIONAL SPECTRUM TWO DETECTED.
HEIGHTENED EMOTIONAL STATE IN PROGRESS.
LET GO!
I SAW IT FIRST!
IT'S MINE!
CHOOOMMM

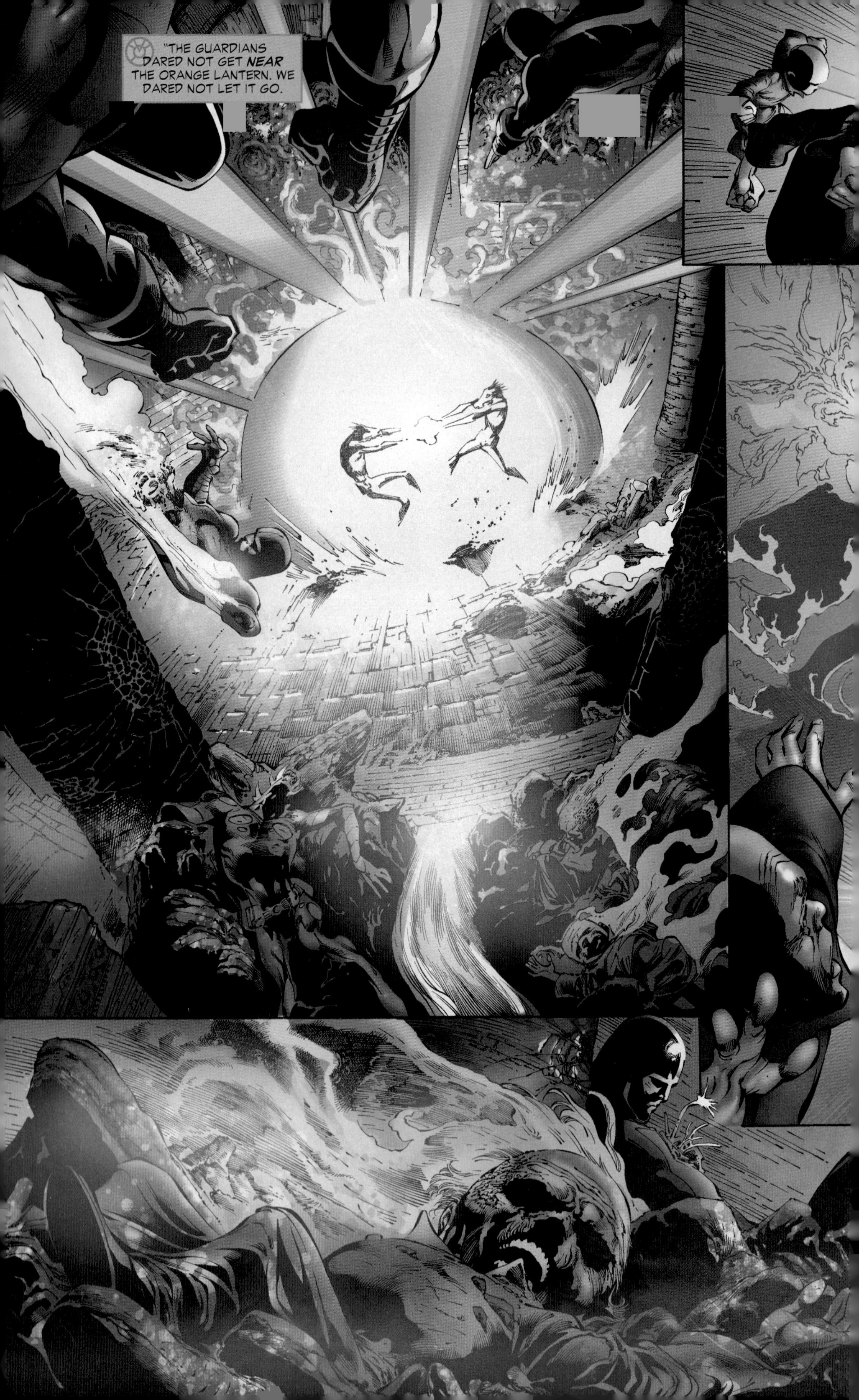
"THE GUARDIANS DARED NOT GET NEAR THE ORANGE LANTERN. WE DARED NOT LET IT GO.

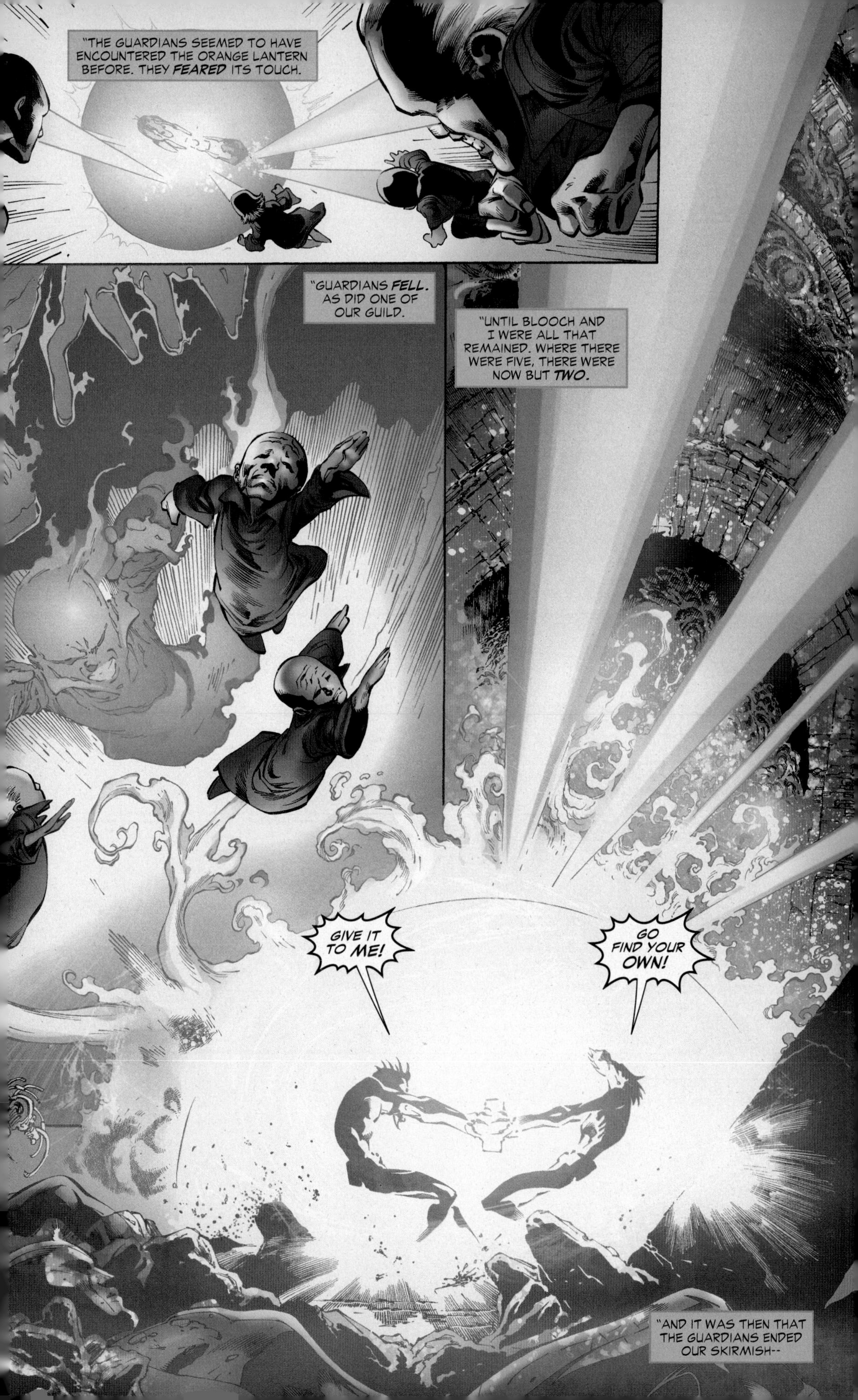
"THE GUARDIANS SEEMED TO HAVE ENCOUNTERED THE ORANGE LANTERN BEFORE. THEY FEARED ITS TOUCH.
"GUARDIANS FELL. AS DID ONE OF OUR GUILD.
"UNTIL BLOOCH AND I WERE ALL THAT REMAINED. WHERE THERE WERE FIVE, THERE WERE NOW BUT TWO.
GIVE IT TO ME!
GO FIND YOUR OWN!
"AND IT WAS THEN THAT THE GUARDIANS ENDED OUR SKIRMISH--

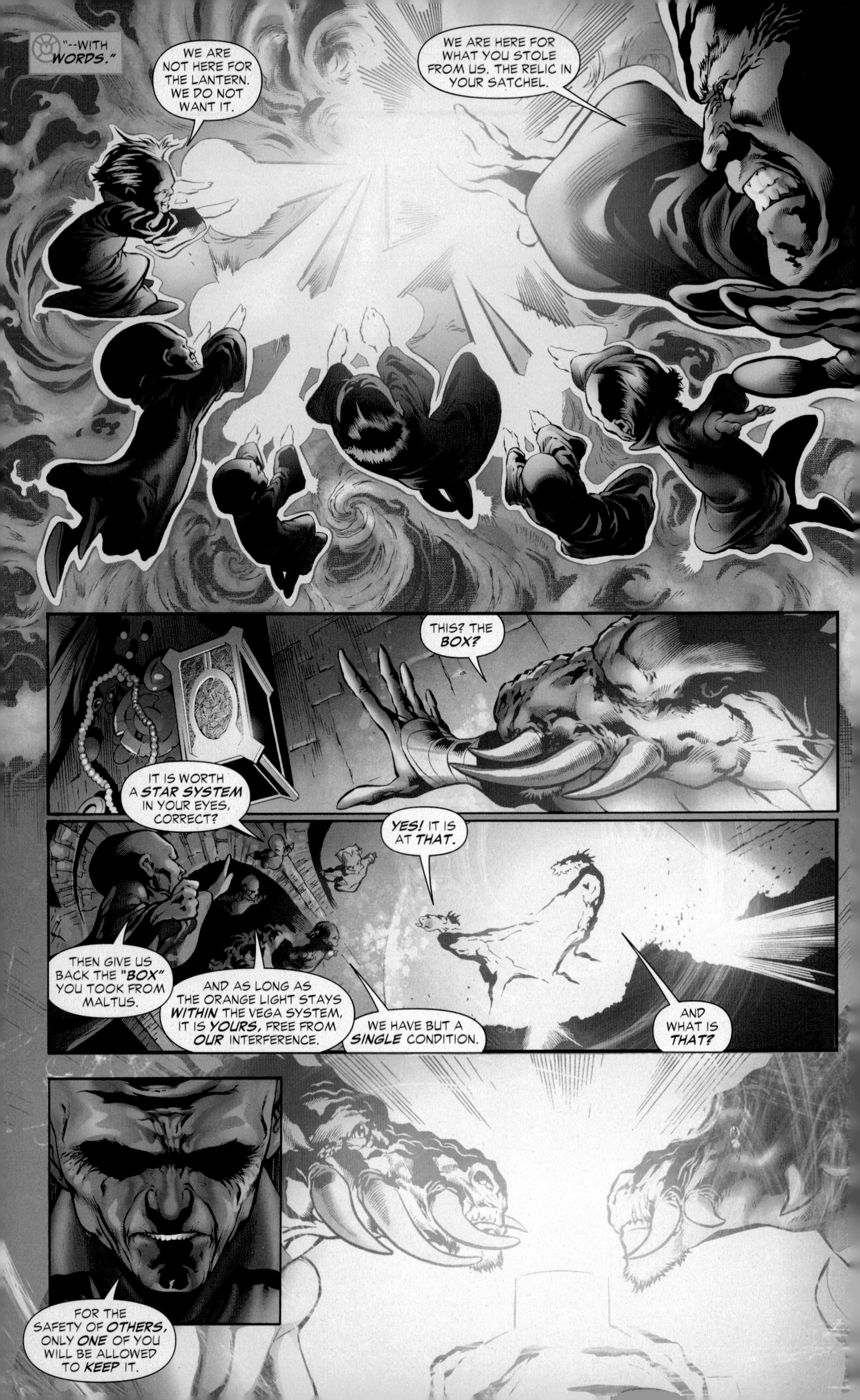
"--WITH WORDS."
WE ARE NOT HERE FOR THE LANTERN. WE DO NOT WANT IT.
WE ARE HERE FOR WHAT YOU STOLE FROM US. THE RELIC IN YOUR SATCHEL.
THIS? THE BOX?
IT IS WORTH A STAR SYSTEM IN YOUR EYES, CORRECT?
YES! IT IS AT THAT.
THEN GIVE US BACK THE "BOX" YOU TOOK FROM MALTUS.
AND AS LONG AS THE ORANGE LIGHT STAYS WITHIN THE VEGA SYSTEM, IT IS YOURS, FREE FROM OUR INTERFERENCE.
WE HAVE BUT A SINGLE CONDITION.
AND WHAT IS THAT?
FOR THE SAFETY OF OTHERS, ONLY ONE OF YOU WILL BE ALLOWED TO KEEP IT.

I WON.

AND THE GUARDIANS *BURIED* OUR PACT IN ORDER TO BURY THE *KNOWLEDGE* OF THE *ORANGE LIGHT.*

JUST AS THEY BURIED THE KNOWLEDGE OF THE MASSACRE OF SECTOR 666 AND PARALLAX.

PARALLAX? WHAT DO YOU KNOW ABOUT PARALLAX?

"WHAT DO YOU THINK WAS IN THE *BOX,* LANTERN?"

YOU HAVE HEARD MY TALE, NOW GIVE ME THE RING--

WAIT--

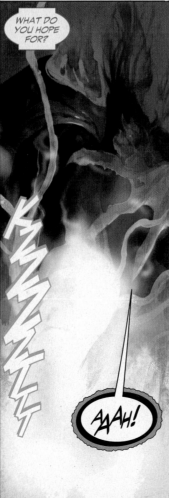

WHAT DO YOU HOPE FOR?

KWWWWWWT

AAAH!

YOU! YOU ARE *WELSHING!* YOU'RE A *WELSHER!*

I'M *TRYING* TO GET IT *OFF.*

ENOUGH BARTERING!

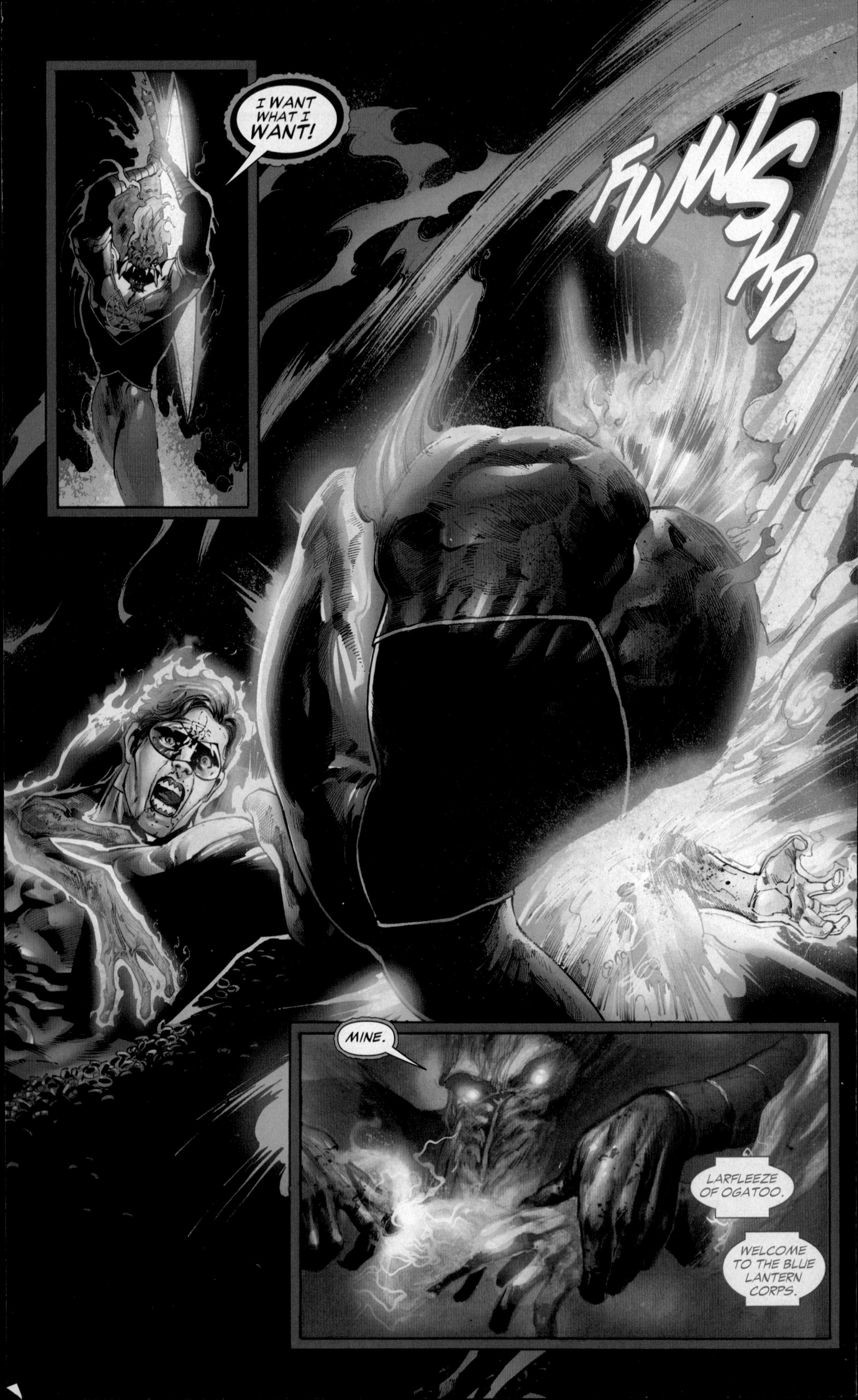
I WANT WHAT I WANT!
FWWSHD
MINE.
LARFLEEZE OF OGATOO.
WELCOME TO THE BLUE LANTERN CORPS.

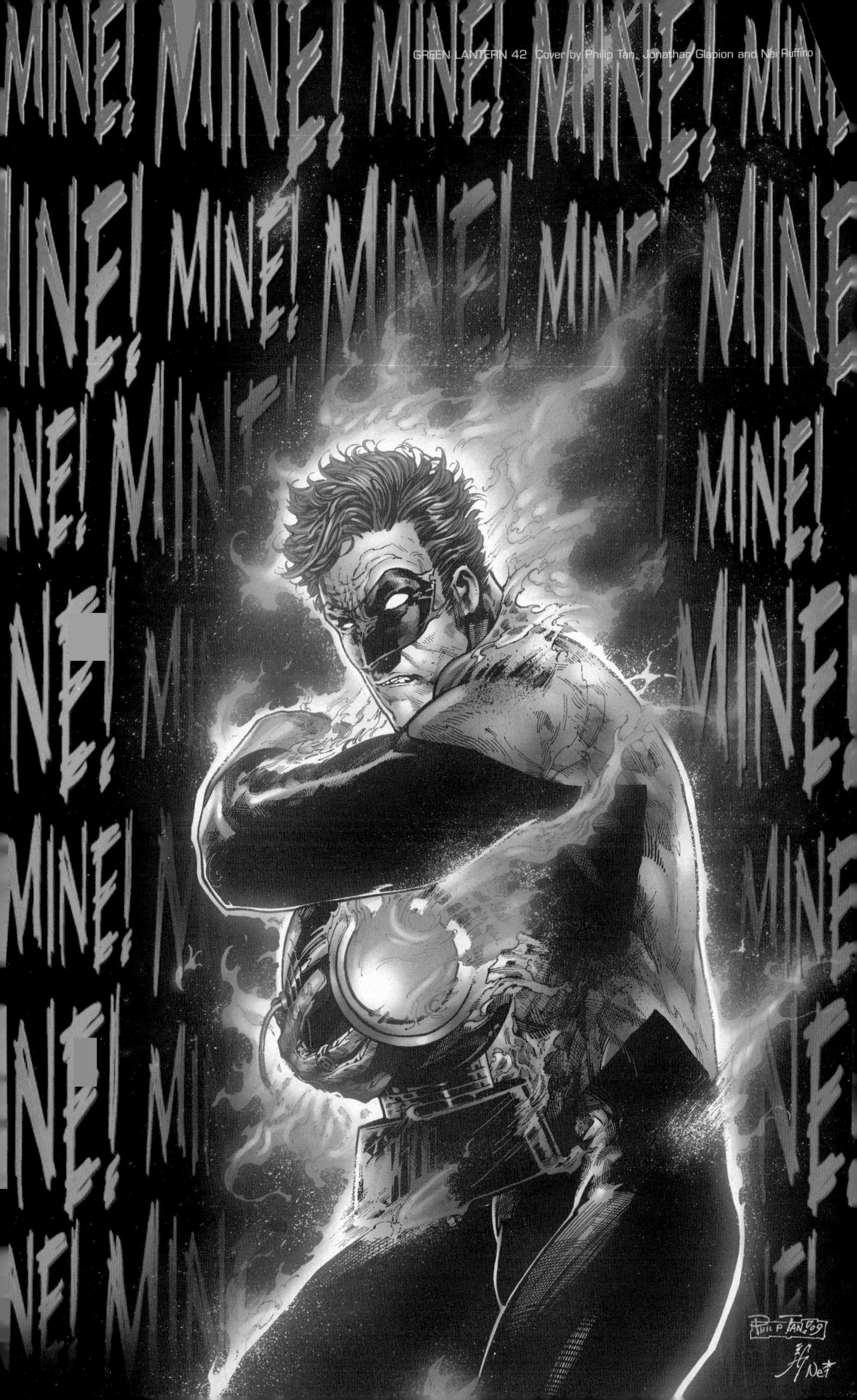
MINE! MINE! MINE! MINE!
MINE! MINE!
MINE!
MINE!
MINE!
MINE!
MINE!
PHILIP TAN '09
Nei

GREEN LANTERN 42 Cover by Philip Tan, Jonathan Glapion and Nei Ruffino

AGENT ORANGE
Part 4

Philip Tan   Eddy Barrows Pencils
Jonathan Glapion   Ruy José Inks

ORIGINS & OMENS

Ivan Reis Pencils
Oclair Albert Inks

TALES OF THE ORANGE LANTERNS: WEED KILLER

Rafael Albuquerque Artist

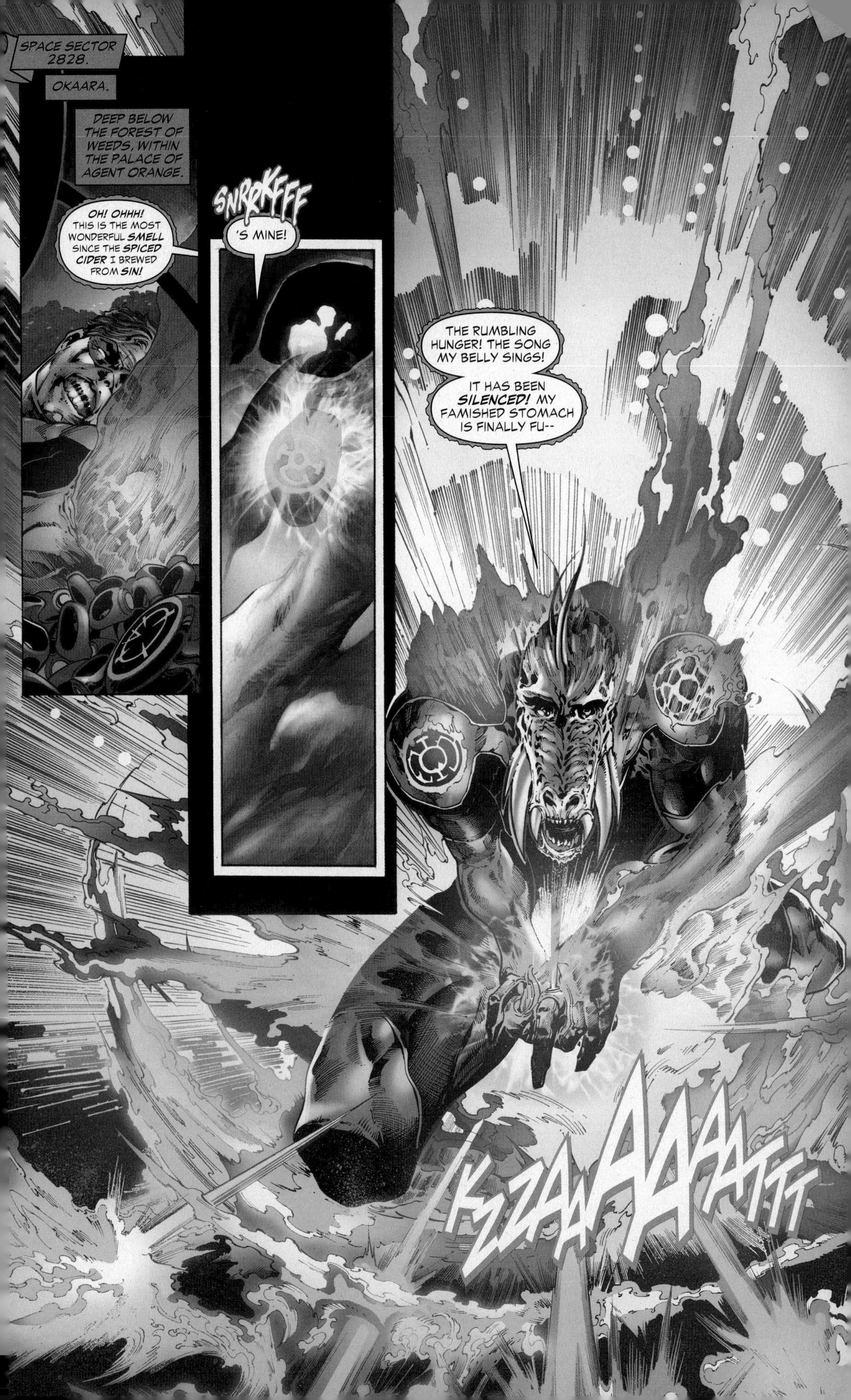
SPACE SECTOR 2828.
OKAARA.
DEEP BELOW THE FOREST OF WEEDS, WITHIN THE PALACE OF AGENT ORANGE.
OH! OHHH! THIS IS THE MOST WONDERFUL SMELL SINCE THE SPICED CIDER I BREWED FROM SIN!
SNRRKFFF
'S MINE!
THE RUMBLING HUNGER! THE SONG MY BELLY SINGS!
IT HAS BEEN SILENCED! MY FAMISHED STOMACH IS FINALLY FU--
KZZAAAAATTT

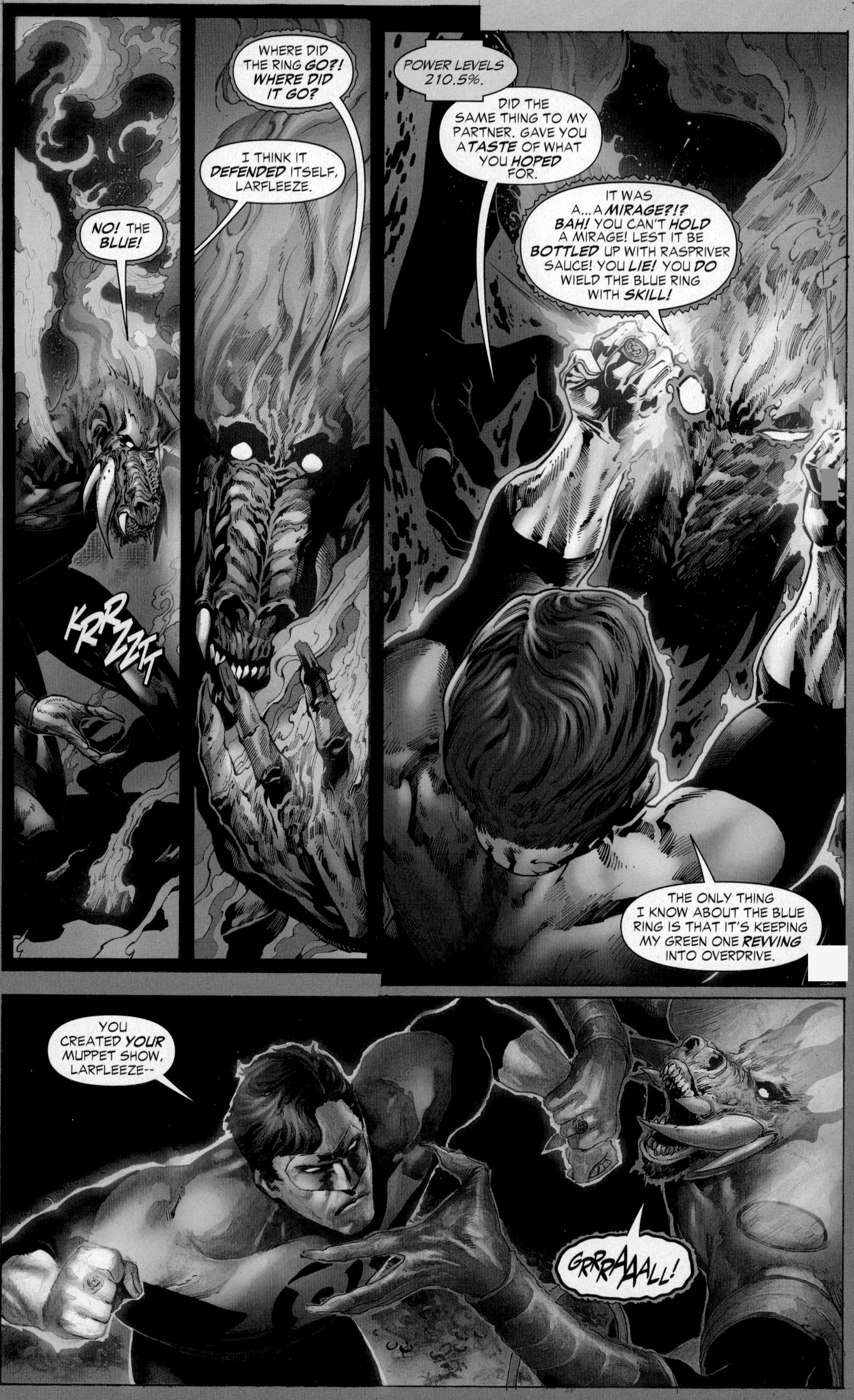
NO! THE BLUE!
KRRZZZK
WHERE DID THE RING GO?! WHERE DID IT GO?
I THINK IT DEFENDED ITSELF, LARFLEEZE.
POWER LEVELS 210.5%.
DID THE SAME THING TO MY PARTNER. GAVE YOU A TASTE OF WHAT YOU HOPED FOR.
IT WAS A...A MIRAGE?!? BAH! YOU CAN'T HOLD A MIRAGE! LEST IT BE BOTTLED UP WITH RASPRIVER SAUCE! YOU LIE! YOU DO WIELD THE BLUE RING WITH SKILL!
THE ONLY THING I KNOW ABOUT THE BLUE RING IS THAT IT'S KEEPING MY GREEN ONE REVVING INTO OVERDRIVE.
YOU CREATED YOUR MUPPET SHOW, LARFLEEZE--
GRRRAAALL!

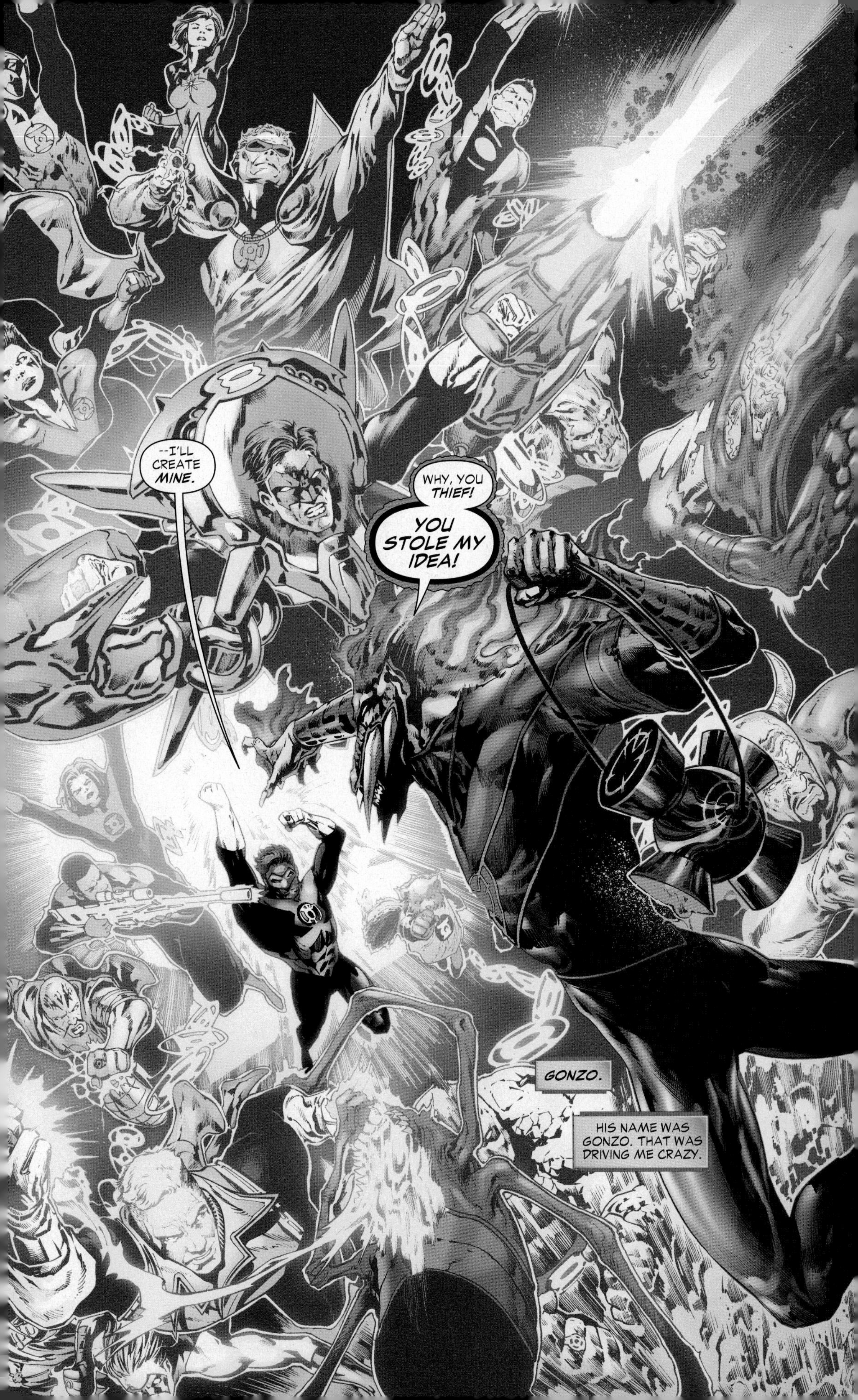
--I'LL CREATE MINE.
WHY, YOU THIEF!
YOU STOLE MY IDEA!
GONZO.
HIS NAME WAS GONZO. THAT WAS DRIVING ME CRAZY.

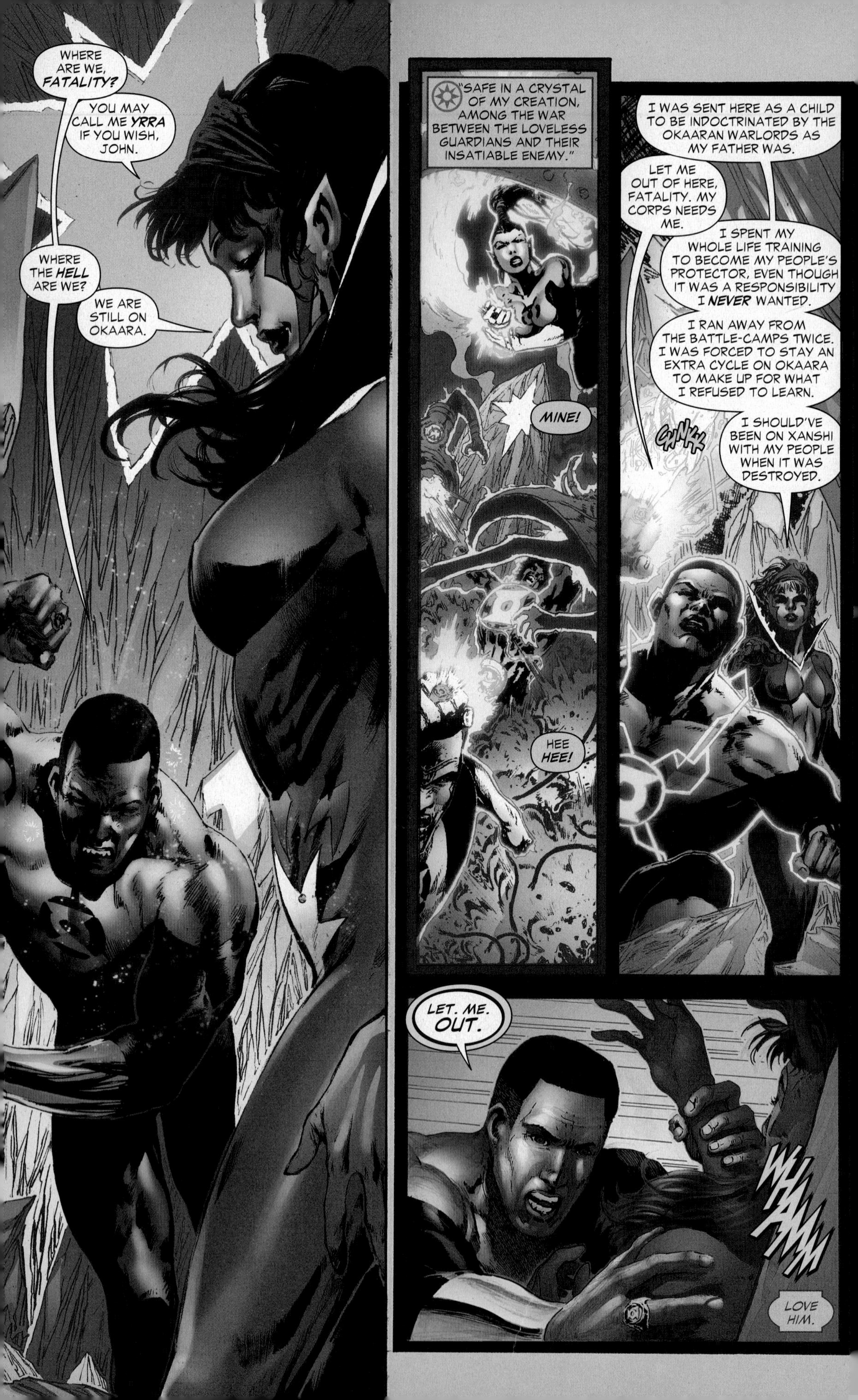

WHERE ARE WE, FATALITY?
YOU MAY CALL ME YRRA IF YOU WISH, JOHN.
WHERE THE HELL ARE WE?
WE ARE STILL ON OKAARA.
"SAFE IN A CRYSTAL OF MY CREATION, AMONG THE WAR BETWEEN THE LOVELESS GUARDIANS AND THEIR INSATIABLE ENEMY."
MINE!
HEE HEE!
I WAS SENT HERE AS A CHILD TO BE INDOCTRINATED BY THE OKAARAN WARLORDS AS MY FATHER WAS.
LET ME OUT OF HERE, FATALITY. MY CORPS NEEDS ME.
I SPENT MY WHOLE LIFE TRAINING TO BECOME MY PEOPLE'S PROTECTOR, EVEN THOUGH IT WAS A RESPONSIBILITY I NEVER WANTED.
I RAN AWAY FROM THE BATTLE-CAMPS TWICE. I WAS FORCED TO STAY AN EXTRA CYCLE ON OKAARA TO MAKE UP FOR WHAT I REFUSED TO LEARN.
I SHOULD'VE BEEN ON XANSHI WITH MY PEOPLE WHEN IT WAS DESTROYED.
LET. ME. OUT.
WHAMM
LOVE HIM.

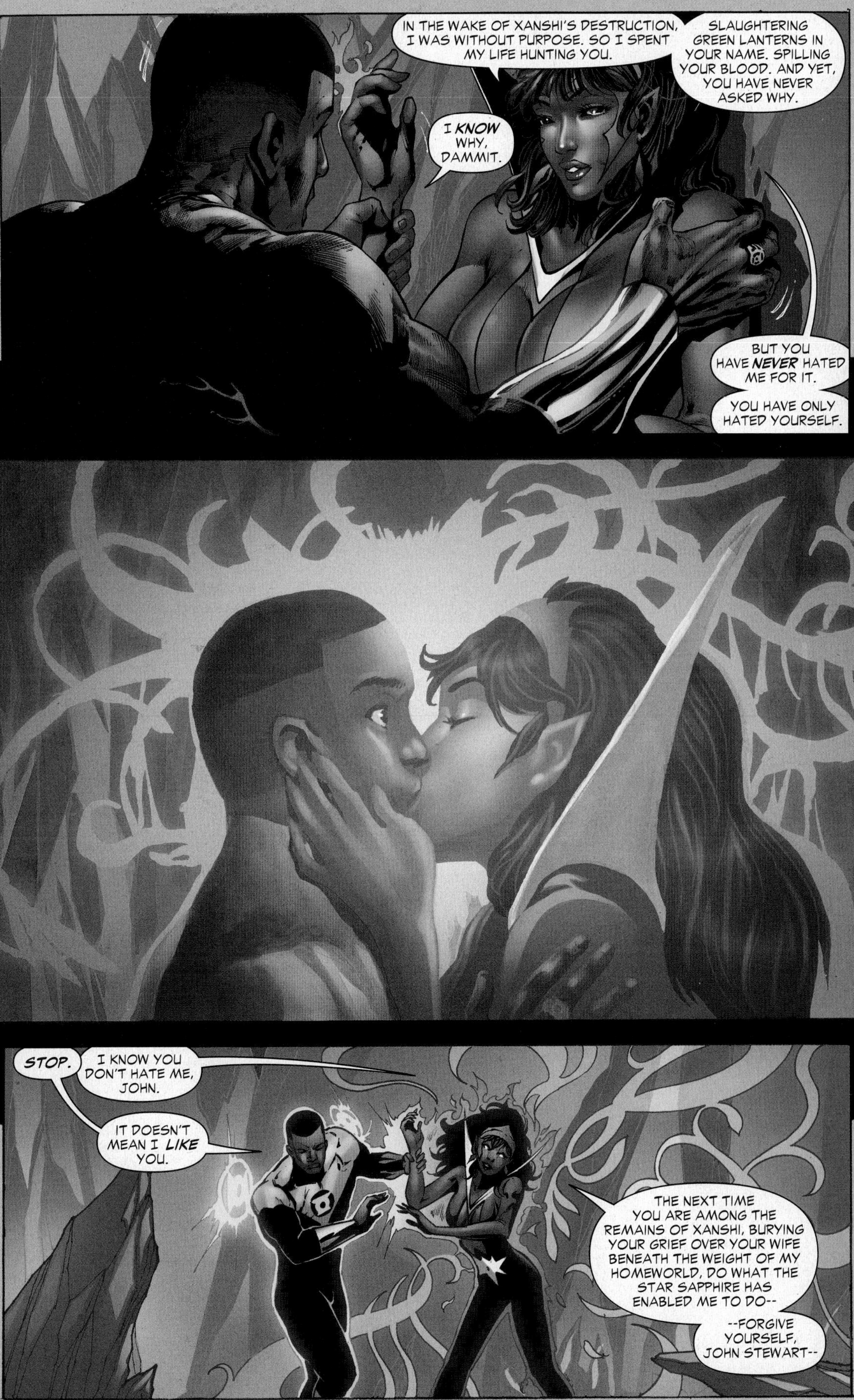
IN THE WAKE OF XANSHI'S DESTRUCTION, I WAS WITHOUT PURPOSE. SO I SPENT MY LIFE HUNTING YOU.
SLAUGHTERING GREEN LANTERNS IN YOUR NAME. SPILLING YOUR BLOOD. AND YET, YOU HAVE NEVER ASKED WHY.
I **KNOW** WHY, DAMMIT.
BUT YOU HAVE **NEVER** HATED ME FOR IT.
YOU HAVE ONLY HATED YOURSELF.
STOP.
I KNOW YOU DON'T HATE ME, JOHN.
IT DOESN'T MEAN I **LIKE** YOU.
THE NEXT TIME YOU ARE AMONG THE REMAINS OF XANSHI, BURYING YOUR GRIEF OVER YOUR WIFE BENEATH THE WEIGHT OF MY HOMEWORLD, DO WHAT THE STAR SAPPHIRE HAS ENABLED ME TO DO--
--FORGIVE YOURSELF, JOHN STEWART--

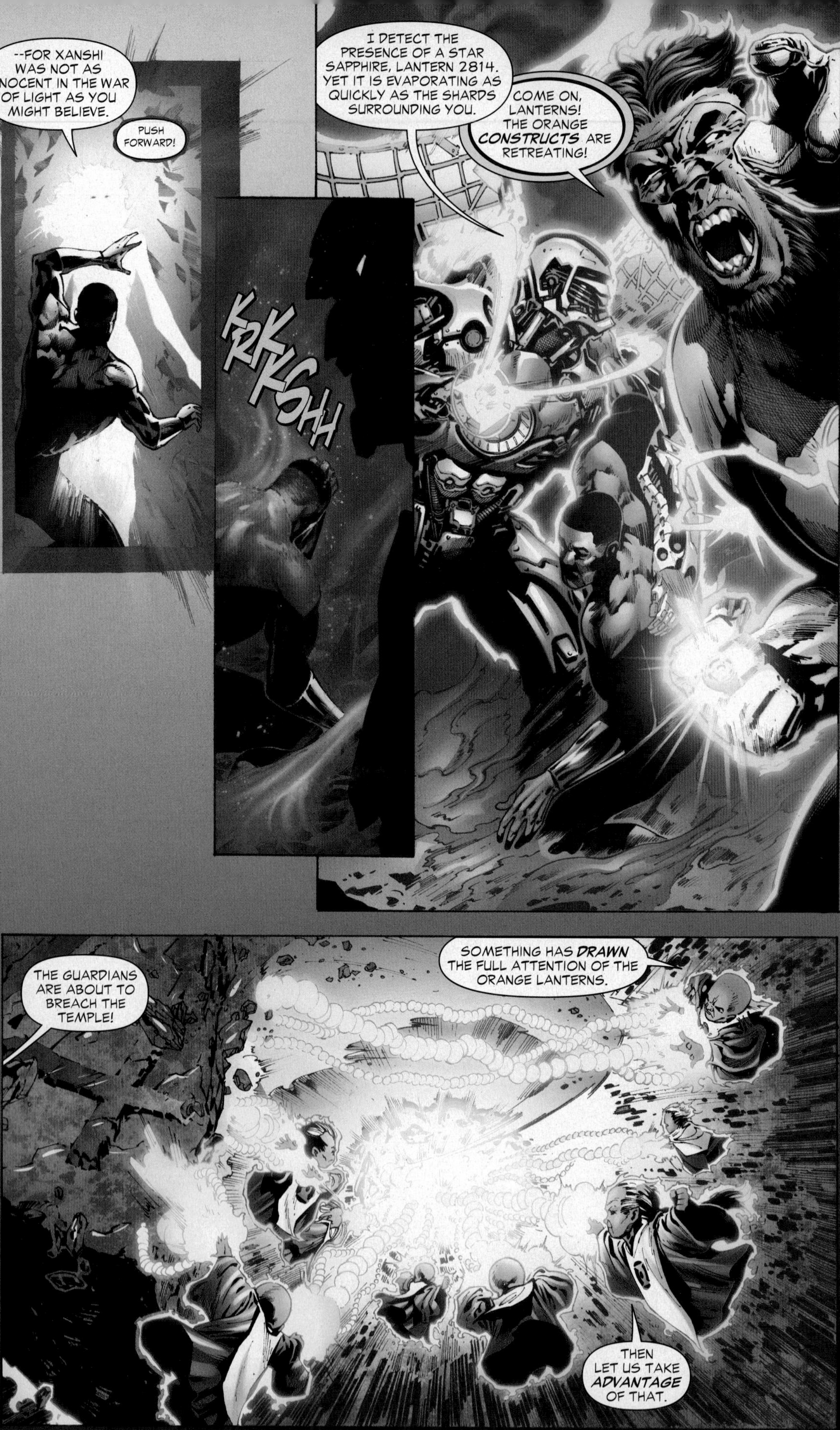
--FOR XANSHI WAS NOT AS INNOCENT IN THE WAR OF LIGHT AS YOU MIGHT BELIEVE.
PUSH FORWARD!
KRKRKKSHH
I DETECT THE PRESENCE OF A STAR SAPPHIRE, LANTERN 2814. YET IT IS EVAPORATING AS QUICKLY AS THE SHARDS SURROUNDING YOU.
COME ON, LANTERNS! THE ORANGE CONSTRUCTS ARE RETREATING!
THE GUARDIANS ARE ABOUT TO BREACH THE TEMPLE!
SOMETHING HAS DRAWN THE FULL ATTENTION OF THE ORANGE LANTERNS.
THEN LET US TAKE ADVANTAGE OF THAT.

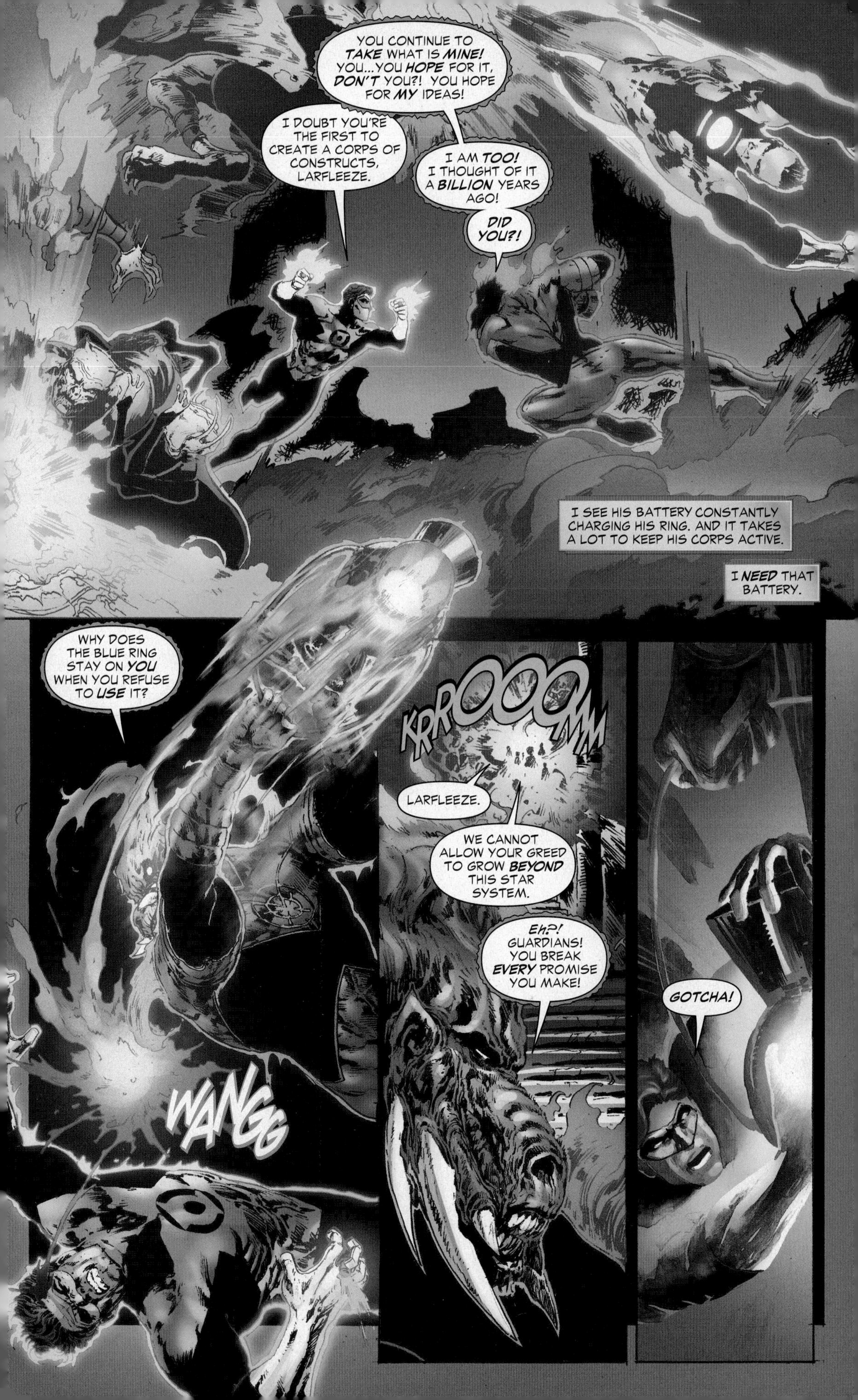

YOU CONTINUE TO TAKE WHAT IS MINE! YOU...YOU HOPE FOR IT, DON'T YOU?! YOU HOPE FOR MY IDEAS!
I DOUBT YOU'RE THE FIRST TO CREATE A CORPS OF CONSTRUCTS, LARFLEEZE.
I AM TOO! I THOUGHT OF IT A BILLION YEARS AGO!
DID YOU?!
I SEE HIS BATTERY CONSTANTLY CHARGING HIS RING. AND IT TAKES A LOT TO KEEP HIS CORPS ACTIVE.
I NEED THAT BATTERY.
WHY DOES THE BLUE RING STAY ON YOU WHEN YOU REFUSE TO USE IT?
WANGG
KRROOOMM
LARFLEEZE.
WE CANNOT ALLOW YOUR GREED TO GROW BEYOND THIS STAR SYSTEM.
Eh?! GUARDIANS! YOU BREAK EVERY PROMISE YOU MAKE!
GOTCHA!

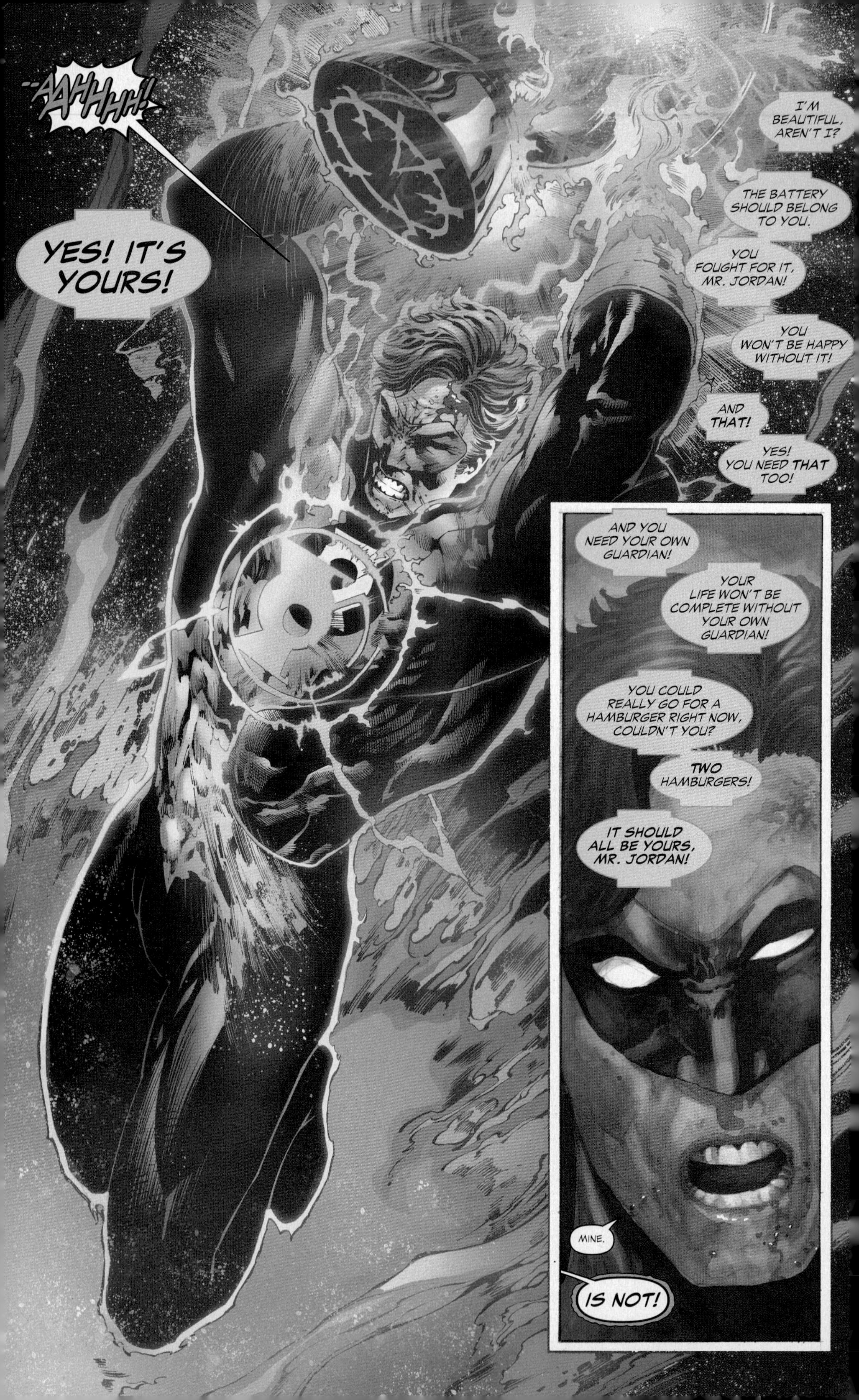
--AAHHHH!
YES! IT'S YOURS!
I'M BEAUTIFUL, AREN'T I?
THE BATTERY SHOULD BELONG TO YOU.
YOU FOUGHT FOR IT, MR. JORDAN!
YOU WON'T BE HAPPY WITHOUT IT!
AND THAT!
YES! YOU NEED THAT TOO!
AND YOU NEED YOUR OWN GUARDIAN!
YOUR LIFE WON'T BE COMPLETE WITHOUT YOUR OWN GUARDIAN!
YOU COULD REALLY GO FOR A HAMBURGER RIGHT NOW, COULDN'T YOU?
TWO HAMBURGERS!
IT SHOULD ALL BE YOURS, MR. JORDAN!
MINE.
IS NOT!

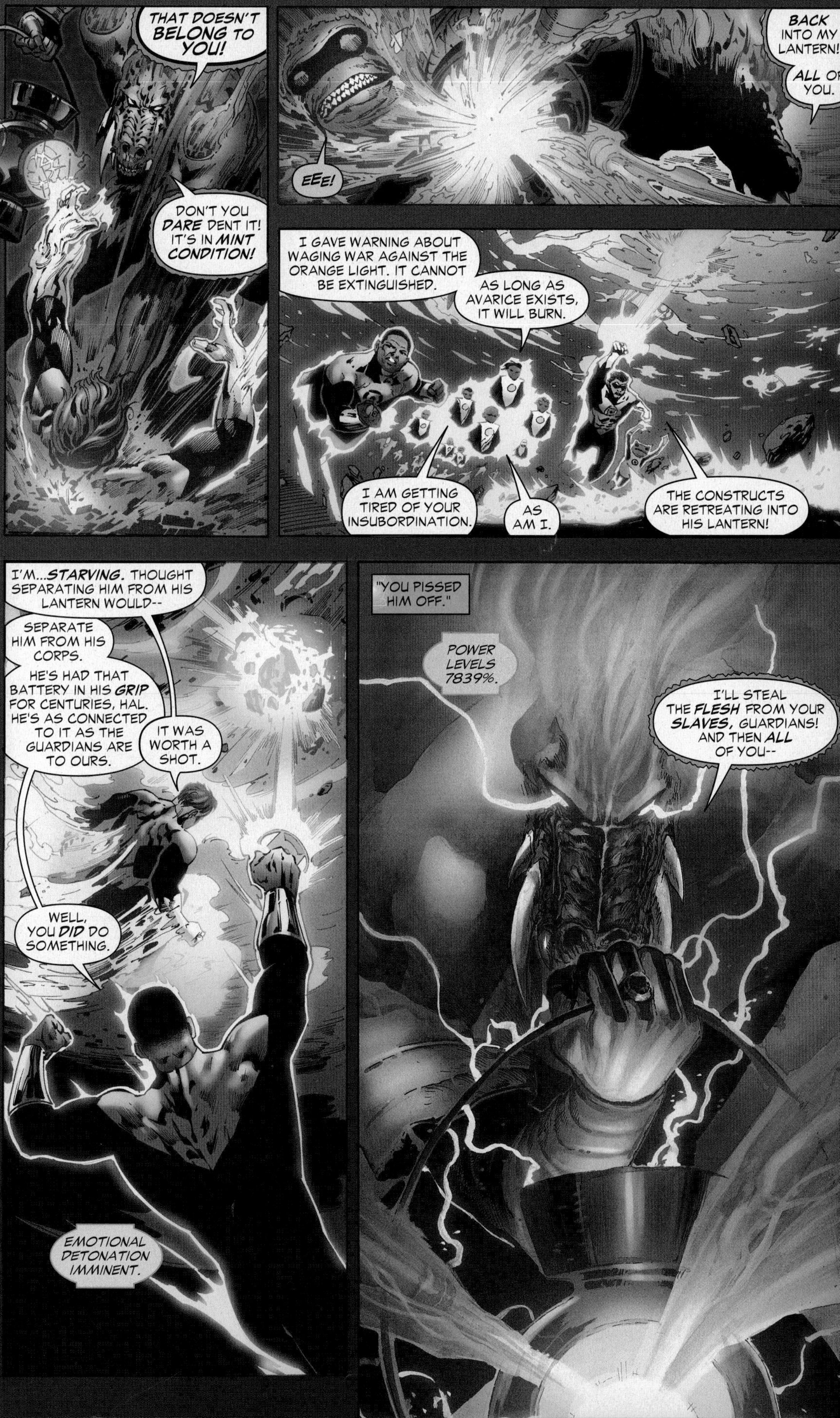
THAT DOESN'T BELONG TO YOU!
DON'T YOU DARE DENT IT! IT'S IN MINT CONDITION!
EEE!
BACK INTO MY LANTERN!
ALL OF YOU.
I GAVE WARNING ABOUT WAGING WAR AGAINST THE ORANGE LIGHT. IT CANNOT BE EXTINGUISHED.
AS LONG AS AVARICE EXISTS, IT WILL BURN.
I AM GETTING TIRED OF YOUR INSUBORDINATION.
AS AM I.
THE CONSTRUCTS ARE RETREATING INTO HIS LANTERN!
I'M...STARVING. THOUGHT SEPARATING HIM FROM HIS LANTERN WOULD--
SEPARATE HIM FROM HIS CORPS.
HE'S HAD THAT BATTERY IN HIS GRIP FOR CENTURIES, HAL. HE'S AS CONNECTED TO IT AS THE GUARDIANS ARE TO OURS.
IT WAS WORTH A SHOT.
WELL, YOU DID DO SOMETHING.
EMOTIONAL DETONATION IMMINENT.
"YOU PISSED HIM OFF."
POWER LEVELS 7839%.
I'LL STEAL THE FLESH FROM YOUR SLAVES, GUARDIANS! AND THEN ALL OF YOU--

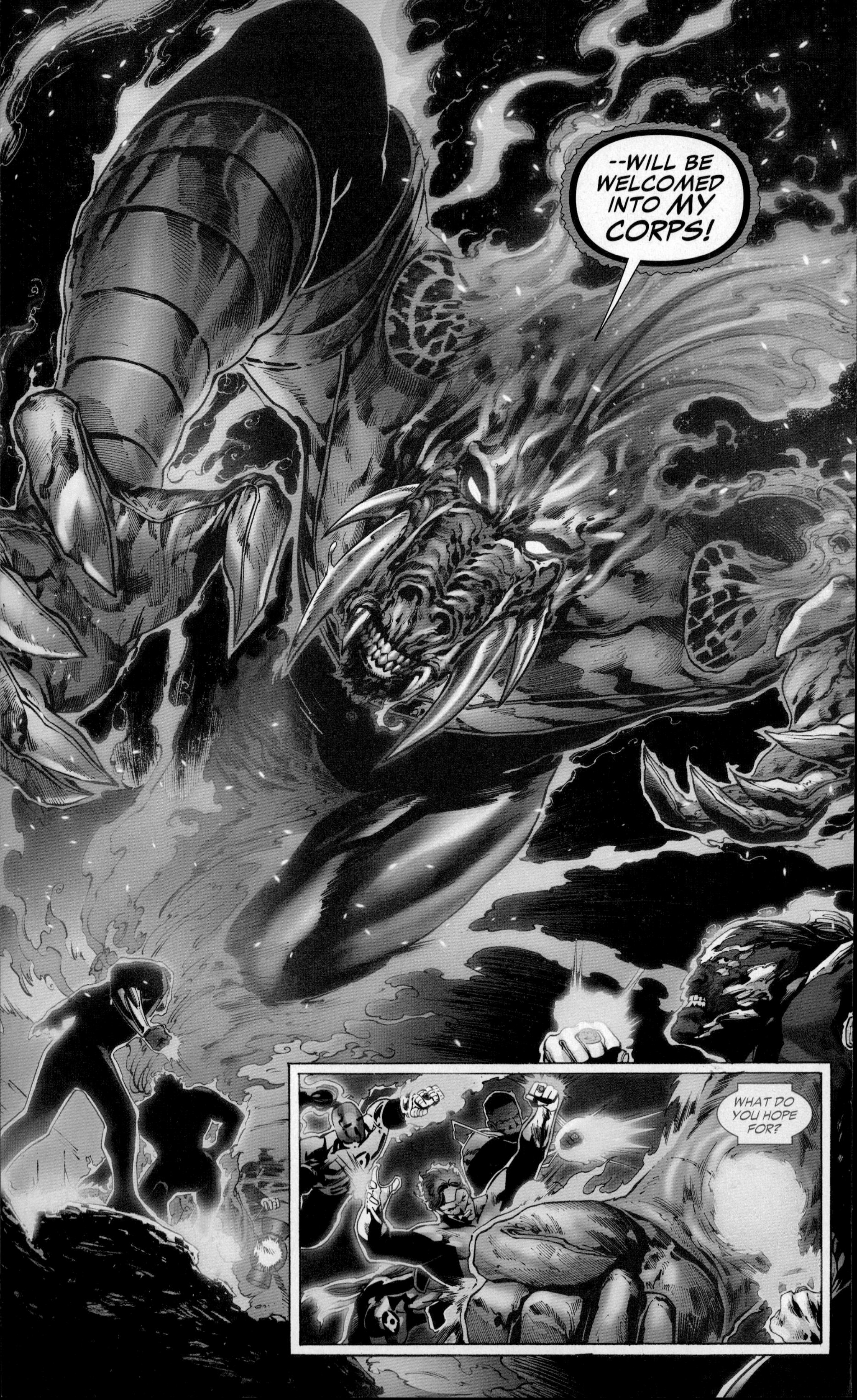
--WILL BE WELCOMED INTO MY CORPS!
WHAT DO YOU HOPE FOR?

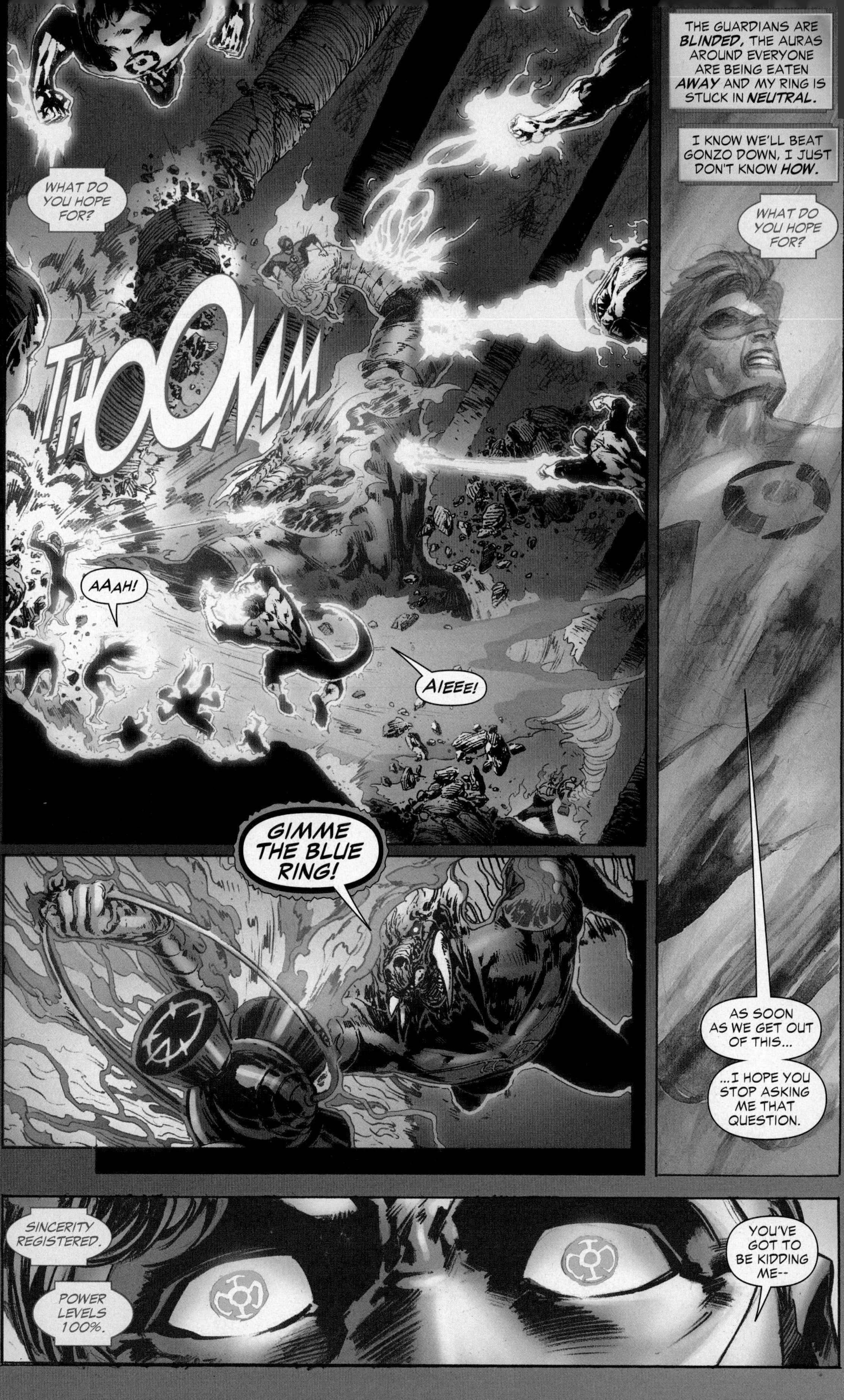
THE GUARDIANS ARE BLINDED, THE AURAS AROUND EVERYONE ARE BEING EATEN AWAY AND MY RING IS STUCK IN NEUTRAL.
I KNOW WE'LL BEAT GONZO DOWN, I JUST DON'T KNOW HOW.
WHAT DO YOU HOPE FOR?
WHAT DO YOU HOPE FOR?
THOOMM
AAAH!
AIEEE!
GIMME THE BLUE RING!
AS SOON AS WE GET OUT OF THIS...
...I HOPE YOU STOP ASKING ME THAT QUESTION.
SINCERITY REGISTERED.
POWER LEVELS 100%.
YOU'VE GOT TO BE KIDDING ME--

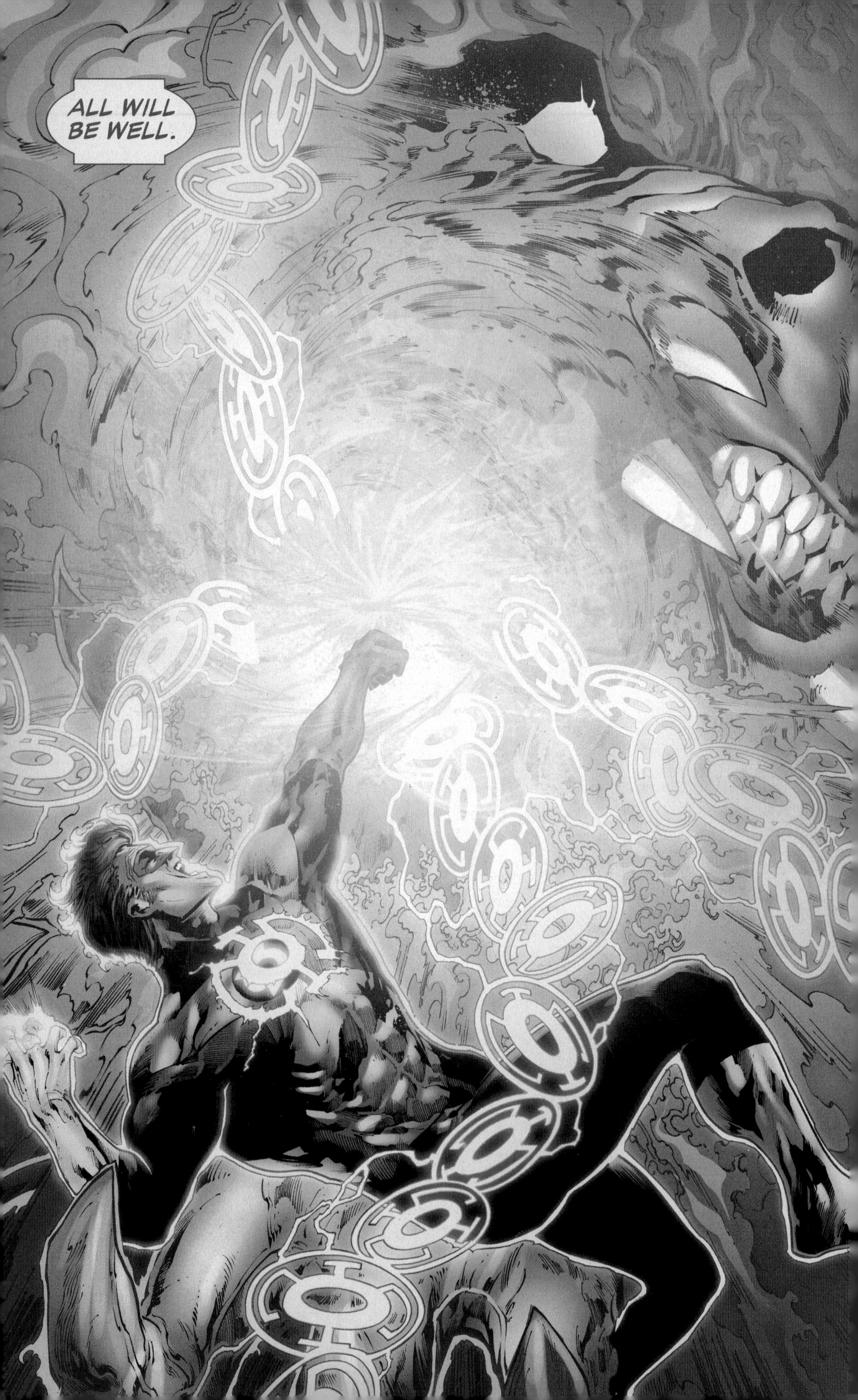
ALL WILL BE WELL.

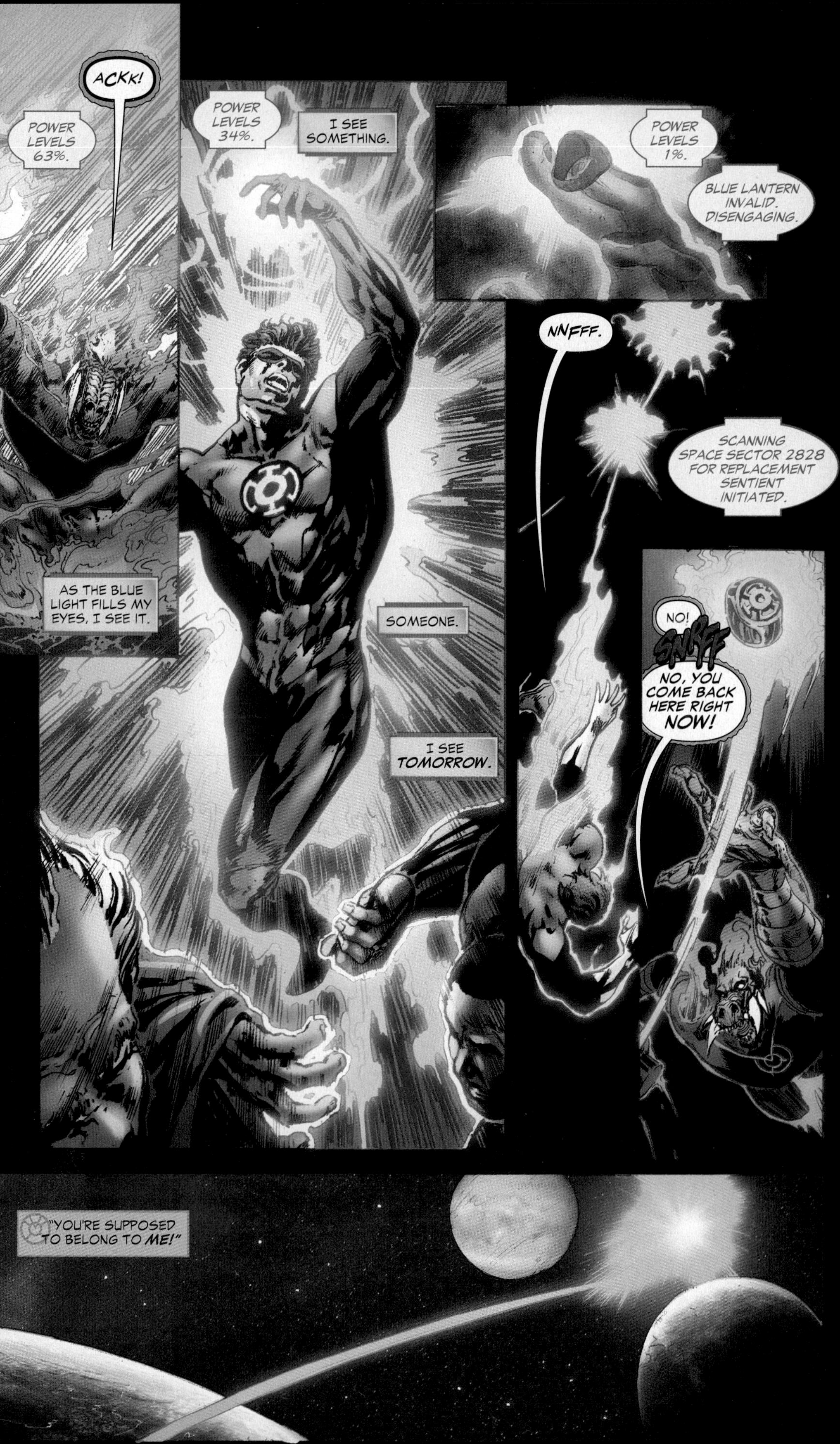
ACKK!
POWER LEVELS 63%.
AS THE BLUE LIGHT FILLS MY EYES, I SEE IT.
POWER LEVELS 34%.
I SEE SOMETHING.
SOMEONE.
I SEE TOMORROW.
POWER LEVELS 1%.
BLUE LANTERN INVALID. DISENGAGING.
NNFFF.
SCANNING SPACE SECTOR 2828 FOR REPLACEMENT SENTIENT INITIATED.
NO!
SNIFF
NO, YOU COME BACK HERE RIGHT NOW!
"YOU'RE SUPPOSED TO BELONG TO ME!"

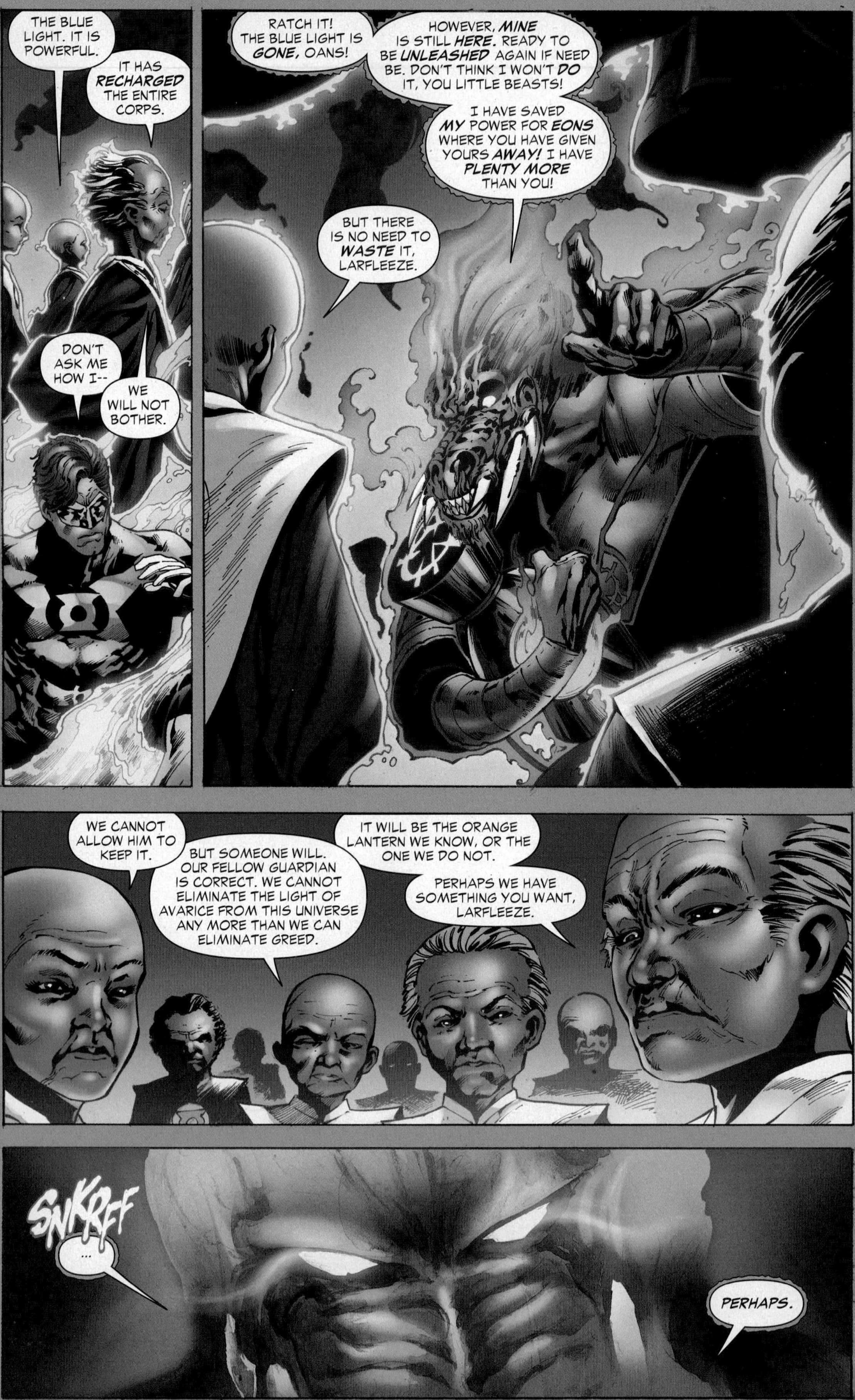
THE BLUE LIGHT. IT IS POWERFUL.
IT HAS RECHARGED THE ENTIRE CORPS.
DON'T ASK ME HOW I--
WE WILL NOT BOTHER.
RATCH IT! THE BLUE LIGHT IS GONE, OANS!
HOWEVER, MINE IS STILL HERE. READY TO BE UNLEASHED AGAIN IF NEED BE. DON'T THINK I WON'T DO IT, YOU LITTLE BEASTS!
I HAVE SAVED MY POWER FOR EONS WHERE YOU HAVE GIVEN YOURS AWAY! I HAVE PLENTY MORE THAN YOU!
BUT THERE IS NO NEED TO WASTE IT, LARFLEEZE.
WE CANNOT ALLOW HIM TO KEEP IT.
BUT SOMEONE WILL. OUR FELLOW GUARDIAN IS CORRECT. WE CANNOT ELIMINATE THE LIGHT OF AVARICE FROM THIS UNIVERSE ANY MORE THAN WE CAN ELIMINATE GREED.
IT WILL BE THE ORANGE LANTERN WE KNOW, OR THE ONE WE DO NOT.
PERHAPS WE HAVE SOMETHING YOU WANT, LARFLEEZE.
SNKRFF
...
PERHAPS.

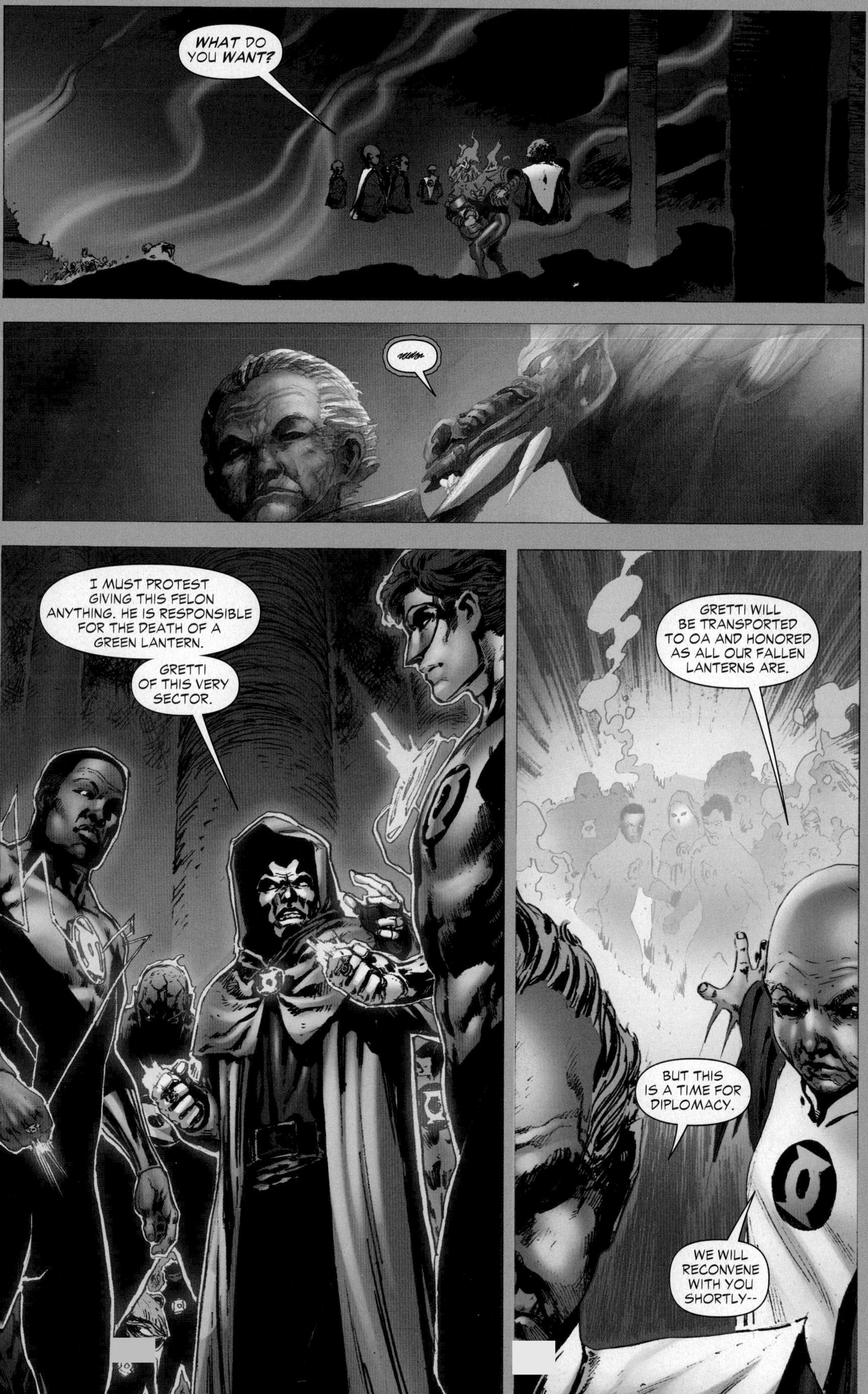
WHAT DO YOU WANT?
I MUST PROTEST GIVING THIS FELON ANYTHING. HE IS RESPONSIBLE FOR THE DEATH OF A GREEN LANTERN.
GRETTI OF THIS VERY SECTOR.
GRETTI WILL BE TRANSPORTED TO OA AND HONORED AS ALL OUR FALLEN LANTERNS ARE.
BUT THIS IS A TIME FOR DIPLOMACY.
WE WILL RECONVENE WITH YOU SHORTLY--

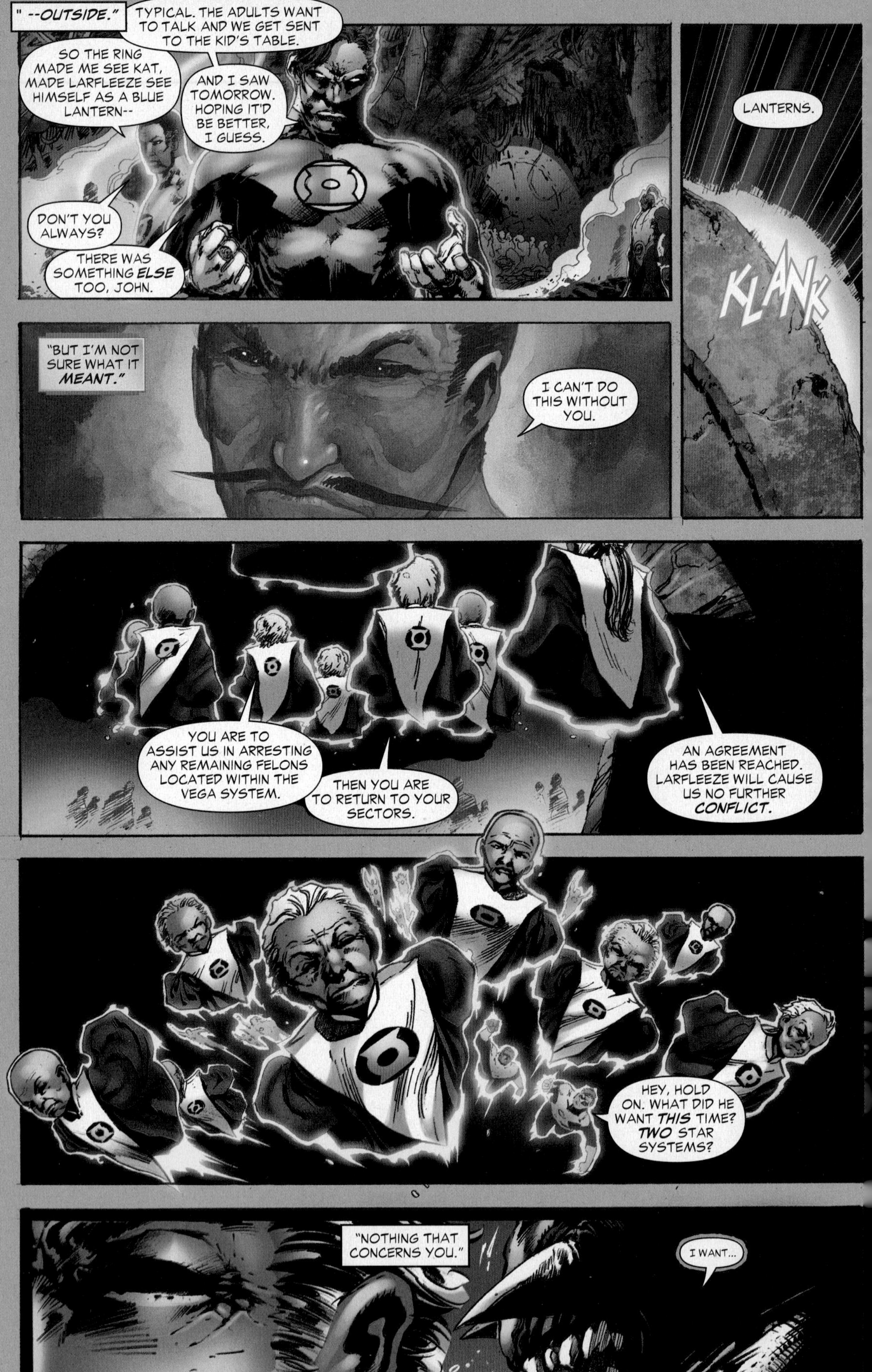
" --OUTSIDE."
TYPICAL. THE ADULTS WANT TO TALK AND WE GET SENT TO THE KID'S TABLE.
SO THE RING MADE ME SEE KAT, MADE LARFLEEZE SEE HIMSELF AS A BLUE LANTERN--
AND I SAW TOMORROW. HOPING IT'D BE BETTER, I GUESS.
DON'T YOU ALWAYS?
THERE WAS SOMETHING ELSE TOO, JOHN.
LANTERNS.
KLANK
"BUT I'M NOT SURE WHAT IT MEANT."
I CAN'T DO THIS WITHOUT YOU.
AN AGREEMENT HAS BEEN REACHED. LARFLEEZE WILL CAUSE US NO FURTHER CONFLICT.
YOU ARE TO ASSIST US IN ARRESTING ANY REMAINING FELONS LOCATED WITHIN THE VEGA SYSTEM.
THEN YOU ARE TO RETURN TO YOUR SECTORS.
HEY, HOLD ON. WHAT DID HE WANT THIS TIME? TWO STAR SYSTEMS?
"NOTHING THAT CONCERNS YOU."
I WANT...

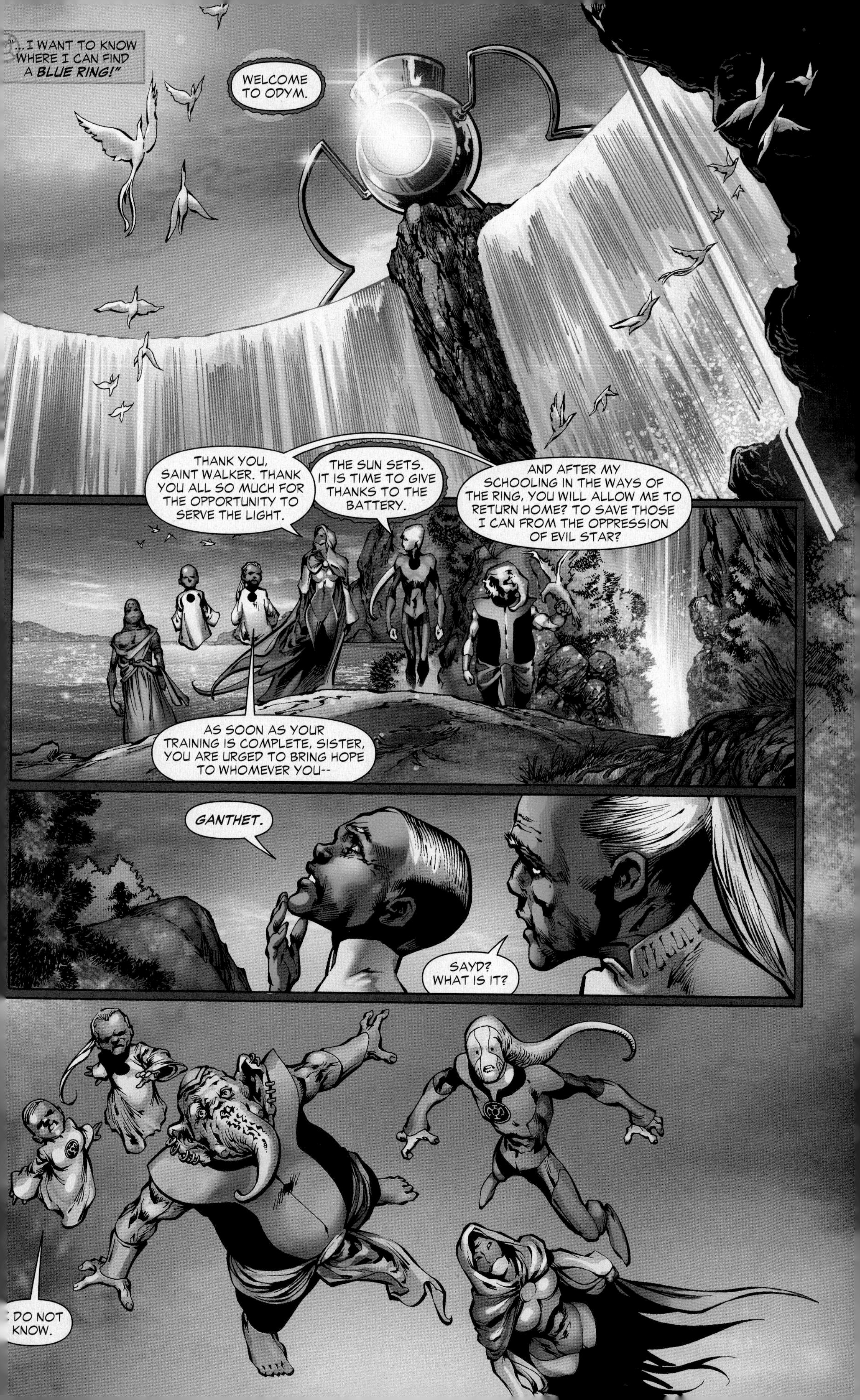
"...I WANT TO KNOW WHERE I CAN FIND A *BLUE RING!*"
WELCOME TO ODYM.
THANK YOU, SAINT WALKER. THANK YOU ALL SO MUCH FOR THE OPPORTUNITY TO SERVE THE LIGHT.
THE SUN SETS. IT IS TIME TO GIVE THANKS TO THE BATTERY.
AND AFTER MY SCHOOLING IN THE WAYS OF THE RING, YOU WILL ALLOW ME TO RETURN HOME? TO SAVE THOSE I CAN FROM THE OPPRESSION OF EVIL STAR?
AS SOON AS YOUR TRAINING IS COMPLETE, SISTER, YOU ARE URGED TO BRING HOPE TO WHOMEVER YOU--
GANTHET.
SAYD? WHAT IS IT?
DO NOT KNOW.

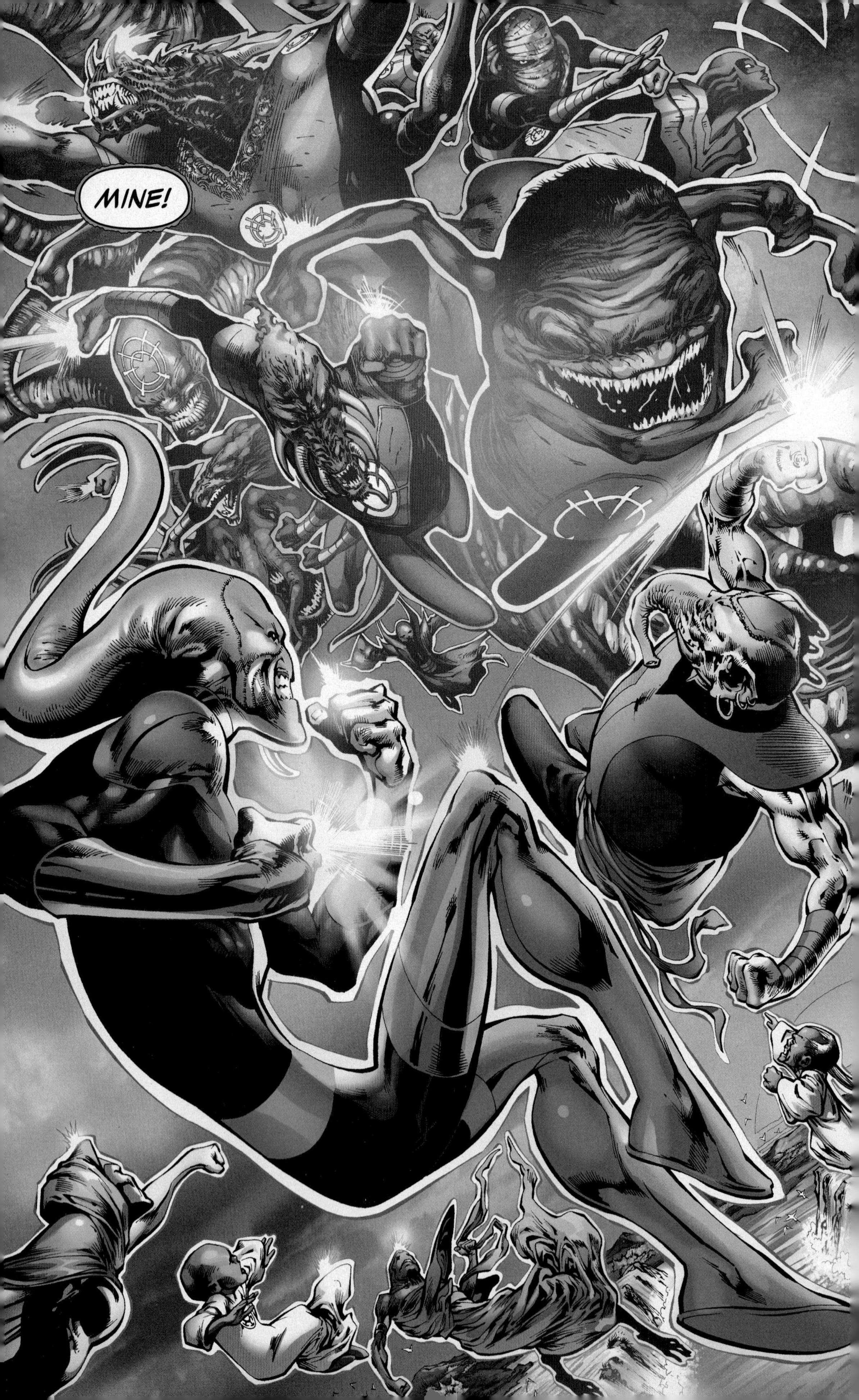
MINE!

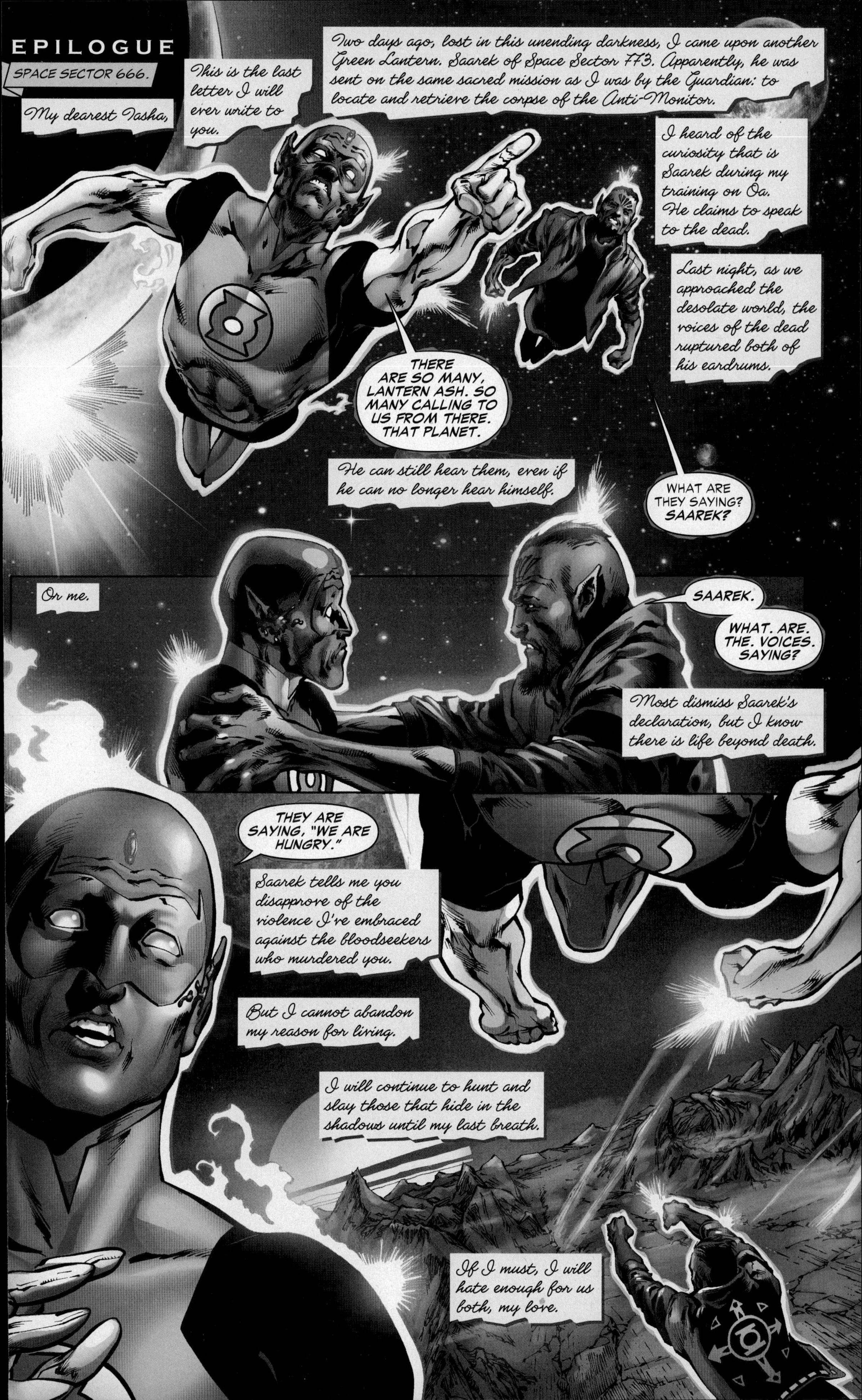
EPILOGUE
SPACE SECTOR 666.
My dearest Iasha,
This is the last letter I will ever write to you.
Two days ago, lost in this unending darkness, I came upon another Green Lantern. Saarek of Space Sector 773. Apparently, he was sent on the same sacred mission as I was by the Guardian: to locate and retrieve the corpse of the Anti-Monitor.
I heard of the curiosity that is Saarek during my training on Oa. He claims to speak to the dead.
Last night, as we approached the desolate world, the voices of the dead ruptured both of his eardrums.
THERE ARE SO MANY, LANTERN ASH. SO MANY CALLING TO US FROM THERE. THAT PLANET.
He can still hear them, even if he can no longer hear himself.
WHAT ARE THEY SAYING? SAAREK?
Or me.
SAAREK.
WHAT. ARE. THE. VOICES. SAYING?
Most dismiss Saarek's declaration, but I know there is life beyond death.
THEY ARE SAYING, "WE ARE HUNGRY."
Saarek tells me you disapprove of the violence I've embraced against the bloodseekers who murdered you.
But I cannot abandon my reason for living.
I will continue to hunt and slay those that hide in the shadows until my last breath.
If I must, I will hate enough for us both, my love.

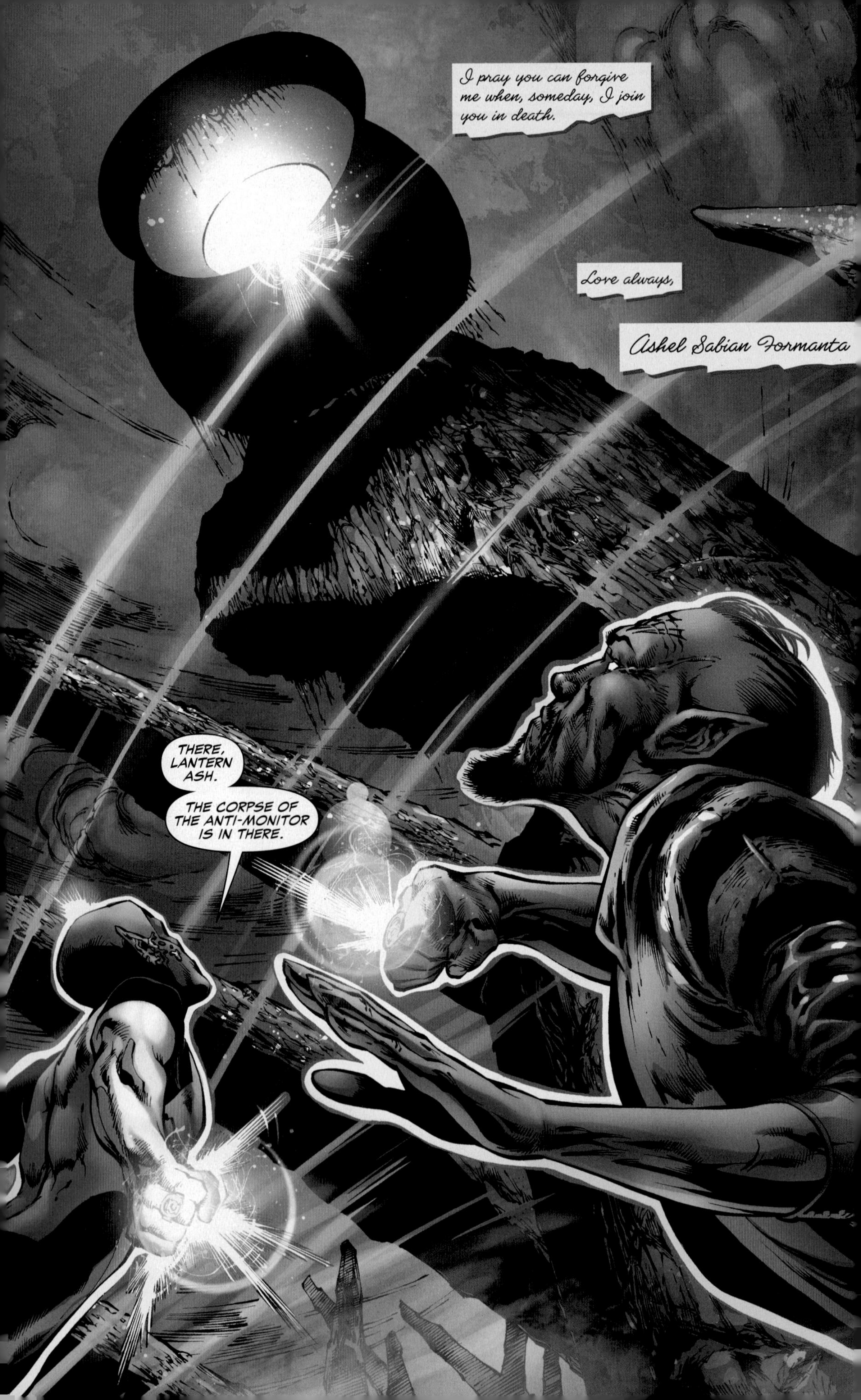
I pray you can forgive me when, someday, I join you in death.
Love always,
Ashel Sabian Formanta
THERE, LANTERN ASH.
THE CORPSE OF THE ANTI-MONITOR IS IN THERE.

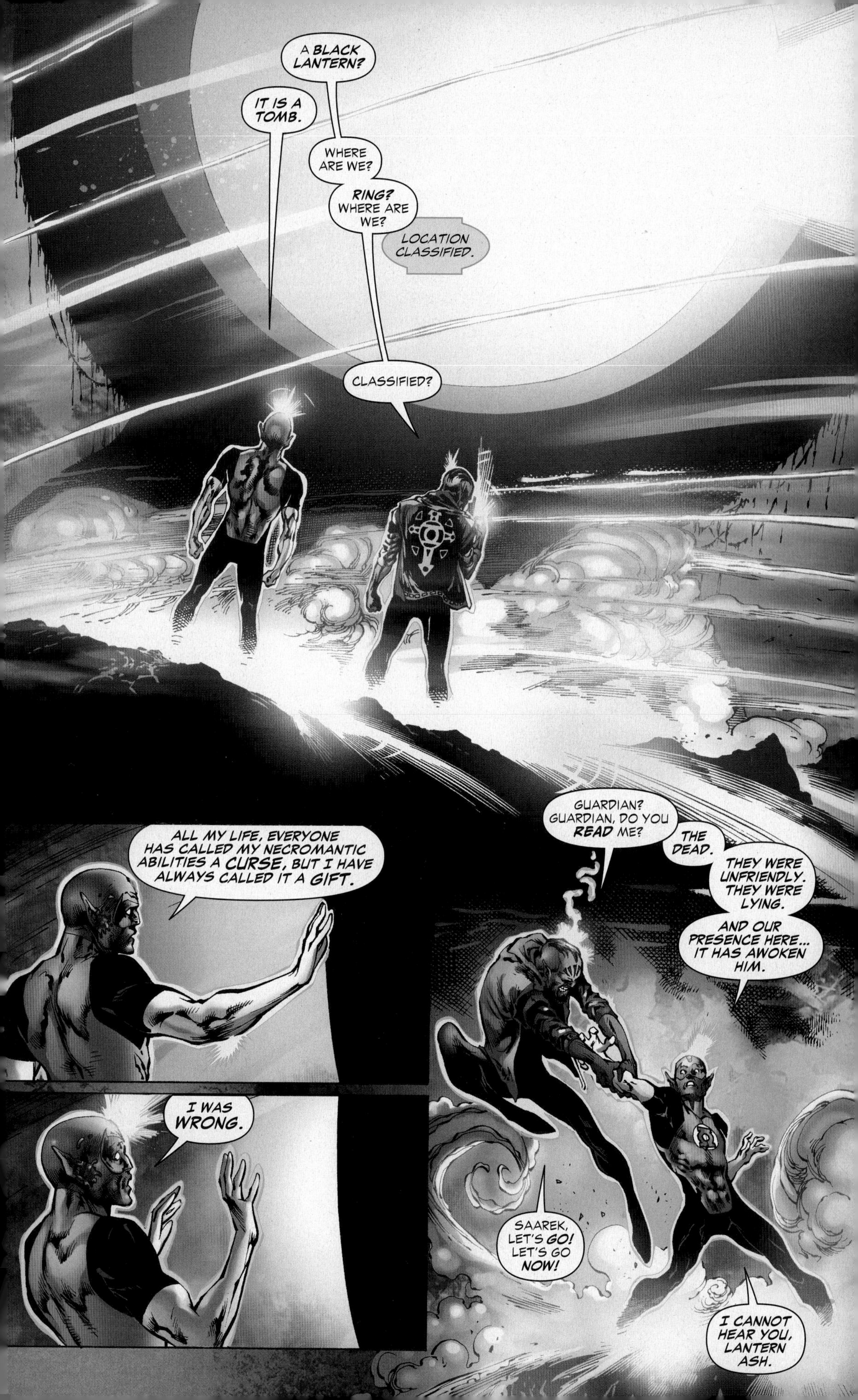
A BLACK LANTERN?
IT IS A TOMB.
WHERE ARE WE?
RING? WHERE ARE WE?
LOCATION CLASSIFIED.
CLASSIFIED?
ALL MY LIFE, EVERYONE HAS CALLED MY NECROMANTIC ABILITIES A CURSE, BUT I HAVE ALWAYS CALLED IT A GIFT.
I WAS WRONG.
GUARDIAN? GUARDIAN, DO YOU READ ME?
THE DEAD.
THEY WERE UNFRIENDLY. THEY WERE LYING.
AND OUR PRESENCE HERE... IT HAS AWOKEN HIM.
SAAREK, LET'S GO! LET'S GO NOW!
I CANNOT HEAR YOU, LANTERN ASH.

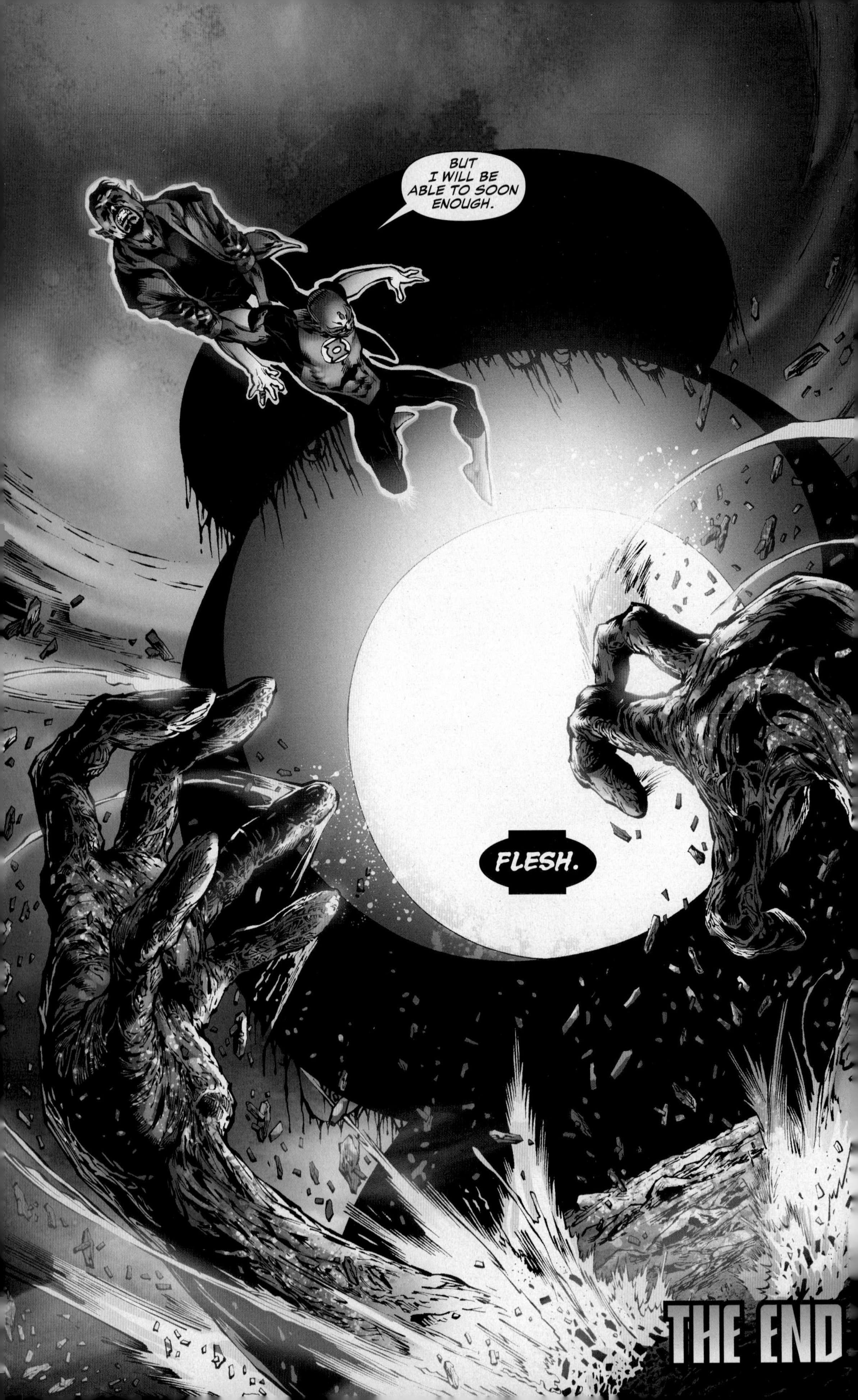
BUT I WILL BE ABLE TO SOON ENOUGH.
FLESH.
THE END

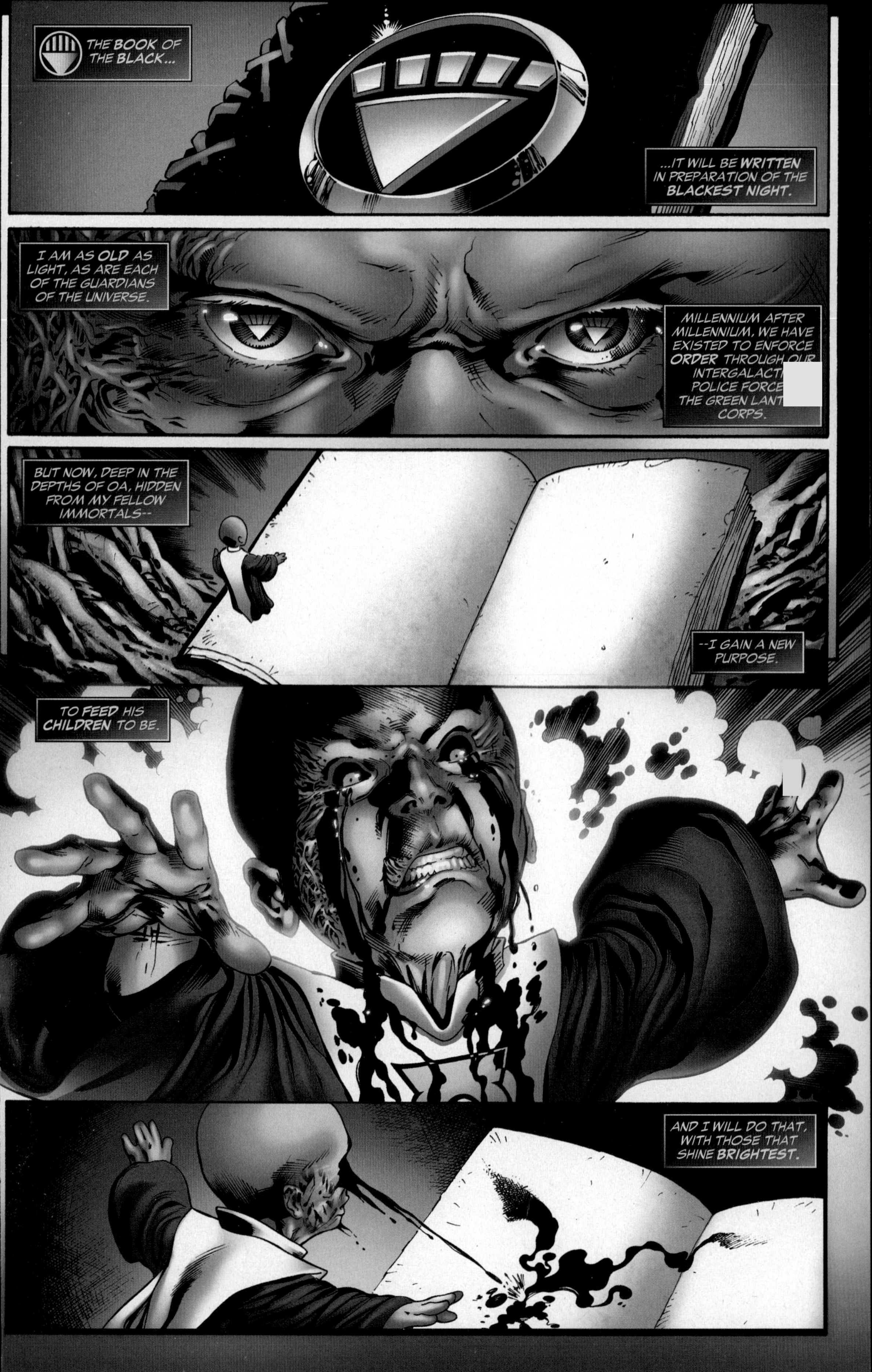

THE BOOK OF THE BLACK...
...IT WILL BE WRITTEN IN PREPARATION OF THE BLACKEST NIGHT.
I AM AS OLD AS LIGHT, AS ARE EACH OF THE GUARDIANS OF THE UNIVERSE.
MILLENNIUM AFTER MILLENNIUM, WE HAVE EXISTED TO ENFORCE ORDER THROUGH OUR INTERGALACT
POLICE FORCE
THE GREEN LANT
CORPS.
BUT NOW, DEEP IN THE DEPTHS OF OA, HIDDEN FROM MY FELLOW IMMORTALS--
--I GAIN A NEW PURPOSE.
TO FEED HIS CHILDREN TO BE.
AND I WILL DO THAT, WITH THOSE THAT SHINE BRIGHTEST.

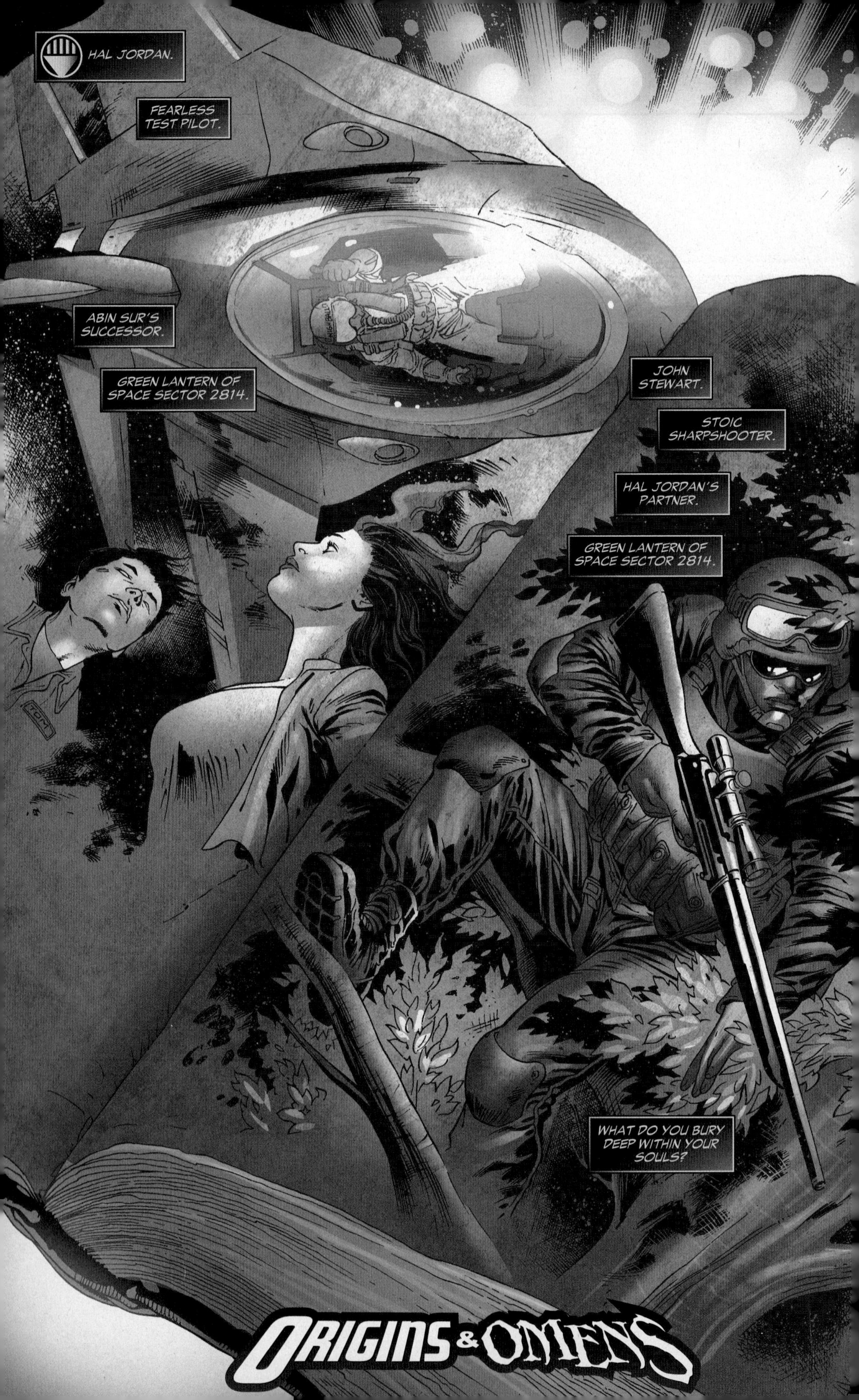
HAL JORDAN.
FEARLESS TEST PILOT.
ABIN SUR'S SUCCESSOR.
GREEN LANTERN OF SPACE SECTOR 2814.
JOHN STEWART.
STOIC SHARPSHOOTER.
HAL JORDAN'S PARTNER.
GREEN LANTERN OF SPACE SECTOR 2814.
WHAT DO YOU BURY DEEP WITHIN YOUR SOULS?
ORIGINS & OMENS

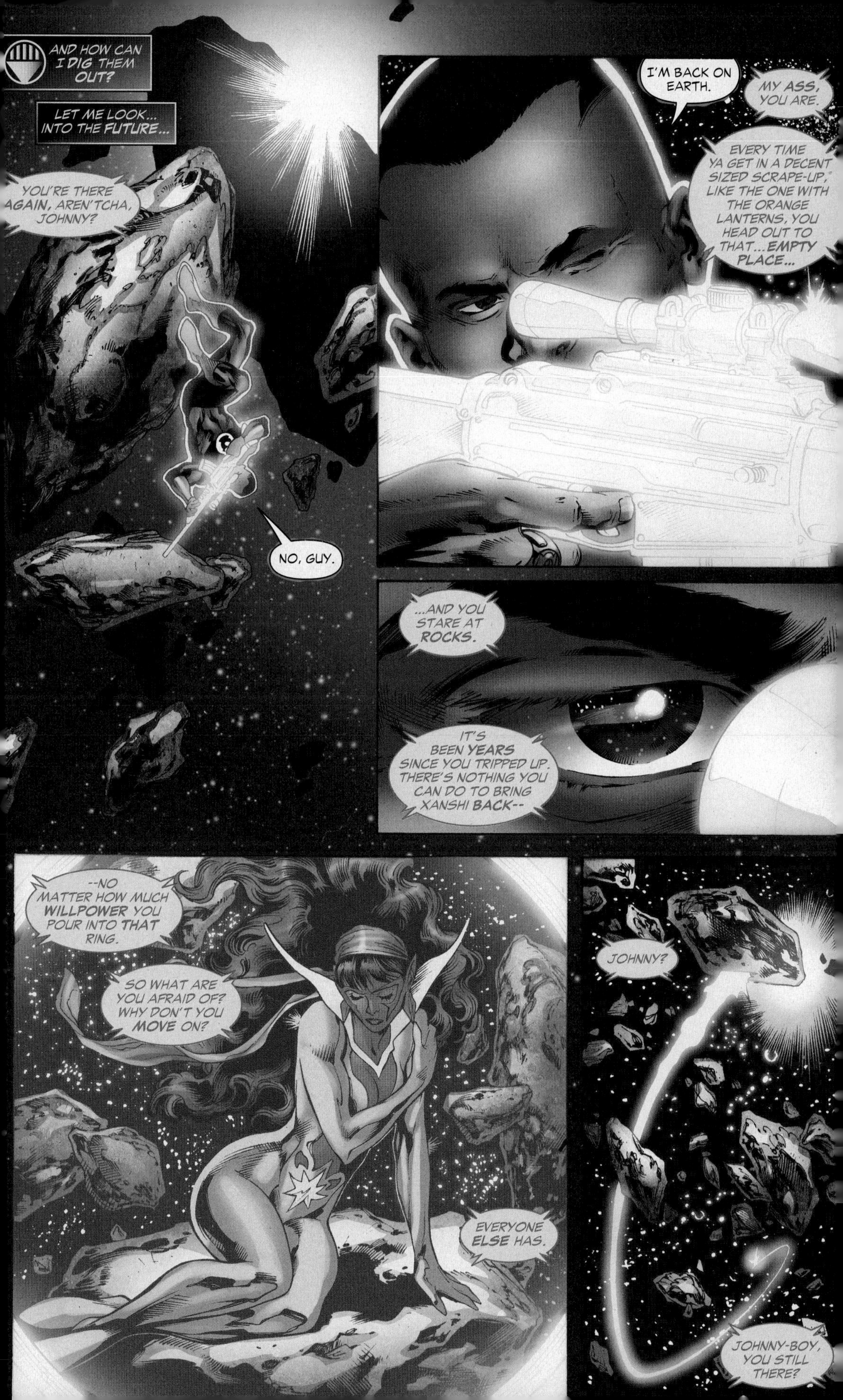
AND HOW CAN I DIG THEM OUT?
LET ME LOOK... INTO THE FUTURE...
YOU'RE THERE AGAIN, AREN'TCHA, JOHNNY?
NO, GUY.
I'M BACK ON EARTH.
MY ASS, YOU ARE.
EVERY TIME YA GET IN A DECENT SIZED SCRAPE-UP, LIKE THE ONE WITH THE ORANGE LANTERNS, YOU HEAD OUT TO THAT... EMPTY PLACE...
...AND YOU STARE AT ROCKS.
IT'S BEEN YEARS SINCE YOU TRIPPED UP. THERE'S NOTHING YOU CAN DO TO BRING XANSHI BACK--
--NO MATTER HOW MUCH WILLPOWER YOU POUR INTO THAT RING.
SO WHAT ARE YOU AFRAID OF? WHY DON'T YOU MOVE ON?
EVERYONE ELSE HAS.
JOHNNY?
JOHNNY-BOY, YOU STILL THERE?

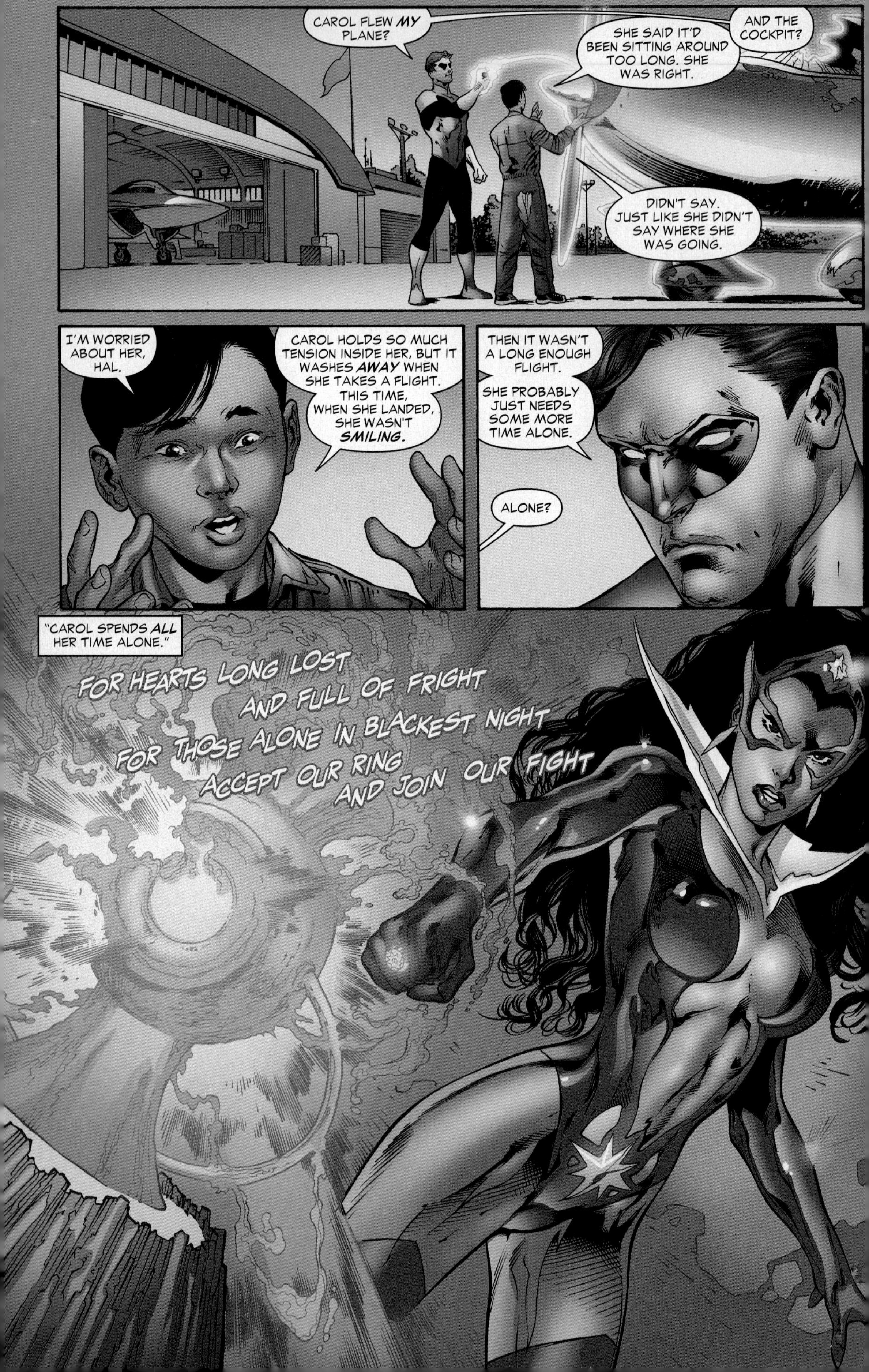
CAROL FLEW *MY* PLANE?
SHE SAID IT'D BEEN SITTING AROUND TOO LONG. SHE WAS RIGHT.
AND THE COCKPIT?
DIDN'T SAY. JUST LIKE SHE DIDN'T SAY WHERE SHE WAS GOING.
I'M WORRIED ABOUT HER, HAL.
CAROL HOLDS SO MUCH TENSION INSIDE HER, BUT IT WASHES *AWAY* WHEN SHE TAKES A FLIGHT. THIS TIME, WHEN SHE LANDED, SHE WASN'T *SMILING.*
THEN IT WASN'T A LONG ENOUGH FLIGHT.
SHE PROBABLY JUST NEEDS SOME MORE TIME ALONE.
ALONE?
"CAROL SPENDS *ALL* HER TIME ALONE."
FOR HEARTS LONG LOST
AND FULL OF FRIGHT
FOR THOSE ALONE IN BLACKEST NIGHT
ACCEPT OUR RING
AND JOIN OUR FIGHT

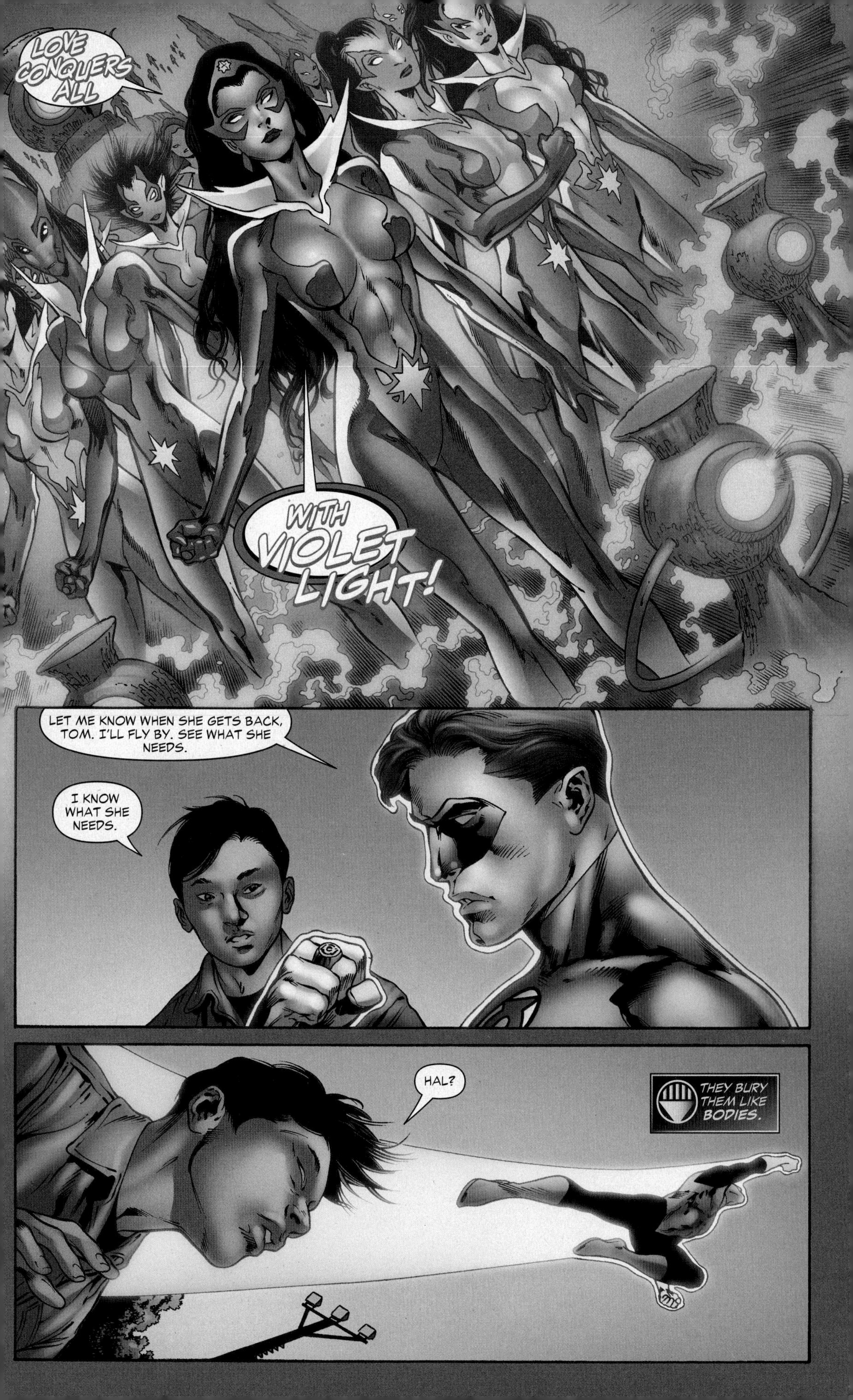
LOVE CONQUERS ALL
WITH VIOLET LIGHT!
LET ME KNOW WHEN SHE GETS BACK, TOM. I'LL FLY BY. SEE WHAT SHE NEEDS.
I KNOW WHAT SHE NEEDS.
HAL?
THEY BURY THEM LIKE BODIES.

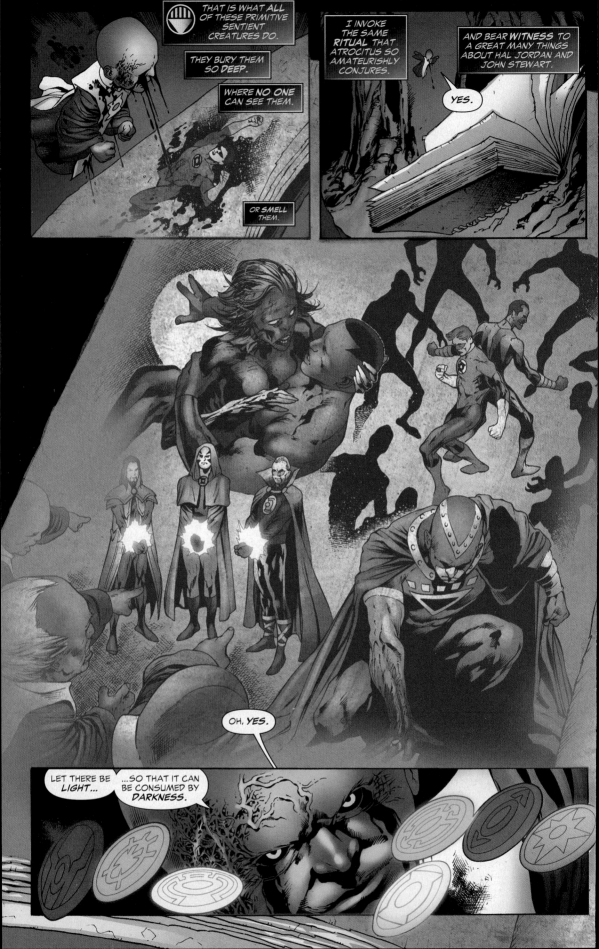

THAT IS WHAT ALL OF THESE PRIMITIVE SENTIENT CREATURES DO.

THEY BURY THEM SO DEEP.

WHERE NO ONE CAN SEE THEM.

OR SMELL THEM.

I INVOKE THE SAME RITUAL THAT ATROCITUS SO AMATEURISHLY CONJURES.

AND BEAR WITNESS TO A GREAT MANY THINGS ABOUT HAL JORDAN AND JOHN STEWART.

YES.

OH, YES.

LET THERE BE LIGHT...

...SO THAT IT CAN BE CONSUMED BY DARKNESS.

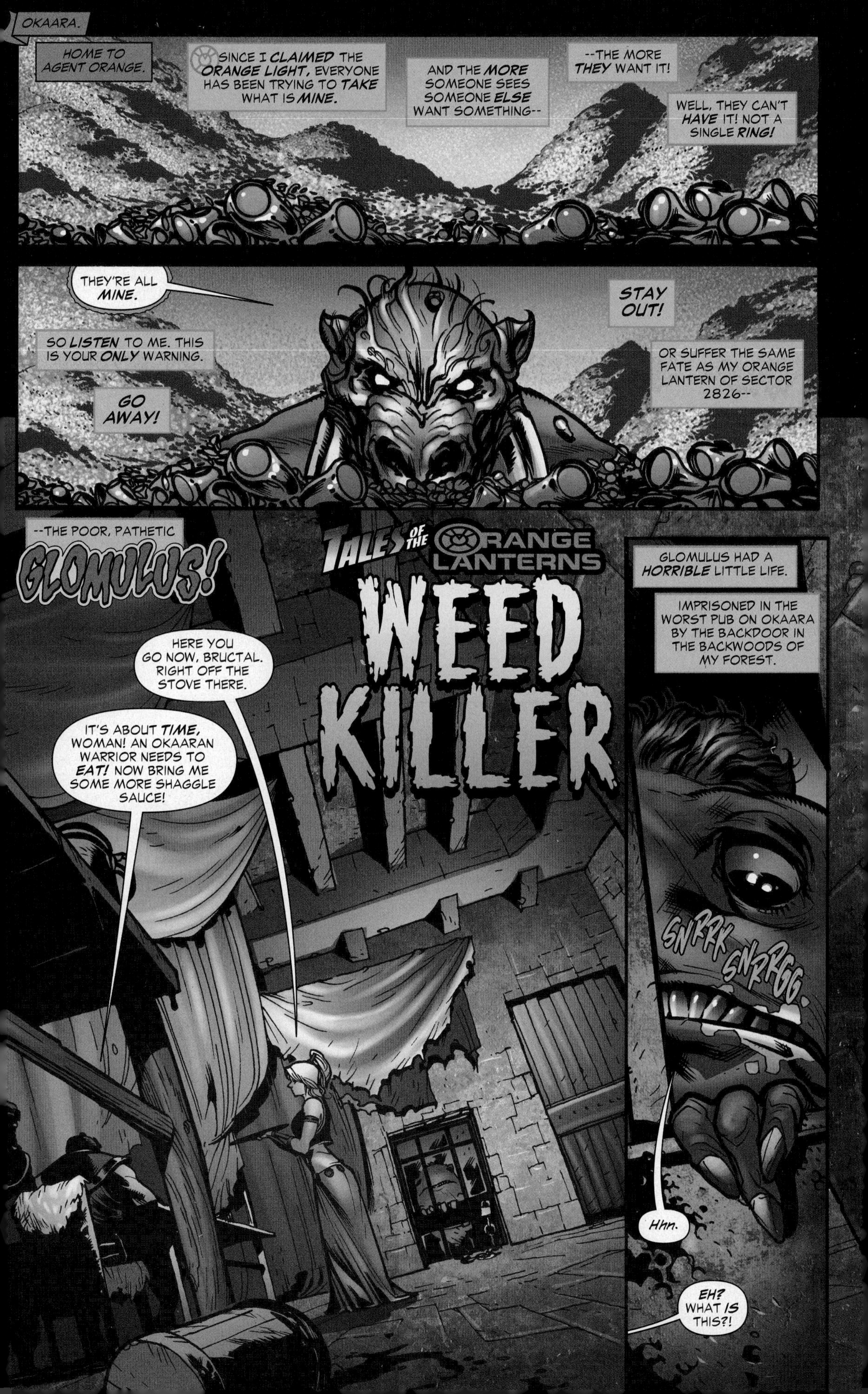

OKAARA.
HOME TO AGENT ORANGE.
SINCE I CLAIMED THE ORANGE LIGHT, EVERYONE HAS BEEN TRYING TO TAKE WHAT IS MINE.
AND THE MORE SOMEONE SEES SOMEONE ELSE WANT SOMETHING--
--THE MORE THEY WANT IT!
WELL, THEY CAN'T HAVE IT! NOT A SINGLE RING!
THEY'RE ALL MINE.
SO LISTEN TO ME. THIS IS YOUR ONLY WARNING.
GO AWAY!
STAY OUT!
OR SUFFER THE SAME FATE AS MY ORANGE LANTERN OF SECTOR 2826--
--THE POOR, PATHETIC
GLOMULUS!
TALES OF THE ORANGE LANTERNS
WEED KILLER
HERE YOU GO NOW, BRUCTAL. RIGHT OFF THE STOVE THERE.
IT'S ABOUT TIME, WOMAN! AN OKAARAN WARRIOR NEEDS TO EAT! NOW BRING ME SOME MORE SHAGGLE SAUCE!
GLOMULUS HAD A HORRIBLE LITTLE LIFE.
IMPRISONED IN THE WORST PUB ON OKAARA BY THE BACKDOOR IN THE BACKWOODS OF MY FOREST.
SNRKK SNRRGG.
Hhn.
EH? WHAT IS THIS?!

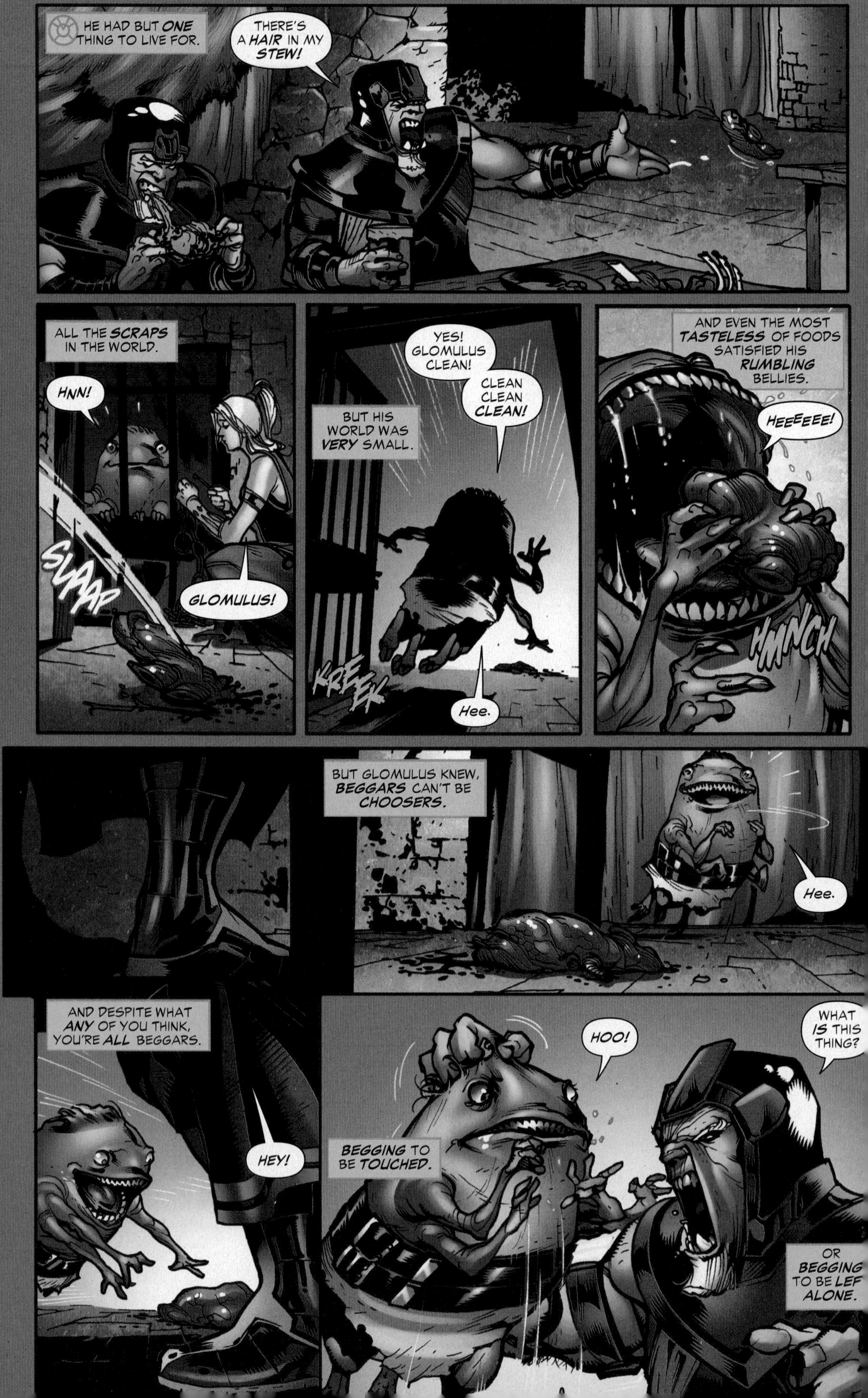
HE HAD BUT ONE THING TO LIVE FOR.
THERE'S A HAIR IN MY STEW!
ALL THE SCRAPS IN THE WORLD.
HNN!
SWAAP
GLOMULUS!
YES! GLOMULUS CLEAN!
CLEAN CLEAN CLEAN!
BUT HIS WORLD WAS VERY SMALL.
KREEEK
Hee.
AND EVEN THE MOST TASTELESS OF FOODS SATISFIED HIS RUMBLING BELLIES.
HEEEEEE!
HMNCH
BUT GLOMULUS KNEW, BEGGARS CAN'T BE CHOOSERS.
Hee.
AND DESPITE WHAT ANY OF YOU THINK, YOU'RE ALL BEGGARS.
HEY!
HOO!
WHAT IS THIS THING?
BEGGING TO BE TOUCHED.
OR BEGGING TO BE LEF ALONE.

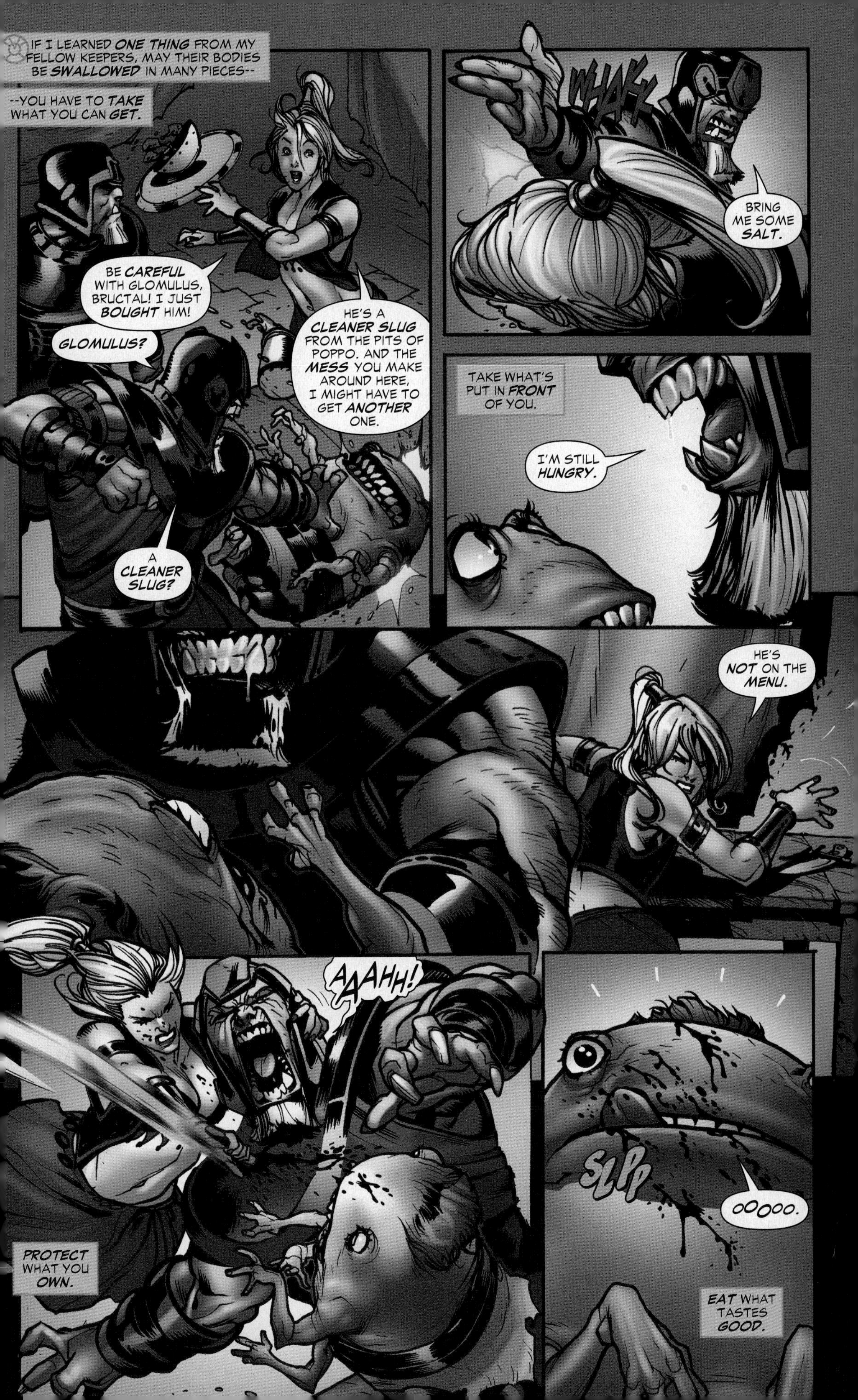
IF I LEARNED ONE THING FROM MY FELLOW KEEPERS, MAY THEIR BODIES BE SWALLOWED IN MANY PIECES--
--YOU HAVE TO TAKE WHAT YOU CAN GET.
BE CAREFUL WITH GLOMULUS, BRUCTAL! I JUST BOUGHT HIM!
GLOMULUS?
HE'S A CLEANER SLUG FROM THE PITS OF POPPO. AND THE MESS YOU MAKE AROUND HERE, I MIGHT HAVE TO GET ANOTHER ONE.
A CLEANER SLUG?
WHAK
BRING ME SOME SALT.
TAKE WHAT'S PUT IN FRONT OF YOU.
I'M STILL HUNGRY.
HE'S NOT ON THE MENU.
AAAHH!
PROTECT WHAT YOU OWN.
SLPP
OOOOO.
EAT WHAT TASTES GOOD.

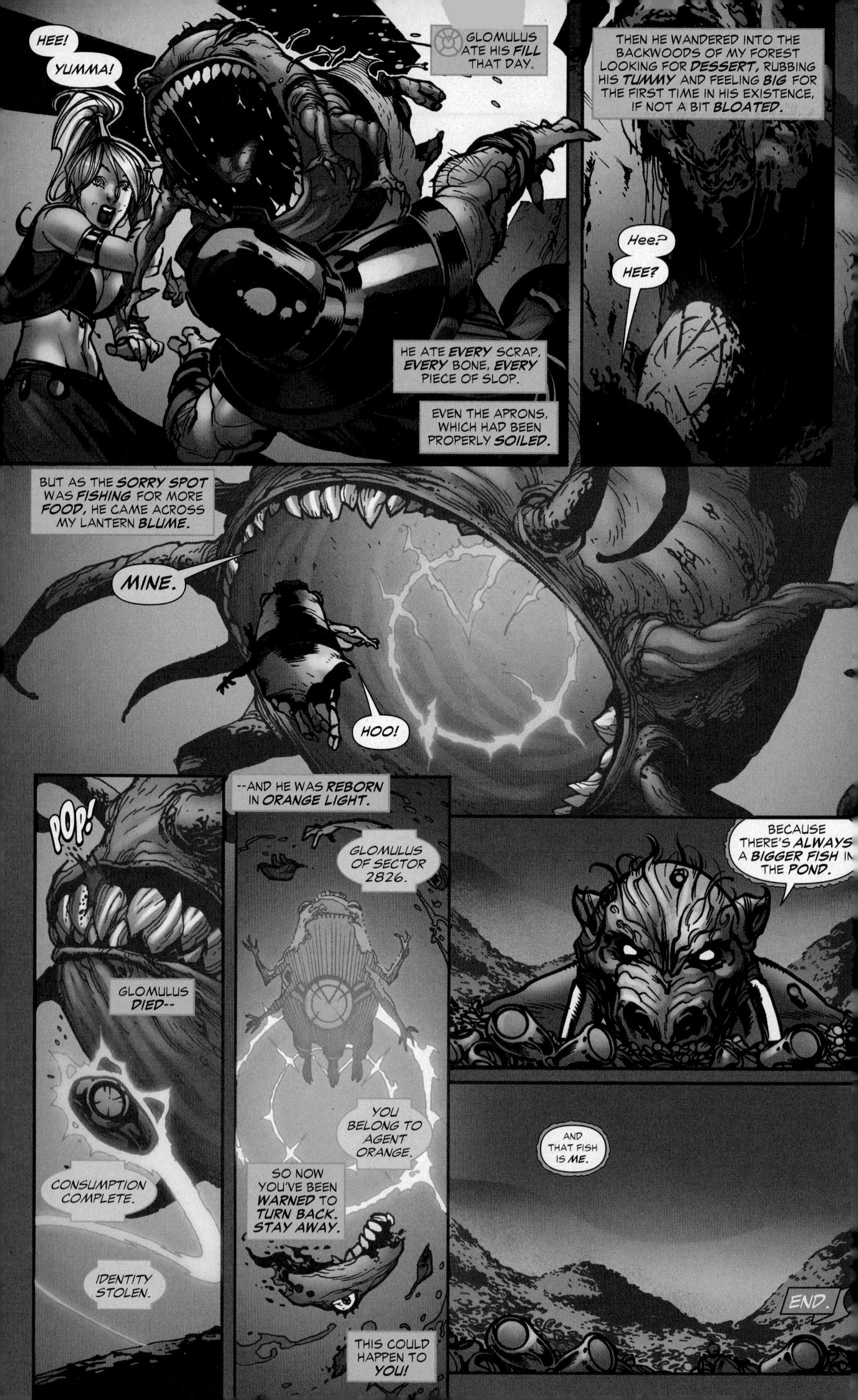
HEE!
YUMMA!
GLOMULUS ATE HIS FILL THAT DAY.
HE ATE EVERY SCRAP, EVERY BONE, EVERY PIECE OF SLOP.
EVEN THE APRONS, WHICH HAD BEEN PROPERLY SOILED.
THEN HE WANDERED INTO THE BACKWOODS OF MY FOREST LOOKING FOR DESSERT, RUBBING HIS TUMMY AND FEELING BIG FOR THE FIRST TIME IN HIS EXISTENCE, IF NOT A BIT BLOATED.
Hee?
HEE?
BUT AS THE SORRY SPOT WAS FISHING FOR MORE FOOD, HE CAME ACROSS MY LANTERN BLUME.
MINE.
HOO!
POP!
GLOMULUS DIED--
CONSUMPTION COMPLETE.
IDENTITY STOLEN.
--AND HE WAS REBORN IN ORANGE LIGHT.
GLOMULUS OF SECTOR 2826.
YOU BELONG TO AGENT ORANGE.
SO NOW YOU'VE BEEN WARNED TO TURN BACK. STAY AWAY.
THIS COULD HAPPEN TO YOU!
BECAUSE THERE'S ALWAYS A BIGGER FISH IN THE POND.
AND THAT FISH IS ME.
END.

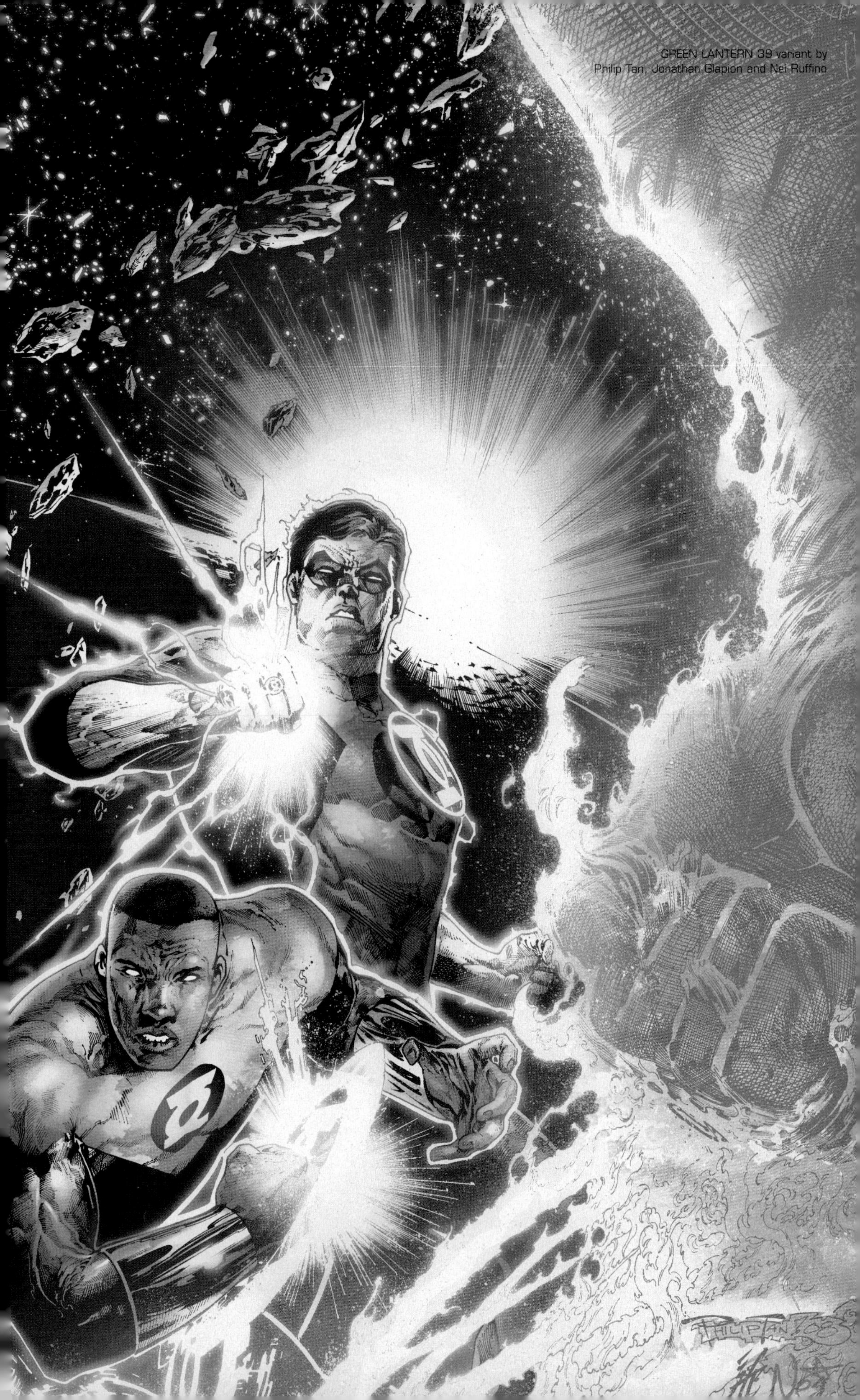

GREEN LANTERN 39 variant by
Philip Tan, Jonathan Glapion and Nei Ruffino

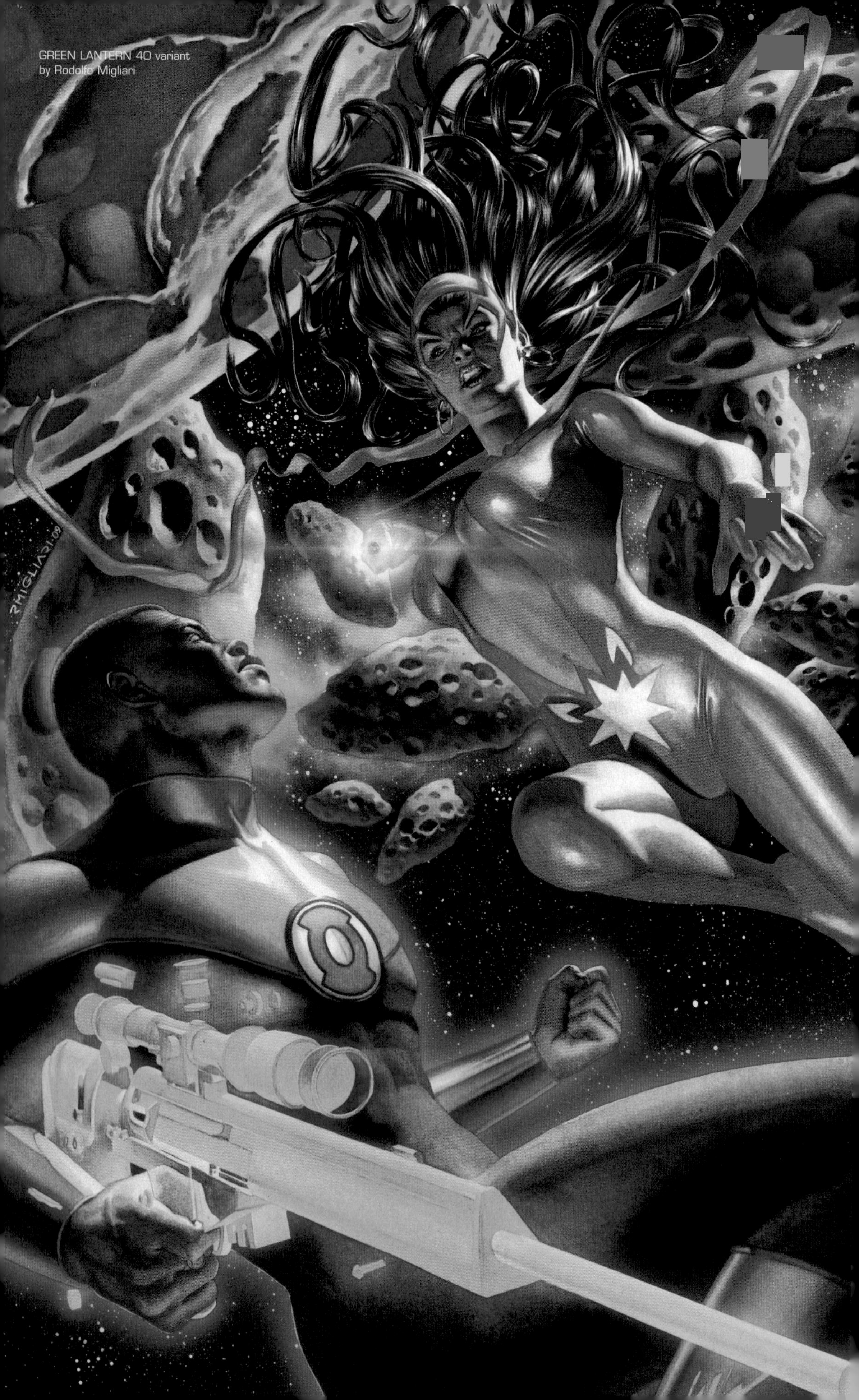

GREEN LANTERN 40 variant
by Rodolfo Migliari

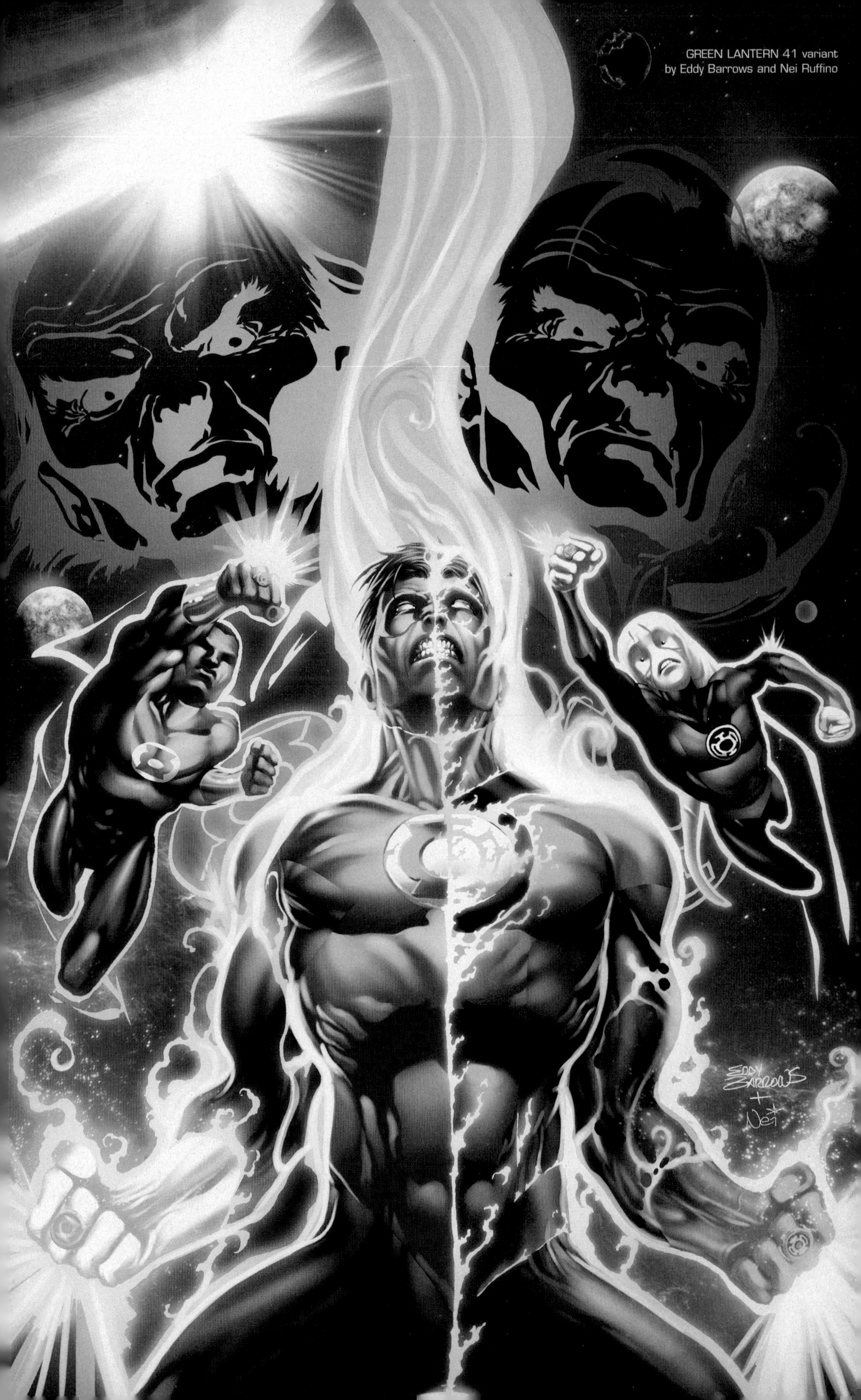

GREEN LANTERN 41 variant
by Eddy Barrows and Nei Ruffino

GREEN LANTERN 42 variant by Eddy Barrows and Nei Ruffino

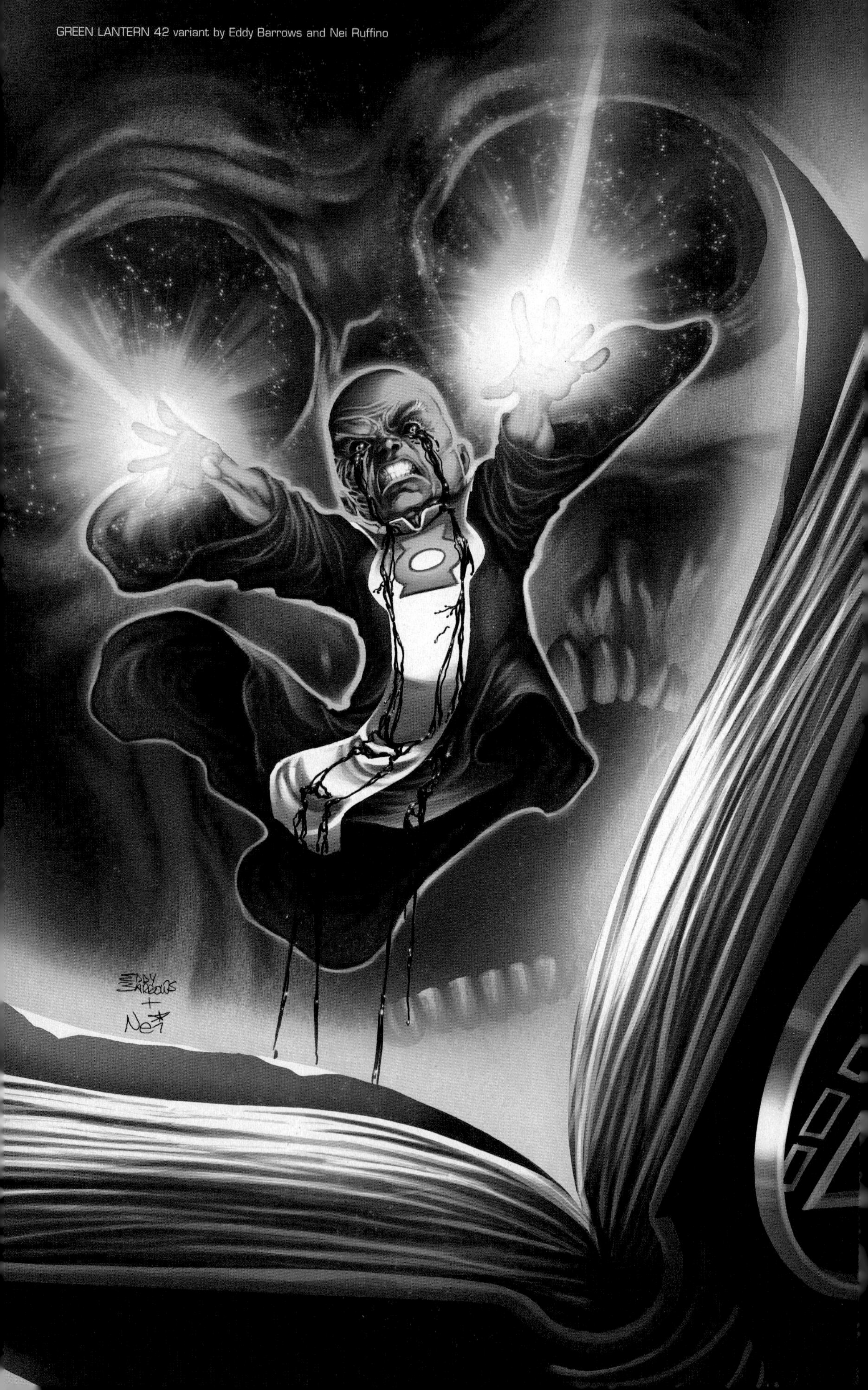

PENCILLER PHILIP TAN   INKER   EDITOR E. BERGANZA/A. SCHLAGMAN

VERTIGO   TITLE GREEN LANTERN   ISSUE # 42   MONTH   TITLE CODE   COVER

AGENT ORANGE SKETCHES
by Philip Tan

What follows is a study of xenobiology from the fevered mind of artist Philip Tan. Given the task of populating the Orange Lantern Corps, Philip went mad — he could not be stopped from creating one fantastical being after another, and no easy bipeds in the lot.

Also included for your reading pleasure (and hard to believe we are sharing something when speaking of the Orange Lantern) are Philip's initial thoughts on some of his creature creations. Their origins are sometimes as unique as their looks, and while not always the ones writer Geoff Johns has chosen to use, they were a great starting point.

—Eddie Berganza

CROP

BLEED

*COLORS = THE ORANGE LIGHT INSIDE THE LANTERN IS VERY BRIGHT & INTENSE.   PRINTED COVER SIZE: 6 5/8 X 10 3/16

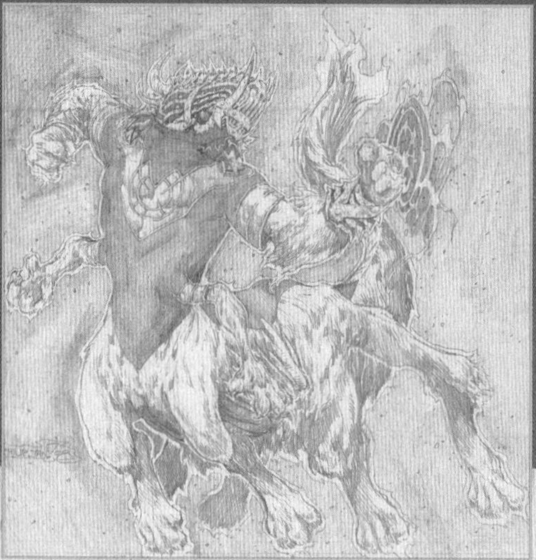

BLUME OF BLOBBA/SPACE SECTOR 2751

Philip: I was thinking about having this creature who cannibalized his whole hive and now hunts others. Their kind dwell on preserved carcasses, so there is only one creature in this hive, but the Orange light gives it power to create whole construct armies of its own kind.

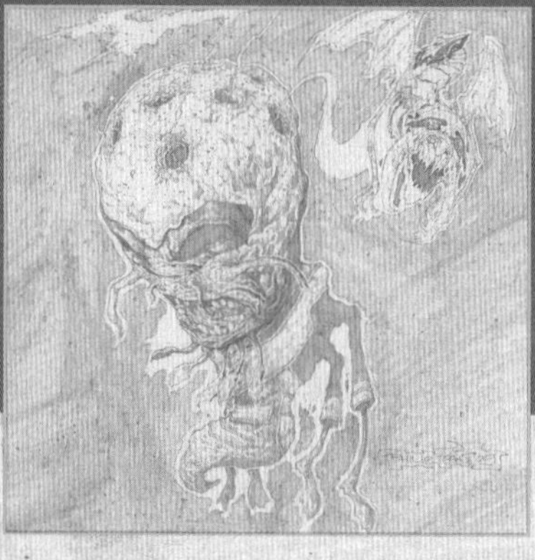

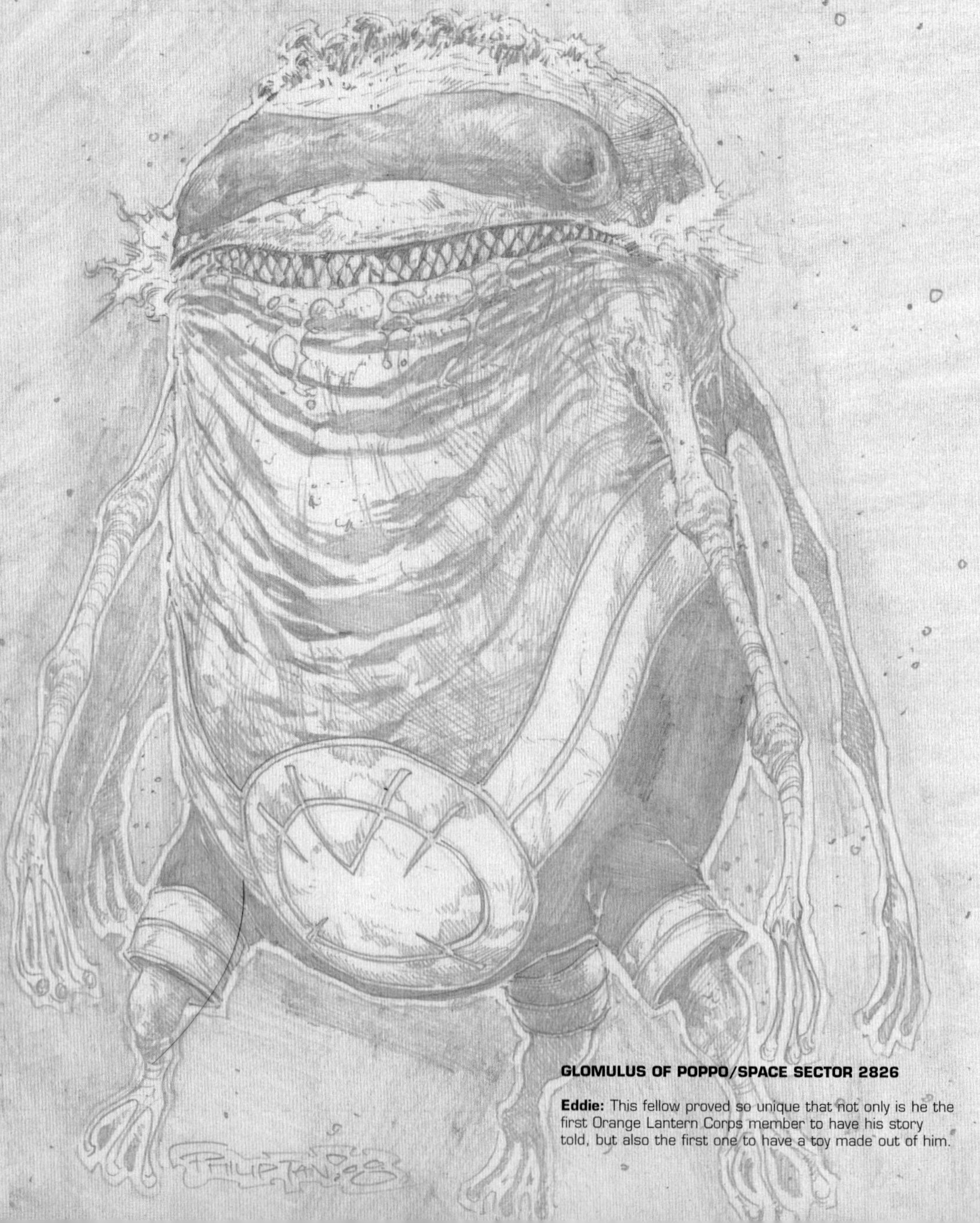

GLOMULUS OF POPPO/SPACE SECTOR 2826

Eddie: This fellow proved so unique that not only is he the first Orange Lantern Corps member to have his story told, but also the first one to have a toy made out of him.

TAMMAL-TAN OF FYLIP/SPACE SECTOR 2813

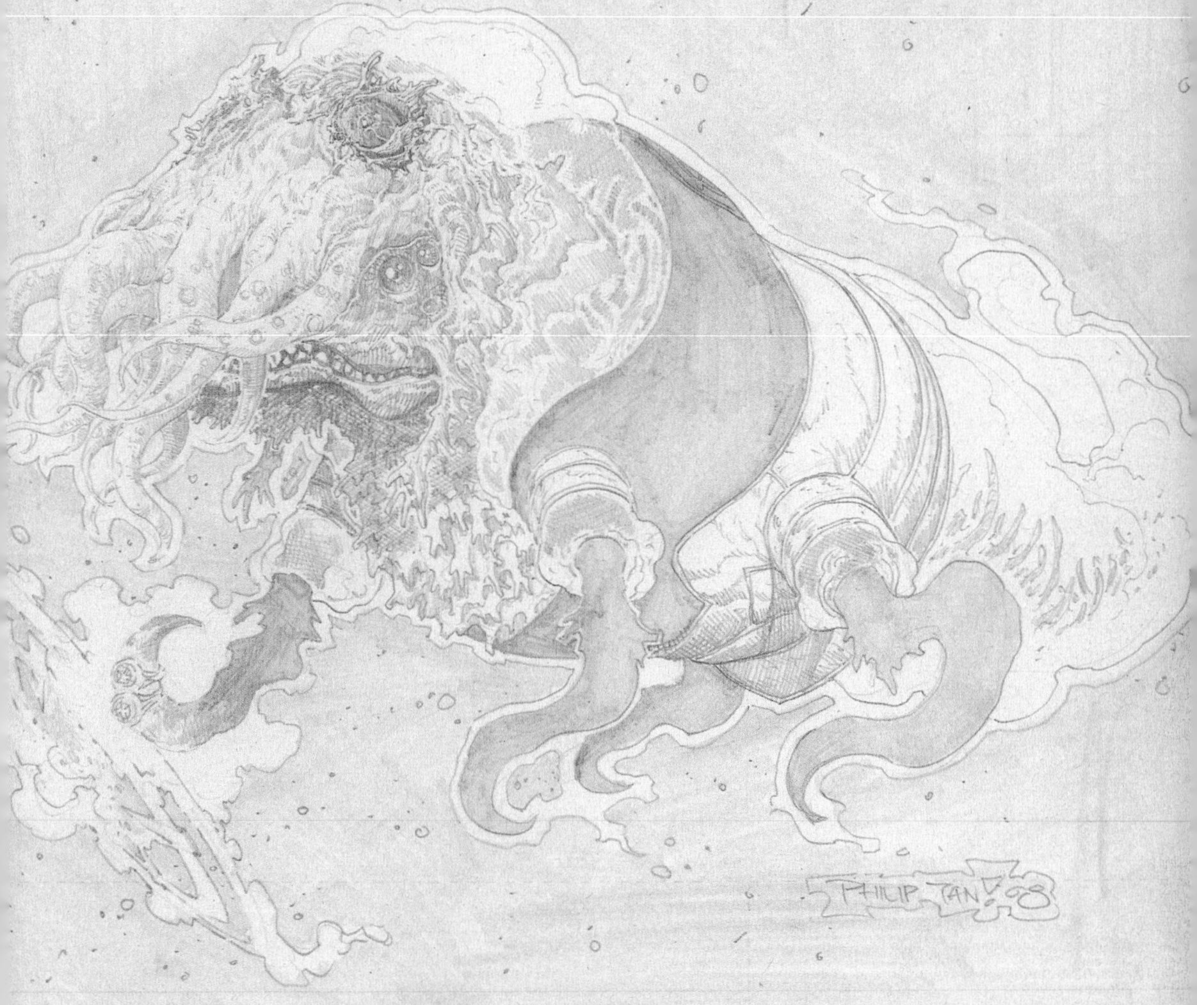

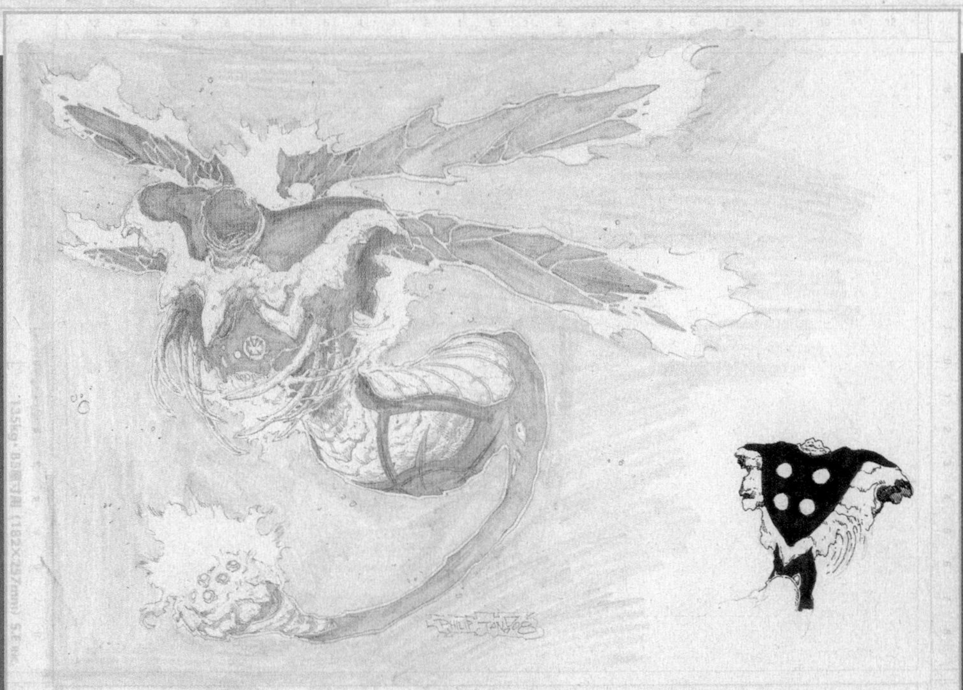

FLAASHA OF MEDUES/SPACE SECTOR 3330

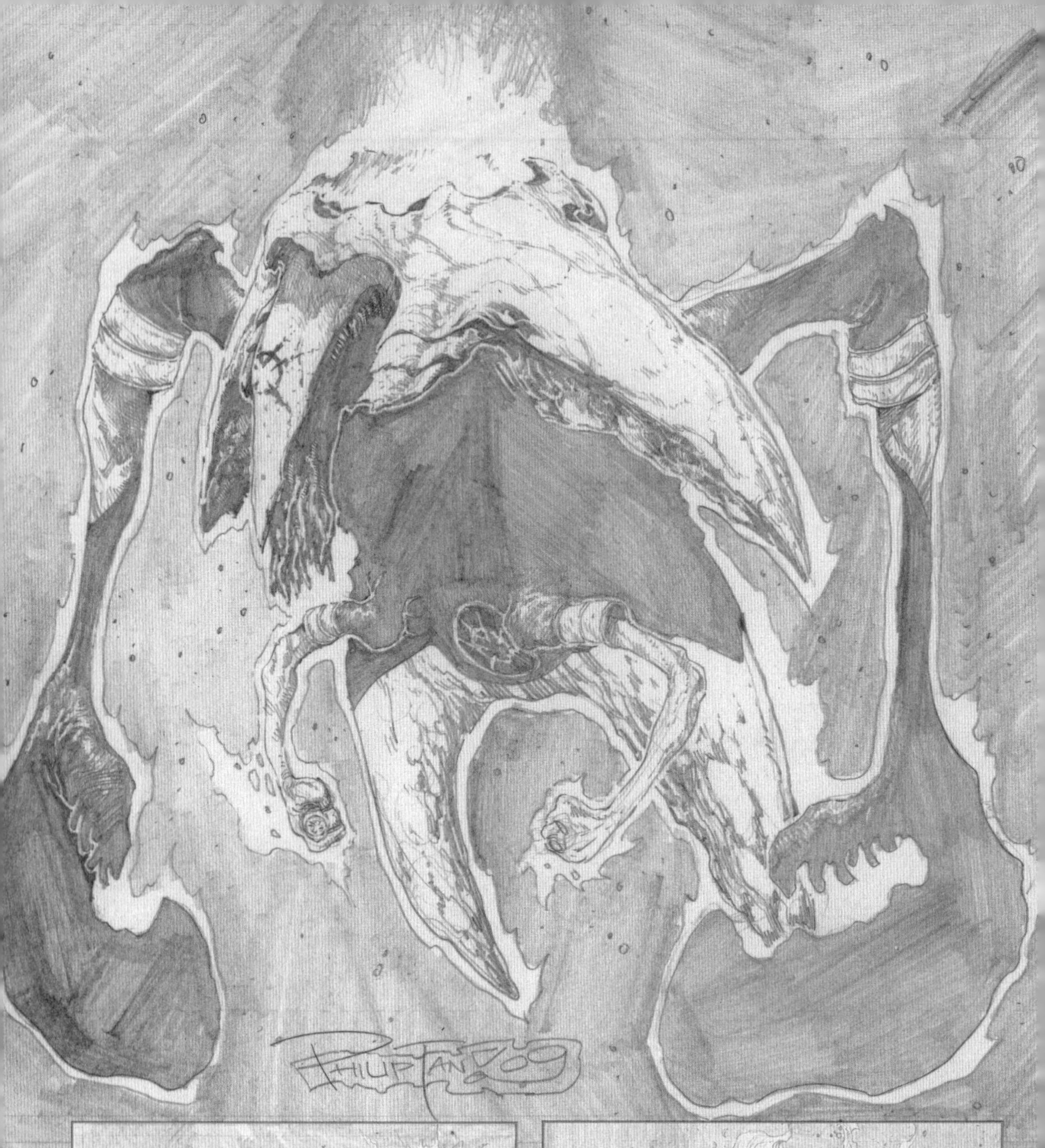
PHILIP TAN 09

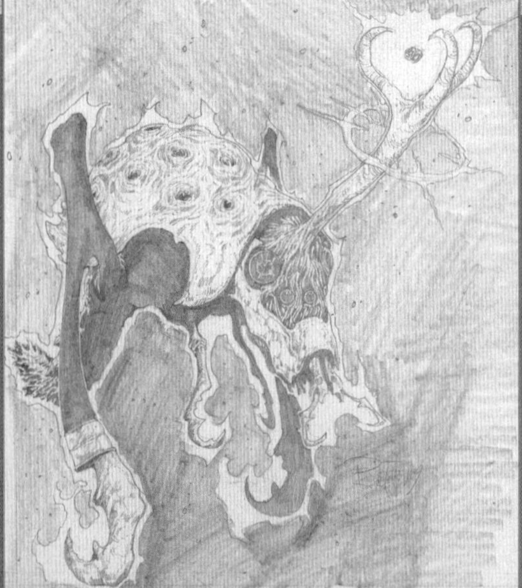

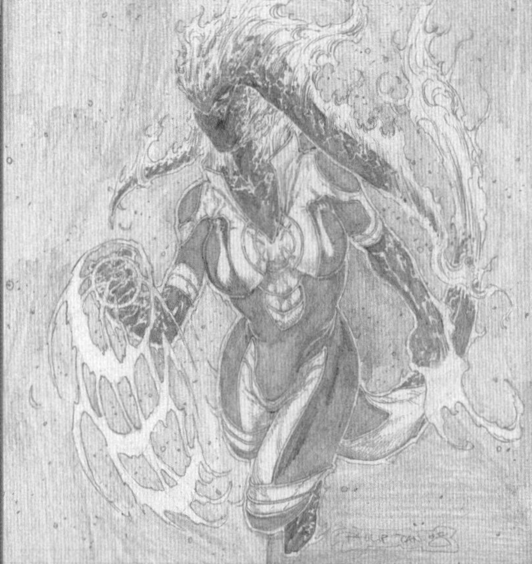

CLYPTA OF THIEVES' WORLD/SPACE SECTOR 2829

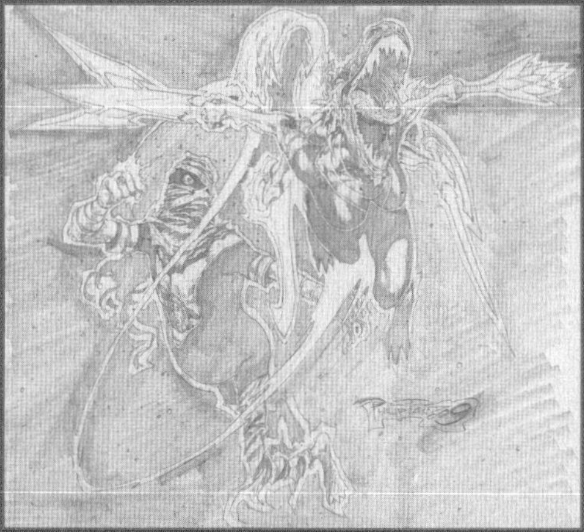

WARP WRAP OF CAIRO/SPACE SECTOR 2

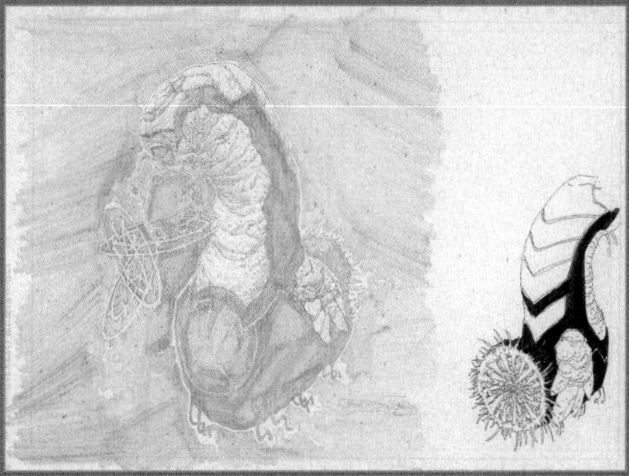

NAT-NAT OF LIMEY ROCK/SPACE SECTOR 228
Philip: A wormlike creature from the Vega System that weaves its traps and manifests its Orange Lantern powers that way. I was thinking of a planet that's more like a cosmic cocoon that breeds these creatures.

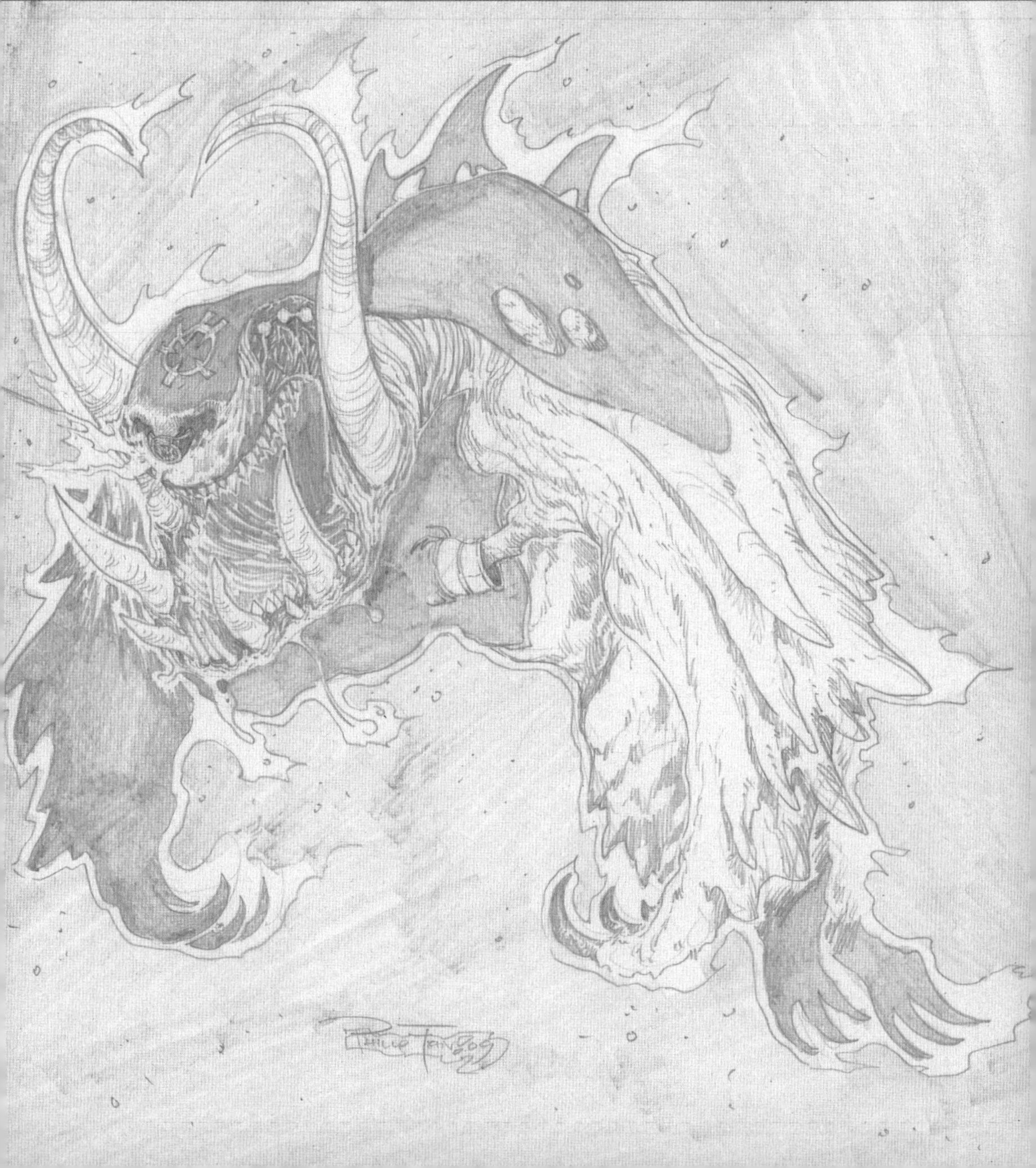

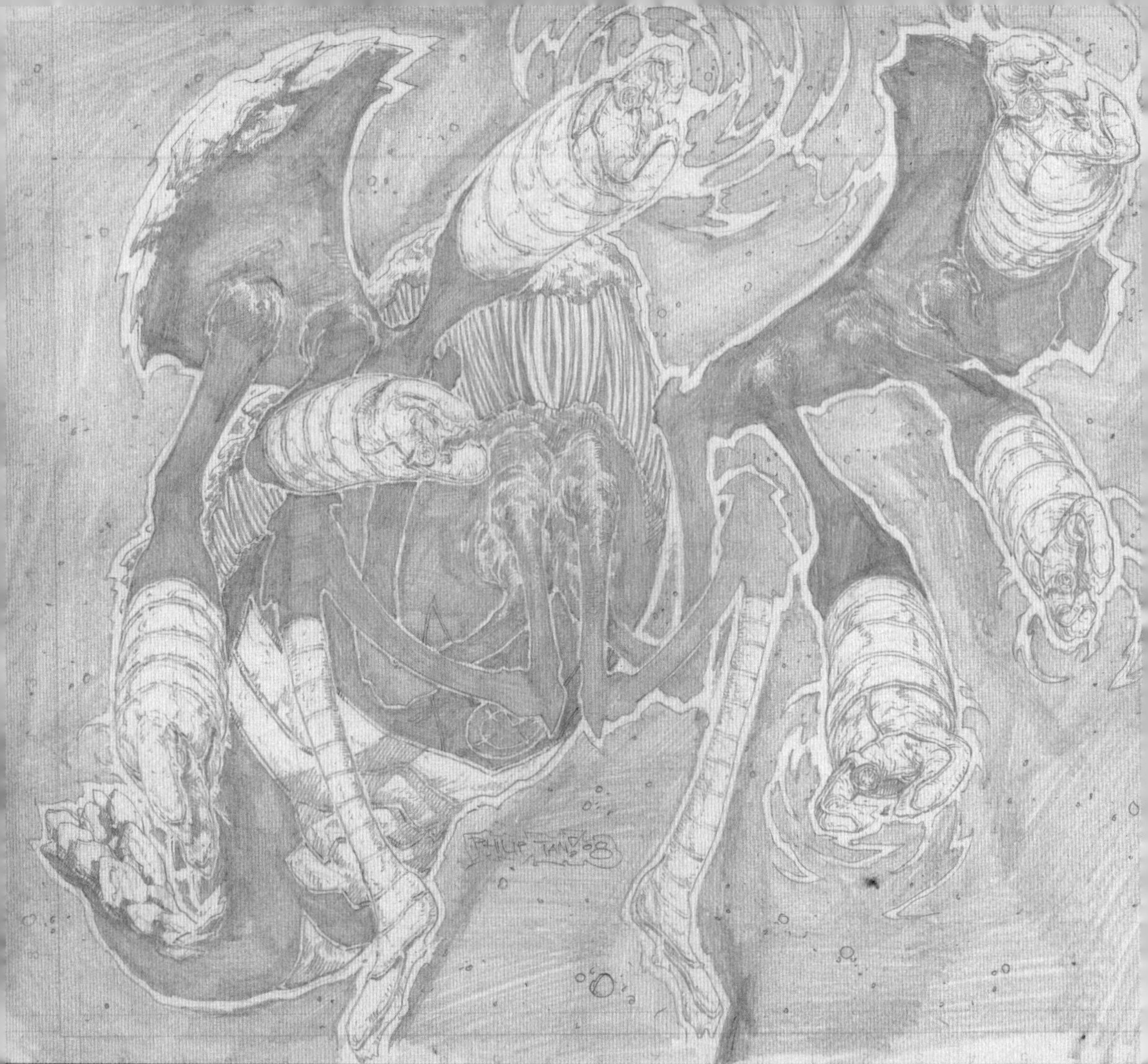
PHILIP TAN '08

Philip: The crocodile looking monster, one who is the size of a spaceship, I was thinking can be the avatar of the Orange Lanterns. Maybe this one actually got a physical form? Maybe he is not sentient and only provides a heavier arsenal for Agent Orange. Geoff was thinking that its mouth can be a mini blackhole. And I just thought, what if the blackhole only sucks in other lights of other rings? That would be so cool!

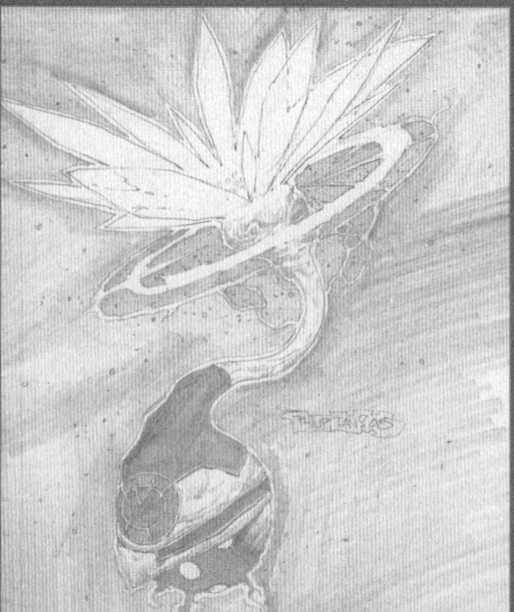

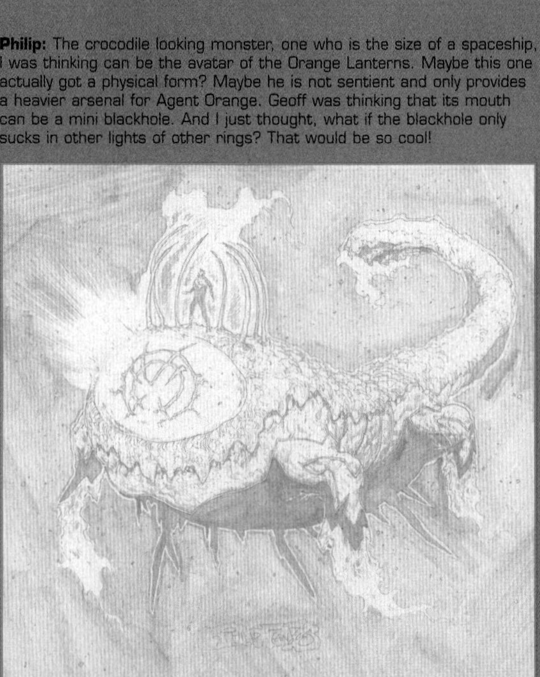

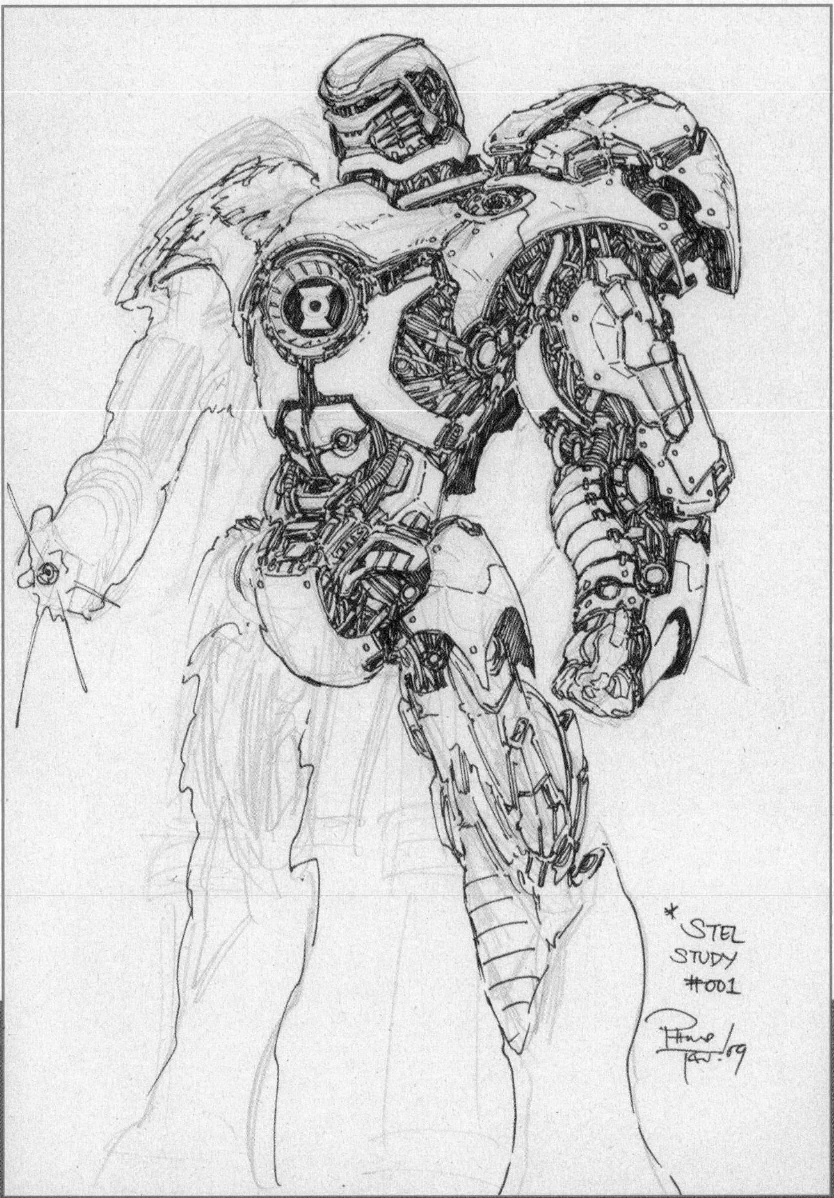
*STEL
STUDY
#001

Eddie: Aside from the Orange Lantern Corps designing, Philip Tan also tricked out veteran robot Green Lantern Stel.

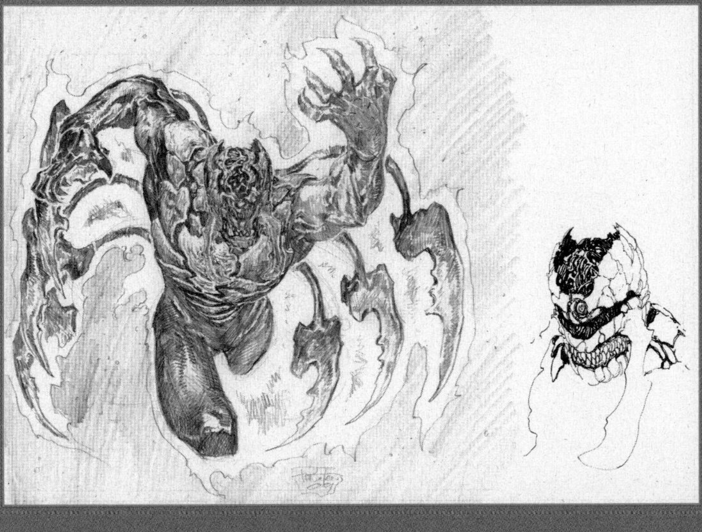

Eddie: Larfleeze, originally designed by Ethan Van Sciver, his name is a combination of two things writer Geoff Johns found disgusting, *Lard and Sleeze.* One of Johns' favorite characters, Larfleeze can be compared to the early Warner Bros. cartoon Daffy Duck: "Mine! Mine! I'm rich! I'm a wealthy miser!"

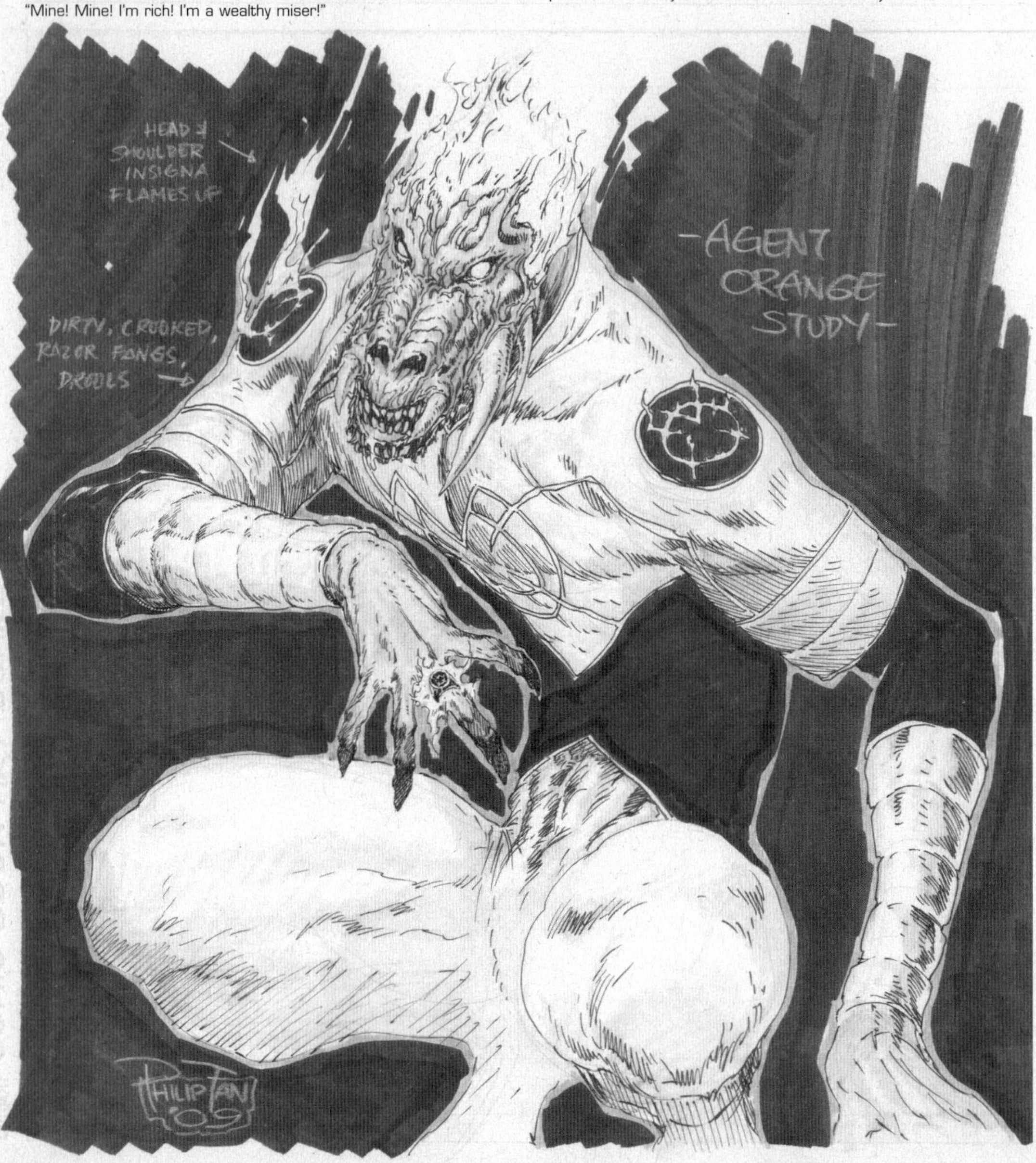
HEAD & SHOULDER INSIGNA FLAMES UP
-AGENT ORANGE STUDY-
DIRTY, CROOKED, RAZOR FANGS, DROOLS
PHILIP TAN '09

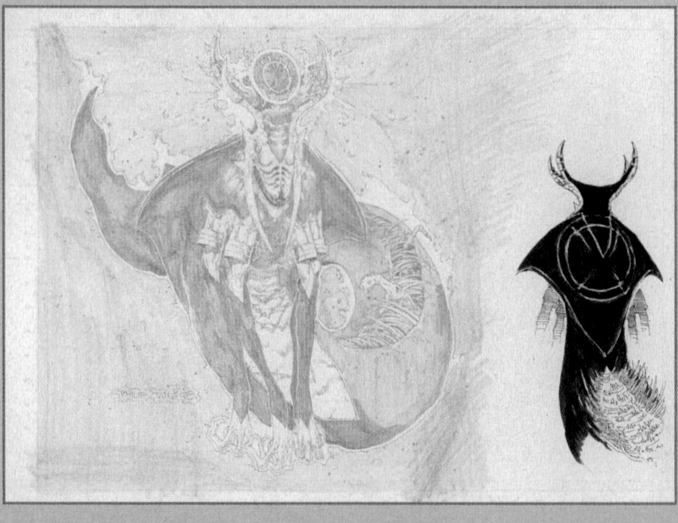

GRUBBER OF NEW BEAG/SPACE SECTOR 2909

Philip: This guy's more of a spider-serpent creature. Without the ring, their kind hunts with a venomous harpoon-like tongue out of their mouth that paralyzes their prey and their mouth is actually the big gap on their back that is full of jagged teeth. They digest their prey alive in the mouth behind them. The rings on its horns amplify its predatory skills with more powers.

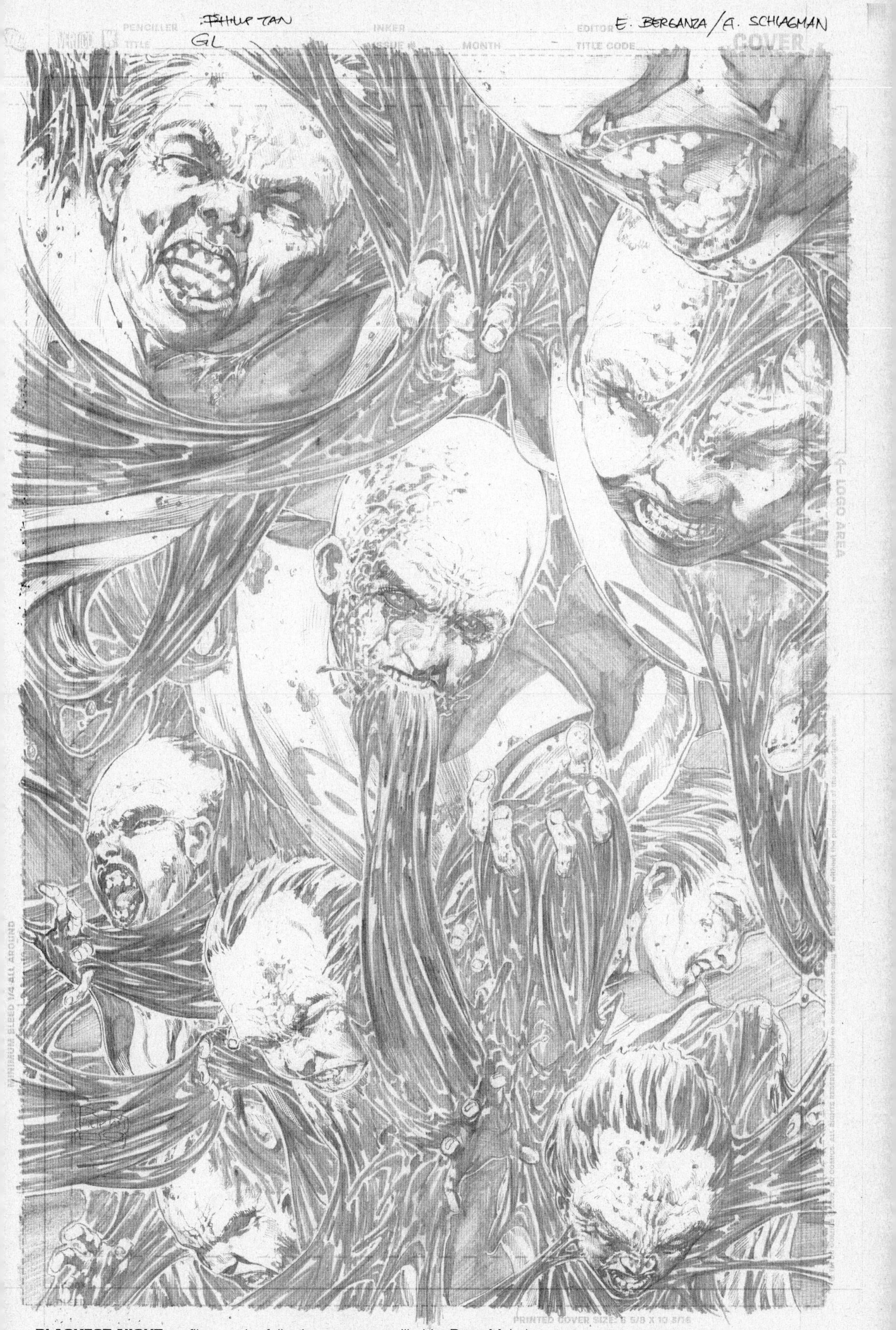
PENCILLER PHILIP TAN
INKER
EDITOR E. BERGANZA / A. SCHLAGMAN
TITLE GL
ISSUE #
MONTH
TITLE CODE
COVER
LOGO AREA
MINIMUM BLEED 1/4 ALL AROUND
PRINTED COVER SIZE: 6 5/8 X 10 3/16

BLACKEST NIGHT profiles on the following pages pencilled by Doug Mahnke.

GREEN LANTERN CORPS

EMOTION: Willpower

HOMEWORLD: Oa

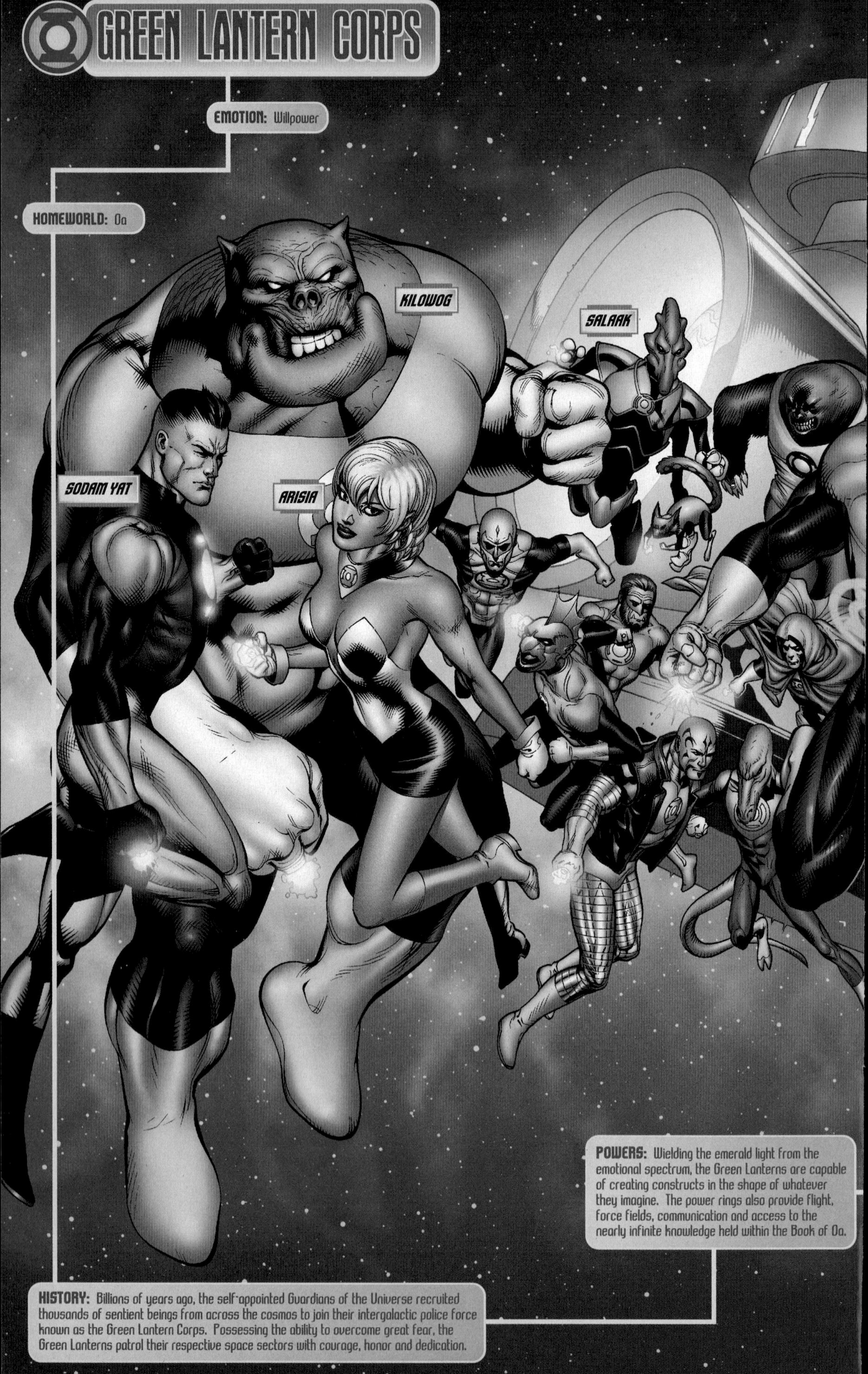
KILOWOG
SALAAK
SODAM YAT
ARISIA

POWERS: Wielding the emerald light from the emotional spectrum, the Green Lanterns are capable of creating constructs in the shape of whatever they imagine. The power rings also provide flight, force fields, communication and access to the nearly infinite knowledge held within the Book of Oa.

HISTORY: Billions of years ago, the self-appointed Guardians of the Universe recruited thousands of sentient beings from across the cosmos to join their intergalactic police force known as the Green Lantern Corps. Possessing the ability to overcome great fear, the Green Lanterns patrol their respective space sectors with courage, honor and dedication.

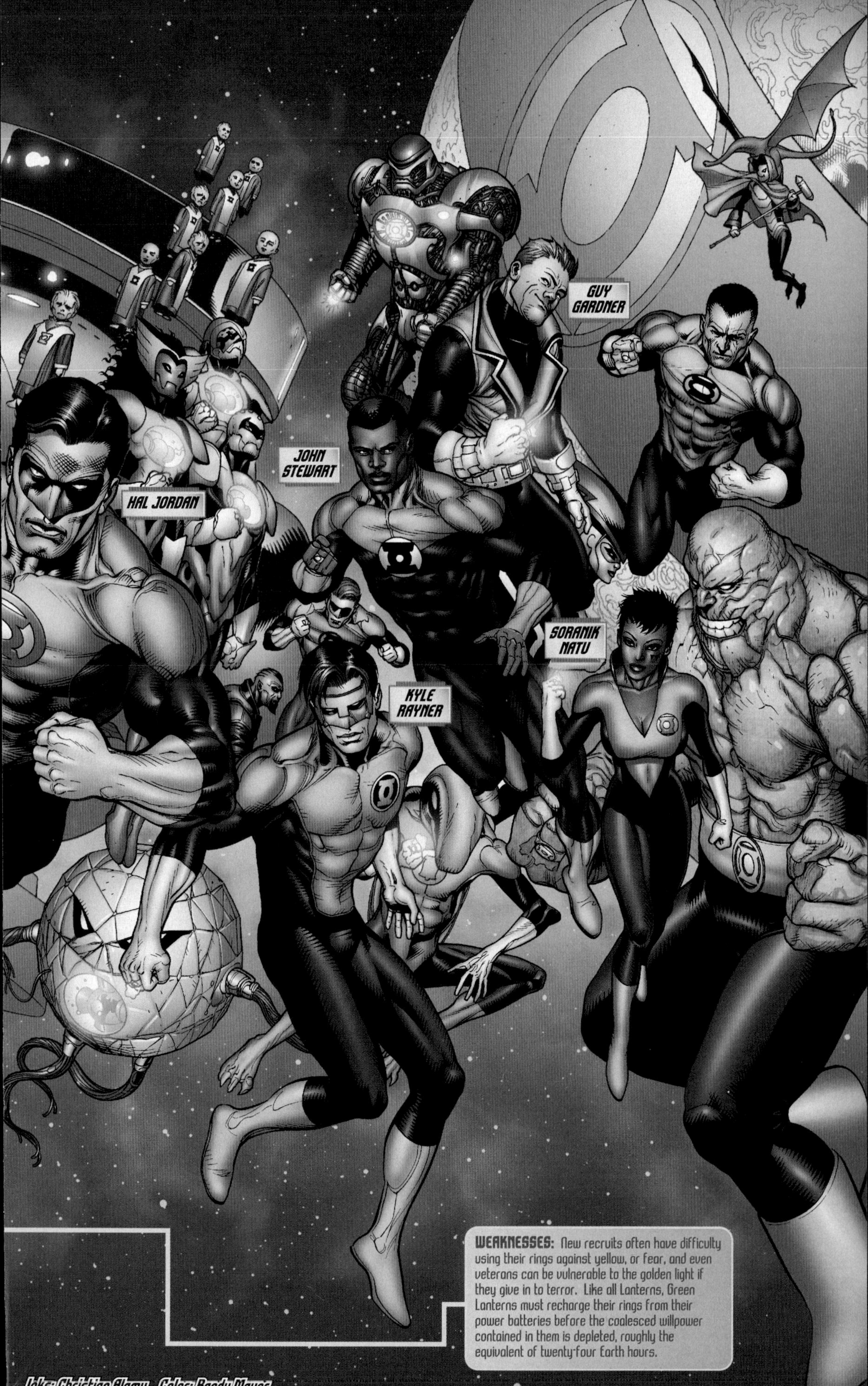
GUY GARDNER
JOHN STEWART
HAL JORDAN
SORANIK NATU
KYLE RAYNER
WEAKNESSES: New recruits often have difficulty using their rings against yellow, or fear, and even veterans can be vulnerable to the golden light if they give in to terror. Like all Lanterns, Green Lanterns must recharge their rings from their power batteries before the coalesced willpower contained in them is depleted, roughly the equivalent of twenty-four Earth hours.

Inks: Christian Alamy Color: Randy Mayor

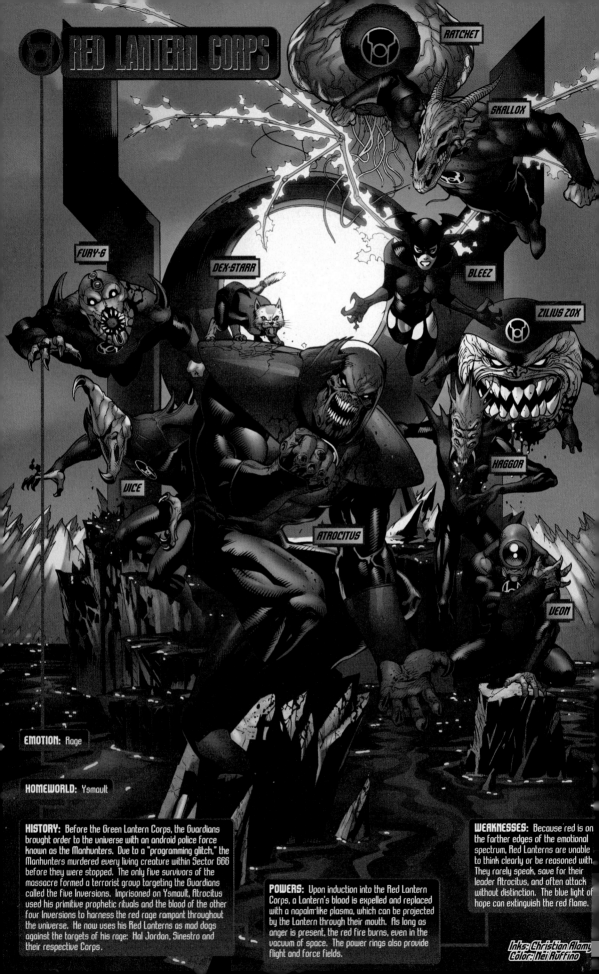

RED LANTERN CORPS

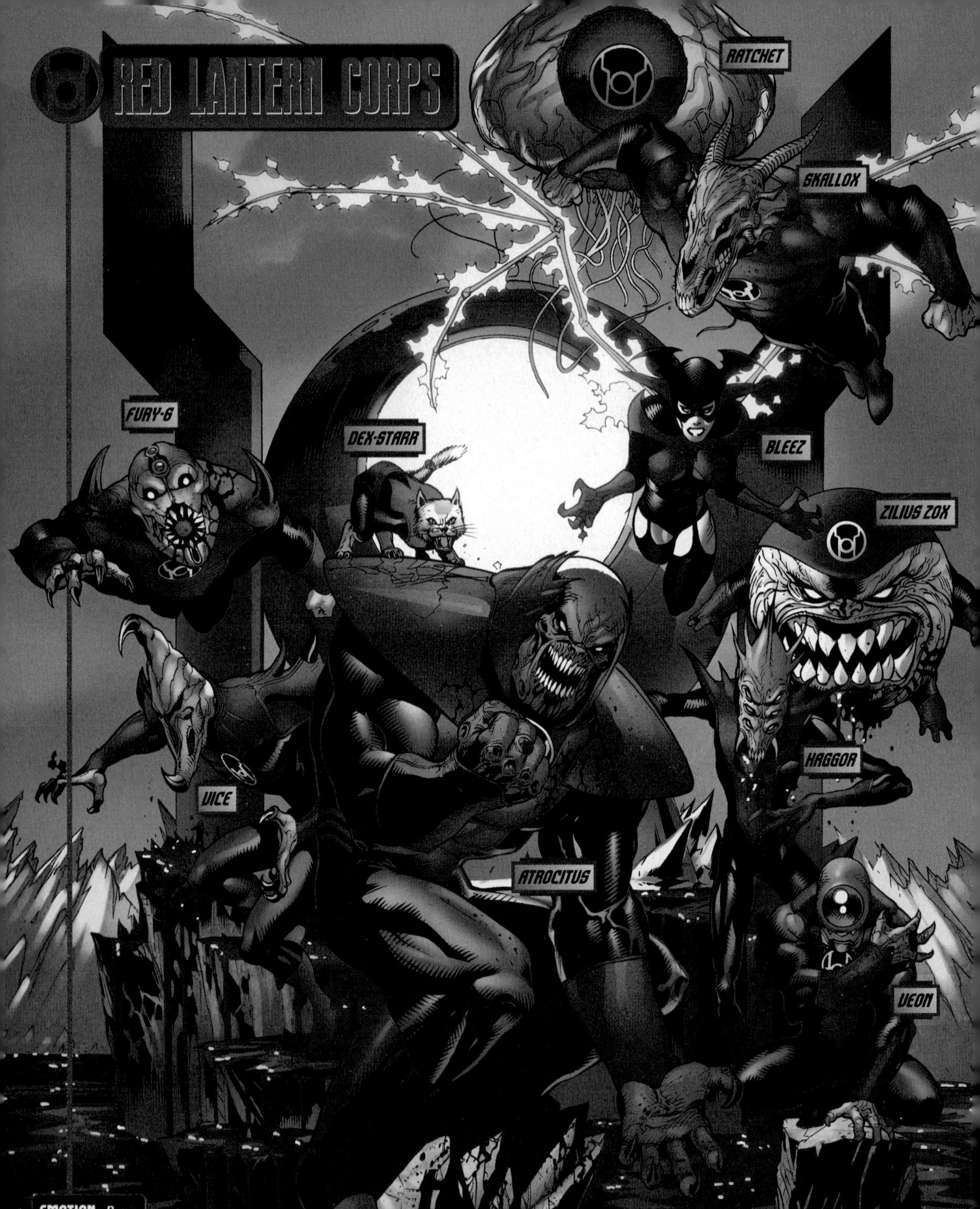

RATCHET
SKALLOX
FURY-6
DEX-STARR
BLEEZ
ZILIUS ZOX
HAGGOR
VICE
ATROCITUS
VEON

EMOTION: Rage

HOMEWORLD: Ysmault

HISTORY: Before the Green Lantern Corps, the Guardians brought order to the universe with an android police force known as the Manhunters. Due to a "programming glitch," the Manhunters murdered every living creature within Sector 666 before they were stopped. The only five survivors of the massacre formed a terrorist group targeting the Guardians called the Five Inversions. Imprisoned on Ysmault, Atrocitus used his primitive prophetic rituals and the blood of the other four Inversions to harness the red rage rampant throughout the universe. He now uses his Red Lanterns as mad dogs against the targets of his rage: Hal Jordan, Sinestro and their respective Corps.

POWERS: Upon induction into the Red Lantern Corps, a Lantern's blood is expelled and replaced with a napalm-like plasma, which can be projected by the Lantern through their mouth. As long as anger is present, the red fire burns, even in the vacuum of space. The power rings also provide flight and force fields.

WEAKNESSES: Because red is on the farther edges of the emotional spectrum, Red Lanterns are unable to think clearly or be reasoned with. They rarely speak, save for their leader Atrocitus, and often attack without distinction. The blue light of hope can extinguish the red flame.

Inks: Christian Alamy
Color: Nei Ruffino

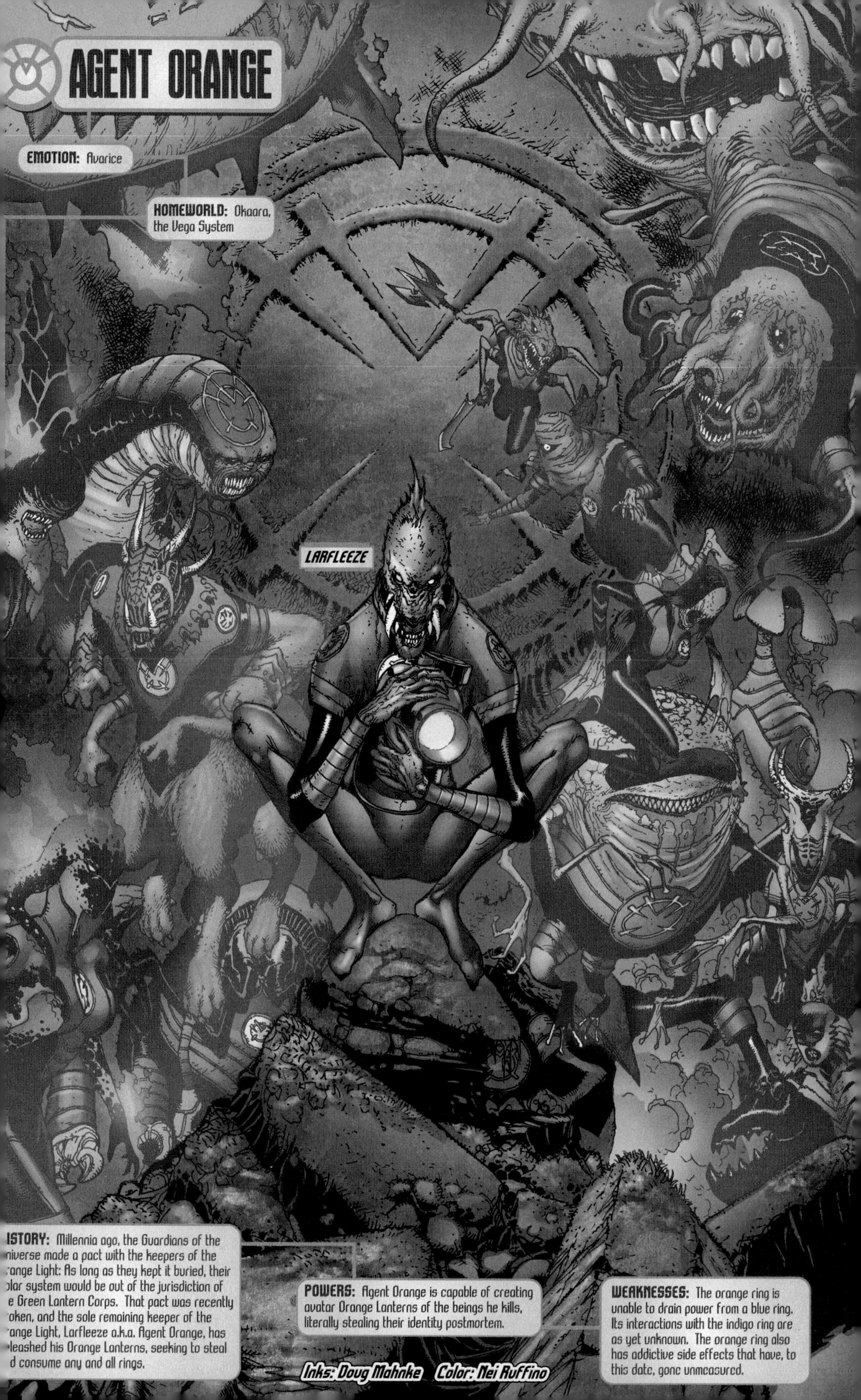

AGENT ORANGE
EMOTION: Avarice
HOMEWORLD: Okaara, the Vega System
LARFLEEZE
ISTORY: Millennia ago, the Guardians of the
niverse made a pact with the keepers of the
range Light: As long as they kept it buried, their
olar system would be out of the jurisdiction of
e Green Lantern Corps. That pact was recently
oken, and the sole remaining keeper of the
range Light, Larfleeze a.k.a. Agent Orange, has
leashed his Orange Lanterns, seeking to steal
d consume any and all rings.
POWERS: Agent Orange is capable of creating avatar Orange Lanterns of the beings he kills, literally stealing their identity postmortem.
WEAKNESSES: The orange ring is unable to drain power from a blue ring. Its interactions with the indigo ring are as yet unknown. The orange ring also has addictive side effects that have, to this date, gone unmeasured.
Inks: Doug Mahnke Color: Nei Ruffino

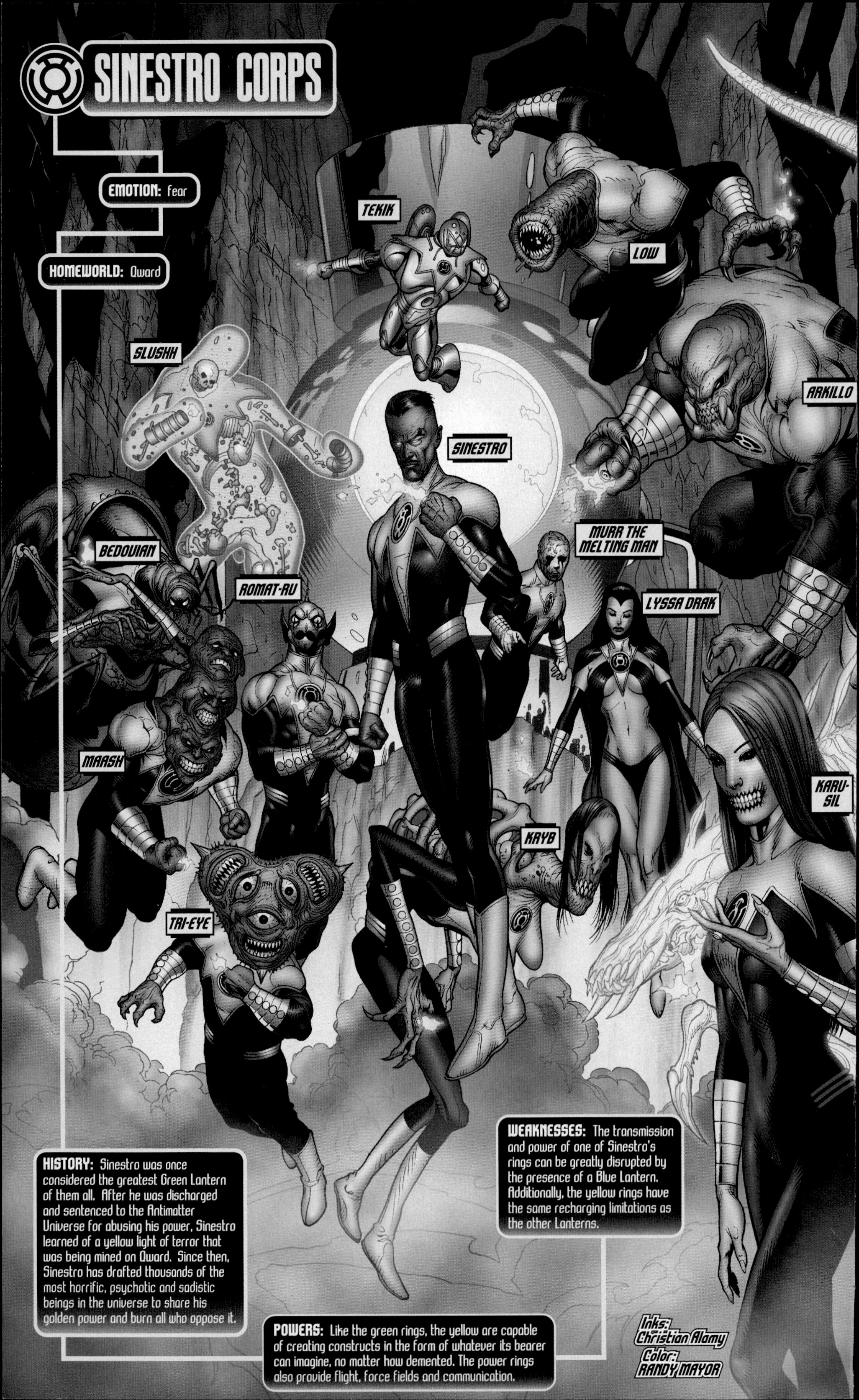

SINESTRO CORPS
EMOTION: fear
HOMEWORLD: Qward
TEKIK
LOW
SLUSHH
ARKILLO
SINESTRO
MURR THE MELTING MAN
BEDOVIAN
ROMAT-RU
LYSSA DRAK
MAASH
KARU-SIL
KRYB
TRI-EYE
WEAKNESSES: The transmission and power of one of Sinestro's rings can be greatly disrupted by the presence of a Blue Lantern. Additionally, the yellow rings have the same recharging limitations as the other Lanterns.
HISTORY: Sinestro was once considered the greatest Green Lantern of them all. After he was discharged and sentenced to the Antimatter Universe for abusing his power, Sinestro learned of a yellow light of terror that was being mined on Qward. Since then, Sinestro has drafted thousands of the most horrific, psychotic and sadistic beings in the universe to share his golden power and burn all who oppose it.
POWERS: Like the green rings, the yellow are capable of creating constructs in the form of whatever its bearer can imagine, no matter how demented. The power rings also provide flight, force fields and communication.
Inks: Christian Alamy
Color: RANDY MAYOR

BLUE LANTERN CORPS

EMOTION: Hope

HOMEWORLD: Odym

SAINT WALKER

GANTHET

SAYD

SISTER SERCY

BROTHER WARTH

BROTHER HYNN

HISTORY: After being banished from the Guardians of the Universe for embracing emotions, Ganthet and Sayd ventured to the sacred garden world of Odym where they established their faith-driven Corps of blue light. Although there are but a handful of Blue Lanterns, their ranks consist of some of the most holy and righteous beings in the universe.

WEAKNESSES: Without a Green Lantern in close proximity, a Blue Lantern's ring will only allow limited flight and protection from the vacuum of space.

POWERS: The blue ring creates constructs that soothe its target based on that target's hopes. Blue Lanterns are also able to de-age dying suns into young, vibrant blue stars that shine in the night sky as a symbol for all to see. Like other power rings, theirs provide flight, force fields and communication. The blue ring charges a green ring and de-charges a yellow.

Inks: Tom Nguyen
Color: Nei Ruffino

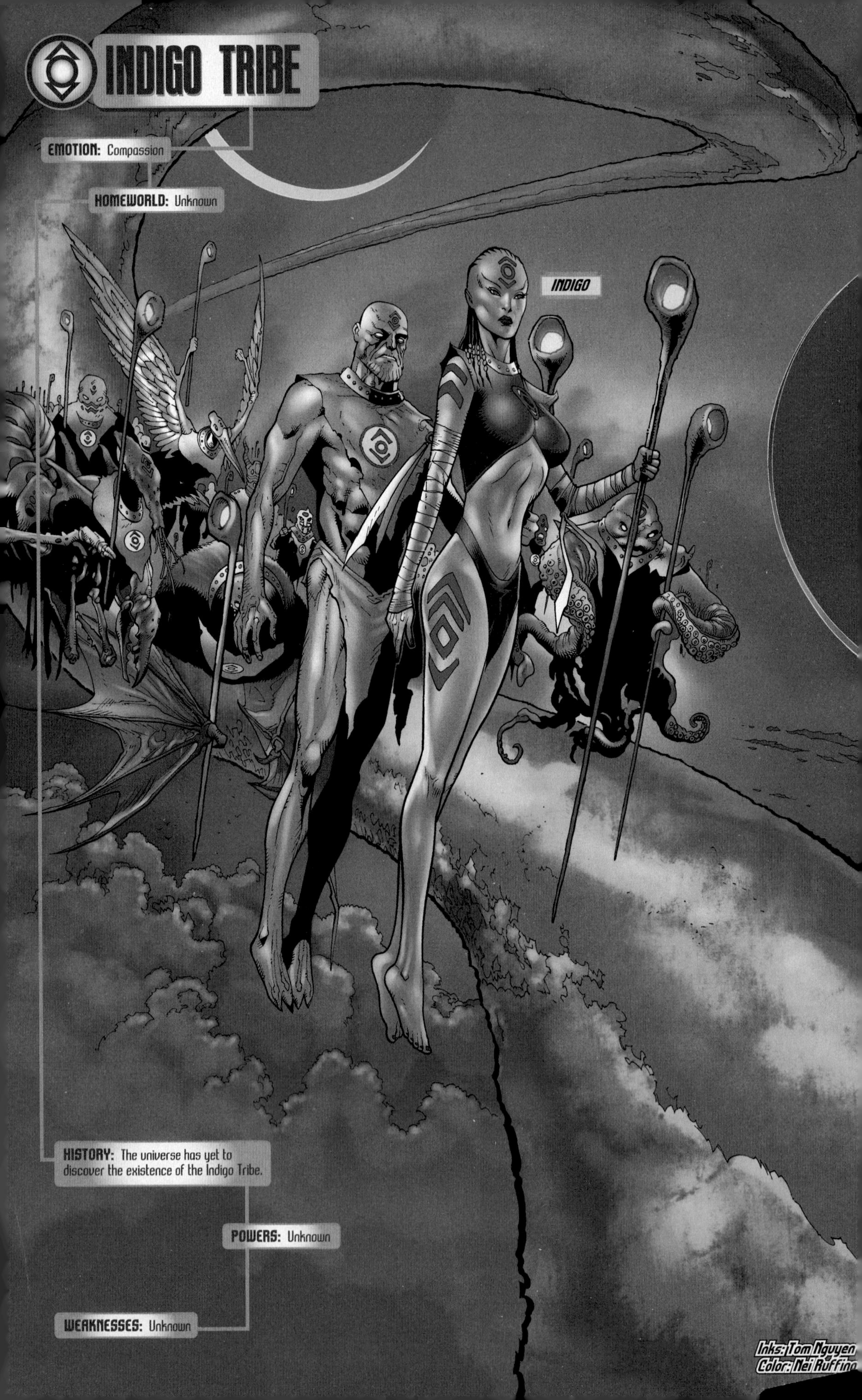
INDIGO TRIBE
EMOTION: Compassion
HOMEWORLD: Unknown
INDIGO
HISTORY: The universe has yet to discover the existence of the Indigo Tribe.
POWERS: Unknown
WEAKNESSES: Unknown
Inks: Tom Nguyen
Color: Nei Ruffino

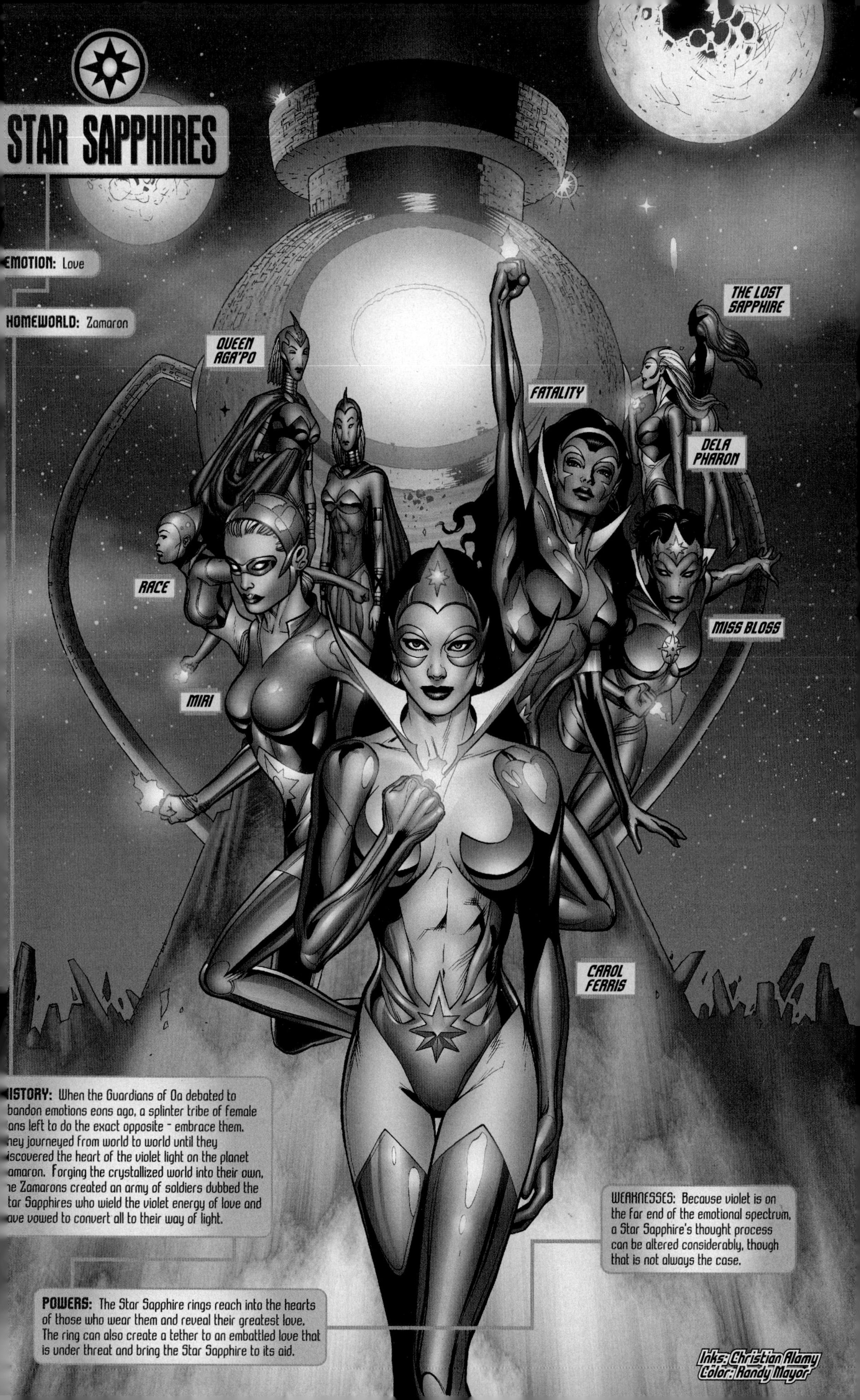

STAR SAPPHIRES
EMOTION: Love
HOMEWORLD: Zamaron
QUEEN AGA'PO
THE LOST SAPPHIRE
FATALITY
DELA PHARON
RACE
MISS BLOSS
MIRI
CAROL FERRIS
ISTORY: When the Guardians of Oa debated to bandon emotions eons ago, a splinter tribe of female ans left to do the exact opposite - embrace them. hey journeyed from world to world until they iscovered the heart of the violet light on the planet amaron. Forging the crystallized world into their own, he Zamarons created an army of soldiers dubbed the tar Sapphires who wield the violet energy of love and ave vowed to convert all to their way of light.
WEAKNESSES: Because violet is on the far end of the emotional spectrum, a Star Sapphire's thought process can be altered considerably, though that is not always the case.
POWERS: The Star Sapphire rings reach into the hearts of those who wear them and reveal their greatest love. The ring can also create a tether to an embattled love that is under threat and bring the Star Sapphire to its aid.
Inks: Christian Alamy
Color: Randy Mayor

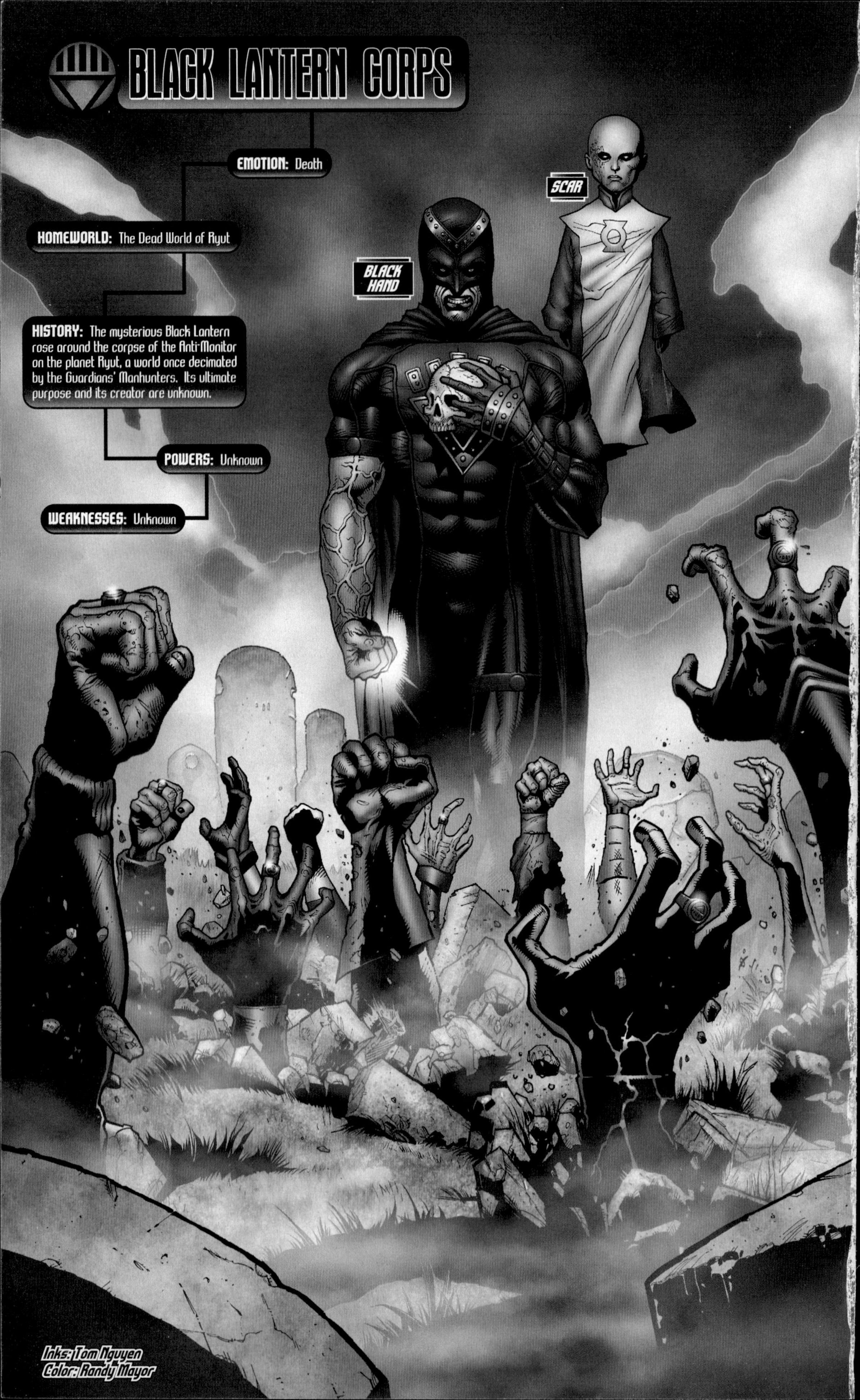
BLACK LANTERN CORPS
EMOTION: Death
HOMEWORLD: The Dead World of Ryut
HISTORY: The mysterious Black Lantern rose around the corpse of the Anti-Monitor on the planet Ryut, a world once decimated by the Guardians' Manhunters. Its ultimate purpose and its creator are unknown.
POWERS: Unknown
WEAKNESSES: Unknown
SCAR
BLACK HAND
Inks: Tom Nguyen
Color: Randy Mayor